A Village
in the Vineyards

The church and the monument

A VILLAGE IN THE VINEYARDS

Thomas Matthews

Photographs by Sara Matthews

Farrar, Straus and Giroux

New York

Published simultaneously in Canada by HarperCollins*CanadaLtd*
Printed and bound in the United States of America
Designed by Martha Rago
First edition, 1993

Library of Congress Cataloging-in-Publication Data
Matthews, Thomas.
A village in the vineyards / Thomas Matthews; photographs
by Sara Matthews.—1st ed.
      p. cm.
      1. Wine and wine making—France—Ruch. I. Matthews, Sara.
II. Title.
      TP553.M36   1993   914.4′71404838—dc20   93-17262

A nos amis Ruchelais

Contents

A Village
in the Vineyards

1

A Village
in the Vineyards

In the summer of 1986, Sara and I left New York with one-way tickets to France. In Paris we bought a twelve-year-old Renault for $850 cash and headed south. Everything we cared about was in the trunk. Our route wound through the vineyards of Burgundy and Beaujolais, down the Rhône Valley to Châteauneuf-du-Pape, then west across mountains and rocky gorges to Bordeaux.

We were looking for a village in the vineyards, a new home, a fresh start. We wanted to explore French wine and country life. First, we needed a place to live. A winemaker friend of a friend sheltered us in a cottage where his grape pickers would bunk for the harvest, fast approaching. We scoured the small towns and the classified ads, but everything available was too small, too dark, or too expensive. Evening found us disappointed again in a town near Saint-Émilion. We stopped at a café for espresso.

Low lamps hung from the ceiling, pooled light on the zinc bar. A beefy fellow in a white apron polished glasses, watching men play cards at a corner table. They stared as we came in, then turned back to the game.

"*Deux cafés, s'il vous plaît.*"

The barman went through the ritual of grinding the beans, filling the steel measure, twisting it into the machine, and snapping the switch. Steam hissed. He put down the cups with a quizzical glance that meant, This isn't the time for coffee. If you belonged here, you would know this isn't the way things are done. We had seen that look before.

Coins clinked and slid across the card table. Sara flipped through our worn copy of the *Gîte Rural* guide. *Gîtes* are old buildings renovated for summer rentals to tourists. We had tried dozens already.

"That place in Rauzan had a view over vineyards and good heat," I said. "Maybe we should take another look."

"No, it didn't feel right," she said. "We'll know it when we find it. What about this one?"

She pointed to a faded photograph of a stone building plain as a blockhouse, a presbytère in a nearby village called Ruch. "It's big, and there's a fireplace. But what's a presbytère?"

"Where the priest lives. Or used to, I guess. I wonder why the church gave it up."

"How do you suppose they say Ruch?"

"Like push?"

"Hutch?"

"Swoosh?"

Sara called the barman over and asked him. He studied the picture, stroked his chin. "Ruch?" The way he said it sounded like spitting a seed: *Rrewshh.* "Never heard of it. It's not French, that."

"Let's find out about it," Sara said. "At least we'll learn a new word."

The barman brought over the phone.

"Mairie de Ruch," sang the voice on the other end of the line. It came out like a birdcall, short and sweet. Roosh.

Sara asked about the *gîte,* whether it was vacant and might be rented for the winter. Her French, like mine, was rusty. She paused. Did the woman understand?

"BON. YOU ARE AMERICAN."

The words boomed from the telephone. The cardplayers turned to listen. "I SPEAK ENGLISH, NO? DO YOU SPEAK FRENCH."

"Well, yes, *un peu,*" Sara replied, a little flustered, thinking she had been speaking French all the while.

"BON. MY NAME IS MADAME TALLON. WHEN WILL YOU COME."

Slowly, painfully, Sara set up an appointment for the following afternoon. When she hung up, the men in the bar were laughing. The barman brought over small brandies and didn't charge us for the call.

Ruch lay east of Bordeaux, away from the sea, through a rolling landscape of woods, meadows, and vineyards called Entre-Deux-Mers. Bordeaux is France's seventh-largest city, but only counts 200,000 inhabitants. The suburbs quickly dwindled into open country, hardly touched by the twentieth century except for power lines that crossed it like the stitching on a crazy quilt.

The region's name, "between two seas," derives from the rivers that form its boundaries, the Dordogne to the north and the Garonne to the south. Once the rivers were highways, and now the highways are built along their banks; traffic and construction have mostly been channeled along them, bypassing the bulk of the region's interior. The only main route that ever crossed Entre-Deux-Mers was the twelfth-century pilgrimage trail from Paris to Santiago de Compostela in Spain. The present roads, still oriented along natural valleys toward medieval refuges, wander and drift in a way quite maddening to a modern driver with a Michelin map.

Entre-Deux-Mers forms a rough triangle, with its point near Bordeaux and its sides following the rivers about 60 kilometers upstream. They are 30 kilometers apart at the eastern boundary, traditionally drawn at the highest point reached by the ocean's tidal flow. But there's little feel of the sea. The steep hillsides are wooded, the fertile valleys planted to corn, wheat, and sunflowers. The plateau, a broad bed of calcium, is better drained, more comfortable for the vine.

Despite the accidental terrain, two unifying factors shape the countryside. The parallel lines of the vineyards weave sprawling patchwork patterns across the rolling hills. And the houses, barns, and churches share an architecture derived from local materials and local weather. Because limestone is so accessible, the villages and farmhouses are built largely of the soft golden stone. Modern buildings, more often of cinder block or brick, are still faced with limestone, or covered with a thin cement *crépis,* a kind of stucco, which takes on the gray-gold tint of the older buildings with time. Summers are warm, so windows are modest; winter brings rain more often than snow, so roof pitches are gentle; storms come from the ocean, so front doors face east or south. The buildings conform in intent but vary in detail, like the eclectic formality of the vineyard rows.

The country was serene under clear skies as the harvest approached. The fields were empty, as if no one wanted to break the spell. Vines and churches keyed a landscape that seemed unscarred by progress; we felt we were driving into the past. The map showed Ruch on a height, and our first glimpse of it came from a distance, east across a valley: a church spire rising from a steep bluff, a beacon blazing in the full light of the afternoon sun.

Cattle grazed in meadows by a stream below the village; we climbed a wooded hill to a rolling plain covered with vines. Through a break in the trees we caught a glimpse of a turreted château. Farmhouses sat near the road, grouped in hamlets of twos and threes. A sign said RUCH. Another sign pointed to the CAVE COOPERATIVE, and tacked below it, one in black and pink advertised LE SCORPION. We passed a soccer field. A small modern school faced a smaller, older post office. In the village the houses became continuous, a gray stone wall tinted gold in the sunlight. Then the road met the main street, where two boys on bikes darted out from a blind corner, causing me to brake and stall.

Ruch looked like all the other villages we had driven through to reach it. There wasn't much sign of life. The houses crowded the streets, protecting themselves with heavy shutters and layers of curtains. Some of the buildings were stuccoed, some bare stone. Moss and cracks veiled weathered walls. On the corner an open shed sheltered a tractor and an ancient Citroën truck. Beyond it, a general store and a garage were silent and still.

We parked the car to explore. The church stood off in a corner of the village. The bell tower rose on the edge of a bluff, turning its back on the community to watch over the valley. From the road, a gravel path

The village

shaded by two rows of chestnut trees led to the portal; we walked fifty yards and left the world behind. Beyond the church, a building joined it at right angles, made of the same ageless stone, austere yet graceful. It too looked over the valley. This must be the presbytère, we decided, ill served by its picture. Together, the buildings and a low wall formed a compound as self-contained and private as a monastery.

At the very edge of the bluff an obelisk commemorated the town's dead from a century of wars. The valley lay below, green meadows and a few golden houses. The cool air carried the sound of distant cowbells. Though it was only the end of September, the chestnuts were rapidly losing their leaves. A thick yellow carpet muffled our footsteps as we walked back toward the village.

The *mairie* stood across the street. The building's original function was illegible, but its age and authority were clear. Three stories tall, it stood well above the houses that pressed close on two sides. Its Gothic windows were large and irregularly placed; the asymmetry gave the building an unsettled and energetic air. Small faces were carved around the windows, simple but vivid, angels and gossips. A hexagonal tower jutted from the central façade, thrusting slightly off center, violent compared to the graceful upreach of the church spire.

A sign said ENTER WITHOUT KNOCKING, but we knocked anyway, then pushed the door open. Bare bulbs lit green walls covered with notices and maps. The floor was plain wood planking, battered cupboards stood around the walls, a new photocopier rested on a spindly table. A small man with thinning gray hair sat across from a plump woman with glasses. He looked up as we entered; she continued scratching on a piece of paper.

"Is this the town hall?" I said in French. "We're the Americans come to look at the *gîte.*"

The woman put down her pen and examined us. *"BON!"* said an unforgettable voice. *"ET VOUS PARLEZ FRANÇAIS."*

"Of course they speak French, Madame Tallon," said the man, rising. "Welcome to Ruch. I'm the Mayor. Bonvoisin is my name."

"It says good neighbor," said the woman in hesitant English. "My name is Denise Tallon."

"Good neighbor. It's a good name for a mayor, don't you think?" asked Bonvoisin.

"You'll be here to see the *gîte,"* decided Madame Tallon, reverting to French. "I'll call Marie-France," she said to the Mayor. "Madame Lunardelli is in charge of the *gîte,"* she said to us. She dialed a number, spoke rapidly to the person who answered.

"Are you on vacation?" asked the Mayor. He hitched at his pants. He had a bad eye that wandered away from our glance, and he was wearing bedroom slippers.

"Not exactly," I answered. "We were living in New York . . ."

"Ah! New York!" They nodded.

"And we tired of it. We met in Paris . . ."

"Ah, Paris!" breathed Madame Tallon. They looked at Sara with interest.

"And we decided to come back to France for a while. We're journalists. I write and Sara photographs. We do articles about food and wine, art and architecture. Where better than France?"

"Well, Ruch has everything you need," said the Mayor. "At least, that's what I've always found."

"Is the *gîte* available for the winter? And might the summer price be negotiable for winter rates?"

They looked at each other for the first time in the conversation. "Madame Lunardelli is in charge of the *gîte*," said the Mayor. "But we'll do everything we can. Won't we, Madame Tallon?" He pulled a battered black beret from his pocket. "Enjoy your look around." And he was out the door.

"So you met in Paris," said Madame Tallon.

We nodded.

"I am Parisian." She nodded. "I grew up there. During the war." She shook her head, frowning. "There was never enough to eat. We were glad to see the Americans, I can tell you. It could have been the Russians. Then France would be Communist!" She nodded toward the door. "Of course, some would like to see it Communist now. You know, the French have a Communist President. But we in Ruch were ahead of the times. We elected a Communist mayor first!"

"Mitterrand? I thought he was a Socialist."

"What difference does it make? The people wanted a change. They were tired of being happy. The French are like that." She shook her head again. "Paris was beautiful then. It's still beautiful, of course, but then it was magical. Ah, the world changes, and not always for the better. But we do what we can."

She sighed. A small fleck of white foam clung to the corner of her mouth. We didn't know what to say, so we gazed around the room. There was a map of the town tacked to one wall. Boundary lines carved the fields into innumerable small polygons, a surveyor's nightmare. The door opened and another woman entered. Younger, she had black curls and a harried air.

"Bonjour, Madame Tallon. A good day, we won both games." She looked at us.

"Bonjour, Marie-France. Here are the Americans." We shook hands. "Madame Lunardelli is in charge of the soccer teams," she said to us.

"Hardly in charge," protested the other. "Just a strong supporter. If a town doesn't encourage its young people, it loses them."

"Marie-France, these young Americans would like to see the presbytère. They're thinking of staying the winter."

Outside, the air was fresh and cool, and somewhere water splashed in a fountain. We walked back along the chestnut path.

The stone house by the church was indeed the presbytère. The last resident priest of Ruch had died in 1962, after serving the parish for half a century. Since then, the priest from a neighboring town had taken charge of Ruch. The presbytère stood empty until 1977, when the town refurbished it to rent as a *gîte*. Madame Lunardelli explained that most of the tourists were British, but once a family of Belgians had lived there for two winters.

"Their children were a bit wild," she said, "and their dogs, too. The damage they did!"

She pushed open the creaky iron gate to the garden and we filed along

The presbytère

a narrow walk lined with rosebushes, their pink blossoms fragrant in the empty air. A gnarled apple tree nestled between the stone buttresses of the church.

The house expanded like a telescope in three sections. Nearest the church, the smallest section had a padlocked door and a small window with stone mullions. The main door was in the central section, with one window beside it and two placed asymmetrically above, out of line with the Gothic window. Then a long, blank wall ran to a low stone boundary wall that came back around the garden, along the edge of the bluff. Judging from the windows, the walls were four feet thick; where the sun fell full, they looked like hammered gold.

Madame Lunardelli opened the door with a black iron key fit for a dungeon. A dark, cool hall ran through the building to another door, daylight around its edges. Down a perpendicular hallway, the kitchen gave onto the garden, and a large room with a fireplace overlooked the bluff to the south. The bathroom was tucked under a wooden staircase that climbed to three bedrooms. The plan was simple, additive, each room a well-proportioned block.

The refurbishment had been simple and cheap. The entire second floor was papered in a dark floral pattern and covered with one strip of thin carpet. Downstairs, all was tan tile and more busy wallpaper, which was in tatters at floor level. "That's the humidity," Madame Lunardelli said. "It climbs right up the walls." The furniture matched the decor. It was serviceable, but there was a certain sadness to the effort, as though a castle had been made up to look like a motel. As the Frenchwoman chattered on about bath towels and spare bottles of cooking gas, we let ourselves sink into the calmness that flowed through the house like the evening breeze.

Suddenly loud bells broke the silence, two deep tones piling up in a long, measured cadence. The notes echoed, amplified through the stone rooms. Conversation was impossible; we looked at each other with helpless smiles. Even when the tolling ended the notes lingered in the air, and as they died, the new silence was deeper than before, charged with a positive quality that held the memory of the bells.

"Angelus," said Madame Lunardelli. "The church bells always rang

Angelus at sunrise and sunset. They used to mark the days for the workers in the fields. Now of course people have watches." She shrugged. "People don't work as long, either. It's loud, isn't it?"

We nodded.

A worried look came into her eyes. "We can turn it off if it bothers you. The British didn't like the morning bells during the summer, so we turned them off. Summer sunrise comes early! They didn't seem to mind the evening bells. But perhaps they would bother you?"

We assured her that we liked bells. But she still seemed uneasy.

"There is another *gîte* in Ruch, farther away from the church. It's smaller, but more modern; we just fixed it up two years ago. Would you like to see that one?"

Sara and I glanced at each other. We didn't want to look anymore. Every choice had drawbacks. If loud bells at sundown was the worst of them here, this place would be paradise. We wanted a fireplace and a view over vines, space and quiet. The presbytère had them all.

All it lacked was an acceptable price. The *gîte* guidebook listed it at 600 francs a week. The franc was trading at around six to the dollar, but we had very few dollars. "Shall I?" I asked Sara in English. She nodded. My negotiating pitch was a set piece by now. I finished with an offer of 1,000 francs a month.

The black curls nodded as Madame Lunardelli heard us out. Then she said, "It's not my position to make such agreements. The Mayor will have to decide, perhaps even ask the municipal council." She smiled.

"But the harvest is beginning," I said. "We have to leave the place we're in. We have to know now. Can we talk with the Mayor again?"

The worried look came back into her eyes. "I'm not sure where he is." She checked her watch. "The *mairie* is closed." Then another smile. "There is a dinner for the soccer team tonight. The Mayor will be there, he always is. Can you stay and join us? Then you could talk to him."

We agreed. She locked the presbytère behind us. The sun was setting, and from the bluff the whole western rim of the sky was pink. We sat on the low wall by the bluff and watched the stone houses turn from gold to gray. Sheep bells tinkled on the slope below us. Our shadows were long, reaching for the big house.

"Could you live here?" I asked Sara.

"I love it."

"It's not heated very well. We might be cold. But I could have an office, a view of the sunset from my desk. A change."

Sometimes lives need change. Not necessarily out of desperation, but from a sense that satisfaction can come too easily, that one day satisfaction might not be enough. For four years, we had lived in a brownstone apartment on the Upper East Side of Manhattan. The kitchen was part of the living room. So were the dining room, the office, the guest room, and the study. The bedroom just barely held a bed. We paid $700 a month for it and considered it a good deal.

New York boomed in the eighties. Money was everywhere. Sara had studied architecture, but moved into interiors and facilities management. Every year she changed her job, for wider horizons and a larger salary. But she wanted more independence, more creativity. I had always been a wanderer, and was surprised to find myself settling down in New York, cobbling a life out of part-time jobs and the small joys of free time at odd moments. I was writing, but my efforts were too diffused. Maybe in a new place I could find fresh subjects.

Wine had become a serious interest for both of us. I stumbled on Bordeaux in 1979 after a year in Spain; out of money, I came for the harvest and found work picking grapes in Entre-Deux-Mers. The enormous crop left me with scarred hands and an aching back, but I made friends and returned with Sara a couple of times. We had met in Paris, and traveled widely through France; in the vineyards, we discovered a world that gave equal weight to work and pleasure. In New York, I worked as a bartender and wine buyer, and the more I tasted good wine, the more I wanted to learn about it. I thought France would be the best of all schools.

The evening air chilled. The church tower had turned to copper and rose. No one in the world we knew, knew where we were. The light dimmed and stars came out. At the other end of the chestnut path, cars stopped. Doors slammed, people called, a streetlight came on and threw pink light over the *mairie* tower.

"The Mayor said that Ruch had everything we needed," Sara said.

"Who would know better?"

I stood up, pulled Sara to her feet. "Let's go meet these people of Ruch."

We picked our way gingerly along the dark pathway. A car pulled in front of the cemetery and three young men climbed out. We followed them through a gateway by the *mairie* and into a courtyard where more cars were parked and laughter sounded through a closed door.

"This is where they keep the people," I murmured. "That's why the streets were empty today. They only come out for special occasions."

"What do you suppose they call them? Ruchians?"

"Ruchettes?"

"Ruchers."

"Ruchini. Ruchelais."

We climbed concrete steps. The building looked like a warehouse. Light leaked around the edges of a plywood door. We pushed through to a large room bright with bare fluorescent bulbs. Trestle tables were set in a long row, with folding chairs scattered around. Children tore across the room laughing. Women sat in a line against a wall, watching them. Young men in a group looked at the women. Old men watched it all.

Two girls careened to a stop at our feet. Curiosity struggling against shyness, they stole a look at us. *"Eh alors!"* said a dark-haired fellow, then *"Bonsoir."* He smiled at Sara, a look between a welcome and a leer. She blushed. The girls giggled and fled. No one else seemed to notice our entrance. We spotted the Mayor among the older men and drifted his way.

"Bonsoir," we said.

He smiled amiably. "So. How did you like the presbytère? It's old, but it has heart. Like me," he added to the others.

"That's about all you've got left," snorted a thin-lipped man.

"What would you like to drink?" asked the Mayor, ignoring him. "Tonight there's sangria." He led us over to the bar; a teenager at a card table poured sangria for us and swapped his empty beer for a full one.

I sipped the sweet wine punch. "We do like the presbytère. We'd like to live there. But we need to talk about the rent."

The Mayor waved his hand. "Oh, there's time for that. There's two things we always have time for in this world, pay bills and die."

"But we want to move in tomorrow. We have to leave our house in Branne."

"You're in Branne now?"

"Well, nearby."

"Where?"

"A village called Guillac."

"Sure." He nodded. "The Lurtons own all the vines around there."

"Yes, we're staying in one of their houses. But the pickers are coming soon."

"You know the Lurtons?"

"Well, a little."

He took a long pull at his beer. We sipped sangria.

"We could offer a thousand francs a month. We'd pay for the heat, of course."

He took another swallow of beer. Smoke thickened the air, and the children's voices echoed like the church bells. A girl clung to the old man's leg and he talked with her, their chatter unintelligible to me. Then he turned to us.

"We don't set the prices for the *gîte*. The *gîte* organization in Bordeaux does that. I can't promise they'd agree to that price even if we asked for it." He paused. "But I do agree in principle, and I'm sure it will work out. At any rate, you can move in and we'll come to some arrangement."

Sara gave a happy laugh. He smiled at her. "Now enjoy your dinner," he said. "I'm paying for this one. I promised the teams a ham if they won today, and so they did."

Sheets of rough paper had been thrown over the tables and two dozen places set. Women carried plates loaded with bricks of pâté, sliced tomatoes, small pickles.

"Isn't it time to eat yet?" he called.

"We're waiting for the bread," someone responded.

Just then a tall man appeared with an armful of long loaves. Everyone moved to the tables. We sat next to an old man who spoke in a harsh croak. We introduced ourselves but couldn't understand his name and weren't sure he understood ours. The fellow with the two girls sat down next to Sara.

"I'm Serge. Were you at the soccer game today?"

"No."

"Too bad. I scored a goal. Then what brings you to Ruch? We're not exactly on the main road."

"We want to live here."

"*Bien sûr!* Doesn't everyone?" He said something to the young woman across from him that made her smile.

Wine bottles, big magnums without labels, made their way down the table. The men filled plastic cups to the rim.

"What's the wine?" I asked my gray-haired neighbor.

"Red," he croaked.

I repeated my question to Serge.

"It's from the *cave*. Wine from Ruch. My grapes are in there. I have the smallest vineyard in town. Five rows."

He drank freely. Most of the men did. The few women who took wine cut it heavily with water. After the pâté came steaming casseroles of macaroni and cheese. Men cut bread with pocketknives, mopped their plates. When the ham was served, the Mayor made a short speech, greeted by cheers and catcalls. We couldn't catch much. We let ourselves sink into a little bubble of English.

Two groups of soccer players traded taunts and laughter. A piece of bread whizzed down the table. Someone started a chant: *Allez les bleus, allez les blancs,* go blue and white. There were cheers, there were gestures, more bread thrown. A tomato flew through the air and splashed against the white shirt of a red-faced man.

"*Ah, zut alors!*"

Sara and I giggled—we had never heard that actually said before. He said more, loudly, and as he got angrier, the crowd laughed harder, and finally he stomped out of the hall.

We decided to leave, too. We said goodbye to the Mayor, who paid little attention, and arranged with Madame Lunardelli to meet at the presbytère the next morning. Outside on the steps we met the red-faced man coming back. He had changed his shirt. As the door closed behind him a cheer went up.

The night air tasted like mineral water. The black sky was dense with stars. The pinkish glow of the lamp washed over the *mairie*. Inside the hall, there was singing and rhythmic pounding, but the streets were empty and dark. In the distance, a dog barked. An owl swooped through the light, eyes gleaming, and vanished. We had found it: our new home.

2

A Stranger in the Cave

Inside, the presbytère was clean but stale, like a motel room empty for weeks.

Behind the decor, though, was a fortress. In the sixteenth century, when the building was begun, the Wars of Religion ravaged Entre-Deux-Mers and every church was a battleground. The priests and their patient masons built thick stone walls and made few windows. We wanted air and light. Our first morning, we opened all the windows; an instant later, all the doors slammed shut. We jumped at the attack, but it was only the house teaching us a lesson about buildings on bluffs and powerful drafts. We adjusted until the house gave us a steady airing breeze.

We had never had so much room, or so little baggage. We mopped the tile floors, washed the dishes, and sharpened the knives. In the big room downstairs we set an oak table by the window, pulled armchairs near the fireplace. Sara put a pinecone on the mantel. I chose an upstairs room for my office, moved a desk under the west-facing window, and dragged in another for files. We took the mattress off sagging box springs in the largest bedroom and put it on the floor. The room nearest the church would be for guests, we decided, if any came to stay.

The mornings were foggy and dim. We felt invisible, slipping through shrouded streets. We lingered over long breakfasts of fresh bread and café au lait. The damp chill made the strong coffee and steaming milk taste even better.

We discovered that the big crusty loaves of bread and *Sud Ouest,* the local paper, arrived early at the store and sold fast. I got into the habit of going for both before breakfast. If I timed it right, the bread was still warm on the shelf.

The Galeries Ruchelaises, with its plate-glass window and streamlined sign, lay at the heart of the little village. The store could have stocked a desert island. Fluorescent lights flickered on produce, canned goods, a meat and cheese counter, pots and pans, guns, boots, wines and liquors, hardware, stationery, magazines, candy, and an electronic cash register by the door. The bread was stacked in back, near the produce and the meat counter, where a tall thin man with a mustache sharpened his knife and chatted with old women. A sign on the wooden racks asked customers not to touch the loaves, for reasons of hygiene.

More old ladies gathered by the register, where a lively black-haired woman took their money and made them laugh. Young men pulled up in cars for cigarettes and newspapers, put imaginary guns to their shoulders, squeezed imaginary triggers. *"Pam! Pam!"* An old man on an ancient bicycle doffed his beret in greeting and picked up a loaf of bread and a liter of red wine.

I got in line. The woman added up my purchases.

"Three francs fifty for the bread. Three twenty the paper. Six francs seventy, please."

"My name's Thomas," I said, handing her a ten-franc piece. "I'm American. I live in the presbytère."

She nodded. "Welcome to Ruch, Mr. . . . Thomas." She put my change on the counter.

"No, just Thomas. First name."

"Welcome all the same."

One morning the small crowd clustered around a crate of bulbous brown mushrooms. They had the color and size of buns. They were marked at 70 francs a kilo, five times as much as the white button mushrooms they called *champignons de Paris*. I asked the shopkeeper what they were.

"*Cèpes,*" he said. "Don't you have them in America?"

"I don't think so," I said. "What are they like?"

"They're the king of mushrooms!" He waved his arms. "Oh, in Périgord they talk about truffles, but nobody really eats them. They're mostly fake anyway. *Cèpes* grow wild, and when the autumn fog comes, they multiply like little rabbits. The best come from oak forests. Every old peasant knows where to find them. Cook them the same day you pick them, in a little oil with garlic and parsley, and drink the best red wine you have. *Mon Dieu!* Then you'll know what *cèpes* are like."

I leaned over to catch their meaty, earthy smell and was tempted to splurge. A clatter at the door saved me. An old woman had tripped at the entrance, knocked a few cans off a shelf, managed to right herself. "*Merde!*" she growled. "There's no room for old people in this world." Her gray hair was wild around her head. She grabbed a bottle of ruby Port, shouted "Mark it down, Madame," and barged out the door again. I could hear her singing in the street as I made my way to the *mairie*.

"Ah well. She's singing again."

I had stopped in for photocopies. A woman in a black dress was shaking her head at Madame Tallon. "It won't be long before she's sick."

"What's to do?" Madame Tallon shrugged. "If she wants to kill herself . . ."

"She came into the store," I said.

"In the streets or the cemetery or anyplace, making a nuisance," Madame Tallon said. "Madame Pagant lives in the house on the corner, but even when she stays inside she makes a nuisance. People have seen her dancing nude in her garden. Haven't they, Jeanette? Madame Barde lives by the church. She can tell you stories . . ."

"She's really just lonely, I think," Madame Barde said. "She's from Paris. She says her husband was a diplomat in Africa, and when he died she stuck a pin in the map of France and wound up here. That was ten years ago. Life hasn't always been easy."

Madame Pagant and Bill

Madame Tallon sniffed. "I don't believe a word she says."

"I go to the store every morning," I said. "But I still don't know the people who run it."

"Oh yes, the Bretons. She's Marie-Jo, he's Gérard. I rarely go there myself. Do you go, Jeanette?"

Jeanette shrugged. "Sometimes."

"They seem very friendly."

Madame Tallon's fluffy blond hair bobbed. "Some would say too friendly."

During the day, the shopkeepers and the secretary were the only people in town. Almost everyone else was in the vineyards. The buzz of the harvesting machines rose and fell as long as there was light. Tractors rumbled through the village pulling loads of grapes. One evening we saw two or three dozen of them lined up outside the cooperative winery, backed out the driveway and up the hill, engines idling, men talking in small groups. Lined, grimy faces were rosy in the twilight. There was an infinity of fruit.

One sunny morning I followed the road out of town, climbed between vineyards to the crest of a ridge. Grapes littered the roadside, crushed by traffic, nipped by birds, brown, dry, and wrinkled. Dirt clods incised with deep curved lines told of tractor tires, individual as fingerprints. Some vineyard parcels were still heavy with grapes, others had been picked clean. Magpies hopped as if drunk through the rows. Crushed cigarette packs glittered in the ditch by the road. The warming sun infused the air with a sweet, earthy scent. I tried to read the fallen grapes like tea leaves.

Ruch lay on a broad ridge running east and west, with the village built on its southern edge. The north slope dropped steeply to the Gamage, a stream that met the Dordogne ten kilometers farther north. On the very edge of the bluff, the gray stone pile of the Château de Vaure commanded a view of the Dordogne River plain to the west and north. The cooperative was just below it.

The main buildings sat back from the road, concrete painted white with red accents. A huge old oak stood halfway down the drive, its crown sixty feet high, its muscular branches seventy-five feet across. Behind the tree, a concrete slab carved into the hillside anchored a dozen gleaming steel vats, blinding contrast to the weatherbeaten cement. The winery buildings, modest from the front, expanded as the hill dropped away to a lower driveway. Red lettering on a long wall proclaimed CAVE COOPERATIVE DE RUCH, 1936.

At nine o'clock, the cooperative was peaceful, picturesque. The wide cement loading dock looked like a veranda. Young men in blue work-suits stretched in the sun, glanced at a blond woman who sat in a glass-walled booth. A tractor with a trailer full of black grapes was backed up to one of the bins.

"What kind are they?" I asked the farmer who sat on the tractor. A small man in his forties, he had a red, deeply lined face and sad, tired eyes.

"Merlot."

Merlot is one of the three principal red-wine grape varieties grown in Bordeaux, along with Cabernet Sauvignon and Cabernet Franc. It dominates the vineyards of nearby Saint-Émilion and Pomerol, whose wines sell for high prices, so it has become very popular in northern Entre-Deux-Mers. The grape ripens early, but it is thin-skinned and susceptible to rot. Its big red-purple berries grow in loose, irregular bunches. The bunches gleamed in the sun. A few bees crawled over the load.

"Picked by hand?"

He nodded.

"They must be hard workers. It's still early."

"Not that early." He called to one of the blue-suited fellows. "Hey, let's get going here!" The man shrugged and walked into the building. The farmer snorted. "They only work three weeks a year, and they can't even do that right. We started early this morning because there's rot setting in. It was too wet last week, and too hot now."

I made a motion toward the grapes that meant could I try some and he nodded. I picked up a small bunch and ate one. The skin was tough, but the pulp was juicy and sweet. It was cool and fresh.

"You like it?"

I nodded.

"Are you English?"

"American. I'm in the presbytère."

"On vacation?"

"I'm a journalist, interested in wine. I'm going to stay in Ruch for a while."

He thought that over. A deep horn sounded, then a loud clanging bell. A big screw set in the bottom of the bin began to turn. The blonde in the booth made a circling motion with her hand.

The farmer waved back and reached for a lever on his tractor. The motor raced and the trailer started to tilt up. He jumped off, hopped to the back of the trailer, and undid the pins that held the gate closed. Juice trickled, then poured under the gate. The trailer rose higher and the mass of grapes broke free, sliding into the bin with a whoosh and a thump. The gate clanged shut, dust rose from the bin, and the horn sounded again. The farmer hopped back on his tractor, raced the engine, and pulled away as the trailer descended. The day had begun.

Four other tractors had arrived to unload. The sad-eyed farmer parked off to the side, then came back to the booth and took a ticket from the woman's assistant. I followed him in. The woman nodded at me.

"What's that?" I asked.

"My score card." He studied it, then handed it to me. It read: 3,700 kilograms, 11.2 degrees. "That's the weight of the load and the degree of sugar in the juice. That's how we get paid. Not too bad, this time. *Chêne Vert* always ripens well."

"*Chêne vert?*" That meant green oak, I thought.

"That's the name of the vineyard parcel."

"Ah. My name's Thomas. What's yours?"

"Bordas. Roger Bordas."

We shook hands. The next tractor swung into the loading bay. The horn sounded, the screw turned, the trailer tilted, and the grapes slid into view, a soupy purple mass marbled with gray mold.

Bordas snorted. "That's the harvesting machine. How'd you like a taste of those, eh?"

The grapes sloshed into the bin, splashing juice onto the concrete deck, a thin dust of mold rising into the air. There were no whole bunches, just loose berries, crushed pulp, and juice. The screw turned, and the weight came up on the control panel: 4,050 kilos. The youth sampling the juice for sugar held his refractometer to the light and whistled. Thirteen point four, he called out. The woman shook her head.

The grower entered the control booth to pick up his slip. The woman looked at him with questions in her eyes. These grapes had gone way beyond maturity; many were rotten. A winery with exacting standards might reject them, for the mold could infect the rest of the wine, turn the vats to vinegar.

"The rain, the heat," muttered the farmer, a stout fellow with wispy gray hair and wide eyes. "A third of the crop in that field is just lying on the ground. I'm working as fast as I can, but you know how fast the rot moves. Most of the fruit is still fine, anyway."

The morning wore on and traffic built up, mostly machine-picked loads. I began to see patterns. Most of the men were wearing blue, for instance, in jumpsuits, jeans, and work pants, T-shirts, lab coats, sneakers or straw-soled slippers, caps. They all seemed to have put on whatever came closest to hand in the morning. But the consistency implied some consensus. I was wearing gray cotton trousers, a maroon warm-up jacket that said *Martell Cognac* on it, and a New York Yankees cap. I felt out of place.

Tractors made another statement, and so did their drivers' hats: green tweed cap driving a red Ford, black beret and a blue Renault, billed rugby cap and a green Massey-Ferguson. The tractors looked newer than the hats. One old fellow boasted that his machine had lasted since the war, but the admiring glances went to the models with Plexiglas cabs, upholstered seats, and built-in stereos.

The unloading operation took about ten minutes. The tractors backed in, the grapes tumbled into the bin, the screw stripped the berries from the stalks, then crushed the fruit. As noon approached, a line built up, but the drivers didn't mind a short wait. They left the motor running, set the brake, and wandered up and down the line to talk with friends. On a bench by the control booth, wine in gallon bag-in-boxes refreshed the thirsty—dry white, sweet white, and an off-dry rosé. Men filled sticky tumblers, drained them, and set them down without ceremony.

A fellow in a blue lab coat brought a foaming jug from inside the winery. It drew a crowd, and he brought me a glassful.

"What is it?"

"The *bourru.*"

"The what?"

"The *bourru,* the new wine. This is the white. It's just been fermenting for two days now."

The liquid was cloudy, tinted green, and fizzy. Its flavors mingled grapey sweetness, lemony tartness, and the sharp heat of alcohol.

"Generally you drink it with roasted chestnuts," the fellow continued. "They ripen about now, and the sweetnesses are nice together. But don't take too much. You'll spend more time at the toilet than the table. Do you like it?"

I nodded.

"I made it. That's my job here. This region could make good white wines, if the *cave* would buy the right machinery."

"Why doesn't it?"

"Farmers don't like to spend money."

He said his name was Chiron, that he had been at the cooperative for two years, after school in viticulture and winemaking. The woman in the booth was his wife, Sylvie. They lived in the small house with the flower garden. He said it made it easy to get to work but hard to get away.

"But you have to be there for the whites," he said. "The reds make themselves. The whites you have to baby along."

He drew me into the winery. We stood on a catwalk above two presses, a dozen enormous vats rising around us. The air was sweet, the concrete floor sticky with juice; motors rumbled and metal clanged. The big dark room vibrated with heat and noise.

Chiron explained that all the grapes were crushed and destemmed in the bins outside. The red grapes were simply pumped into the big vats to steep, like tea, with their skins and seeds. The natural yeasts clinging to the skins would kick off the fermentation and the maceration would turn the juice deep red.

"You just draw it off after a couple of weeks and, *voilà,* you have wine. But for the whites, you press the juice from the grapes first and ferment it by itself. That's called the must. It has to be clean. It's delicate. The temperature must be kept down—that protects the aromas—but the system for that here! We just drip cool water down the sides of the vats. We should have steel tanks with temperature controls, but we can't afford it. The prices for white wine are too low—only a third of the red. The farmers don't care, anyway. People don't join a cooperative because they want to make the best wine possible. They join to sell off their grapes and have the winters free for hunting."

Even Ruch's best wines were at the bottom of the Bordeaux hierarchy, so the growers' insouciance wasn't too surprising. Entre-Deux-

The cooperative during the 1986 harvest

Mers was primarily a source of bulk wine for blending, and it had been that way for centuries.

Long experience has convinced the French that wine made honestly and traditionally would reflect the qualities of the *terroir* that nourished it. *Terroir* translates loosely as character expressed in geography—the combination of soil, slope, sunshine, and rain that distinguishes one place from any other. In 1986, the vineyards around Bordeaux covered a quarter of a million acres and produced 75 million cases of wine. The winemakers and their customers made finely graded distinctions of quality and price on the basis of *terroir*. Over centuries of vintages, certain districts of Bordeaux had become famous—Margaux, Pauillac, Saint-Émilion. Within these small territories, the great châteaux—Lafite-Rothschild, Latour—were the pinnacles of specificity. Connoisseurs claimed these *terroirs* were so singular that their wines could be identified by taste alone.

French wine law assigns *appellations,* formal names, to geographic ensembles that share related *terroirs*. The larger they are, in general, the less distinguished. The biggest *appellation* in Bordeaux is simply "Bordeaux," for red and white, and that's basically what the Ruch cooperative produced, along with "Entre-Deux-Mers," for its dry white wine. Prices for these wines were a long way from Latour. I was curious to know if the *terroir* of Ruch had any specific, distinctive character, whether the people who made wine here searched for it, whether I could find it.

At 1:10 the last tractor in line emptied its trailer and headed home for lunch. During the morning, the cooperative had taken in forty-nine loads, nine harvested by hand. As the dust settled in the driveway, cooking smells wafted from the winery. Chiron explained that they all ate together.

"It smells good," I said.

"Ah, Colette!"

At 1:25 three fellows with grape-stained hands emerged from the winery. *"À la soupe!"* Everybody filed inside. There was sudden quiet. No more grinding, pumping, revving, honking, shouting. Only the tinkle of glasses, and the faint music of a faraway radio.

I walked back home. Sara had tossed a salad of lamb's-lettuce, tomatoes, and the sweetest carrots we had ever tasted, with olive oil and red wine vinegar. We slathered ripe, gooey Camembert over thick slices of bread.

"The store is cute," she said. "But it's deceiving. You think they have everything under the sun, and then you discover that there's only three kinds of cheese and no fresh milk at all. I like Marie-Jo, though. She said my accent was good."

She had spent the morning writing letters, then chatting with the postman.

"His name is Ithier; he's from the north. He makes his rounds on a bicycle and says the harvest season is a pain because there are tractors all over the roads. But when it's over, he'll take a vacation and go hunting. He had some mail for us, but he didn't know where to deliver it. He said he'll slip it under the back door from now on. He lives right there, in the post office. His wife was sitting in the doorway knitting. When he talked about hunting, she rolled her eyes."

I walked back to the cooperative about 2:30. The sky was clear, the sun hot.

Down the hill, a long line of tractors snaked back out the courtyard and into the road, all the trailers full of grapes. There wasn't any noise. Both bins were full of grapes, but the crushing screws weren't turning. Blue-suited workmen crawled over the machinery. A stocky man in blue coveralls pointed and shouted, and I recognized the fellow who had been hit with the tomato at the soccer dinner. He was just as angry now.

Bordas leaned against the loading dock. "What's going on?" I asked him.

"The press for the white grapes clogged and stopped right after lunch. It happens a lot—it's old, that press. Now the red crusher is down. Probably something stuck in the screw. They have to find it before they can turn the machine back on." He nodded toward the fellow shouting. "Chatelier's in charge of that."

Chatelier, short, stocky, and red-faced, shouted at a youth in rubber boots and swimming briefs wading through the purple muck in the crusher. With purple stains on his pale body and a mien of weary distaste, he looked like a medieval martyr being boiled alive for his faith.

"He's digging for whatever's jamming the crusher," Chiron told me. "It could be almost anything. Look what we've already pulled out of there this week." He pointed toward the control booth, where driftwood and scrap metal sat along the top of the weighing machine.

"This rarely happened before the harvesting machines," he went on. "No picker would leave a vine branch or a metal stake in his basket— it'd be too heavy. But the machines scoop up everything, and it all gets dumped in the vats. Next thing, breakdown. Once we found a wrench in there, new, expensive. It was only a little scratched when we pulled it out. No one ever claimed it."

They fixed the machines and it took nearly an hour to work away the backlog of tractors. Then, for a moment, the courtyard was empty, the bins were empty, and the world came to a halt. The sunlight fell thick and warm. The tinkle of a cowbell carried across the valley from a bright green meadow. The young martyr lay stretched out on a wooden bench. In repose, his wiry limbs and stained skin looked even more like those of a figure from some medieval manuscript of the end of days.

The pace picked up through the afternoon, work going smoothly. The farmers' hats were dark with sweat. Their hands were grimy with grapeskins and machine oil. Their teeth were stained by cigarettes. Their clothes were slick with dirt. They said a few words when they collected their tickets but didn't linger, rarely drank the wine. The sun started to slip in the sky. Everyone knew it could rain tomorrow. The grapes would be safe only in the vats.

The hundredth load of the day came in at 6:30, as the light began to fade. The shadow of the oak tree reached out the driveway to the road; across the valley, west-facing buildings on the ridge turned rosy. The Mayor parked his tractor and poured himself a glass of wine. A few jokes later he was in the center of a knot of drinking men.

Watching the group swell with new arrivals, I began to decipher another pattern: the code of greeting. There's a hierarchy of intimacy. It begins with a blankness between strangers, a careful neutrality. Eye contact prompts a nod, short and sharp. Once introduced, people shake hands. Those related by blood or long familiarity, who use the intimate *tu* form of address rather than the impersonal *vous,* exchange kisses on each cheek. Young people kiss friends four times.

This hierarchy is not only well established, it is also iron-clad. Once you have reached the handshake level, you must always shake hands on the first meeting of the day. If you part after a social event, you shake hands again. If thirty people were at a party, and you were on a handshake level with all of them, you would shake hands thirty times when you left. If you only nod to some, those people will think you are cutting them. The rules seemed arcane, but the rough-hewn men acted upon them with sureness and grace. I stood with them on the narrow porch of the loading bay, invisible as a stone is to the stream that flows around it.

"Et alors, Thomas." It was the Mayor. "Everything all right in Ruch?"

"Fine. So far, we like it here just fine."

"Good. Let me know if there's anything I can do." He started to move away.

"Well."

"Eh?"

"I wanted to spend a day with a picking team. But not many people still pick by hand. Could you suggest someone?"

"Oh, that's the way we do it. We're old-fashioned, I guess. You want to come with us tomorrow?"

"Would you mind?"

"Not at all. Come by before eight, though. That's when we leave."

"Thanks."

He nodded. *"C'est pas grand-chose, eh?"*

Fluorescent lights came on over the loading bays, and a green spot flashed to signal the growers to dump their grapes. Headlights dazzled and brake lights flared as the tractors turned into the yard. The air was thick with road dust, tractor exhaust, cigarette smoke, clouds of mold. Night fell. The girls were gone, the boys after them, and only strangers crowded the control booth, their faces hard with fatigue and impatience. The machines banged away. The wooden bench that held the wine cartons was sticky with spills, the glasses lay empty on the concrete floor.

At 8:45, load number 132 tumbled in the bin, and done. All the tractors gone, all the farmers sitting down to dinner. The young men in the jumpsuits hosed down the bins and surfaces, and the noise slowly diminished. The doors to the kitchen opened, incandescent light spilling out warm and welcoming. Time to eat. Another day safely stored away.

I walked back to town in darkness unbroken by streetlights. No moon, but a sky full of stars. Few sounds—dogs barking in the distance, the low throb of cicadas, a snatch of television from an open window. The night had swallowed the day, and nothing remained of its restlessness but the sweet smell of grape juice rising from warm asphalt.

3

Harvesting by Hand

The next morning, mist hung like smoke in the vineyards that bordered
the road, coiled damp against my face and hands. Across a rising field, the
Mayor's house loomed over the village. It hovered faint as a dream,
haloed by the rays of sun that fought through the fog.

The house was built of the same gray stone as its neighbors, but it was
larger and more symmetrical than most. Three ornamental lightning rods
gave it a Victorian dignity. It was a bourgeois embellishment on the local
farmhouse plan, sturdy yet meant at least partly for show.

A girl's laughter sounded somewhere around the back, so I climbed
narrow stone steps to find the front door facing the fields. The yard had
been fenced for a chicken coop and rabbit hutch. Behind it, vineyards
climbed to the horizon. A dozen people were scattered around the door,
adjusting raincoats and boots, talking, smoking, gazing into the fog.

I didn't see the Mayor; I didn't know anyone there. No one greeted
me. I gave a general nod and leaned up against the house. After a little
while, tractor engines fired up, and there was a slow drift down the steps.
A young man I recognized from the soccer team was sitting on one
tractor, the Mayor on another.

"*Ah, bonjour, Thomas. Ça va?*" He smiled and shook my hand. I nodded. "That's my grandson, Claude." He pointed to the other tractor. Claude was talking to two girls in sweatsuits. "Go with him." He raised his voice. *"À la vigne!"*

The girls and two young men climbed into the empty trailer behind Claude's tractor, so I joined them. The trailer was sticky with juice. Crushed grapes, leaves, and twigs stuck to its cold metal sides. Sweet and sharp aromas mingled with the cool moist air. The ride was too bumpy for conversation. We rolled through the village, then west past the soccer field and off the road into the vines. A few minutes' meandering brought us to an open space, and the tractor halted. We climbed out.

They all knew their places. Twelve pickers paired up, two to a row: the girls together, a balding man and his wife speaking Spanish, the Mayor and a tiny old woman wrapped in green rain gear. Claude and two other young men strapped plastic tubs on their backs and leaned against fenceposts at the end of the rows. One lit a cigarette.

I stayed near the tractor, climbing onto a dented fender for the engine's fading warmth and a view of the vines. There were white grapes in this parcel. They grew in long bunches of small golden berries flecked with brown, the color of a translucent banana. I ate some. The fruit was sweet but mealy, the juice almost sugary.

The vines rose about four feet off the ground, their grapes tucked under the foliage close to the gnarled trunks, obliging the cutters to stoop and kneel and squat. Their interlocking movements were a dance, set to the music of murmured conversation, the sharp click of the scissors, the rustle of branches. They snipped away the bunches of grapes, dropped them into small plastic baskets. The panniers held two dozen bunches or so, the fruit of three or four vines. The porters patrolled the rows, and pickers emptied panniers into their big plastic tubs. After four or five, the tubs were full and the porters dumped them into the trailer at the end of the row. The cycle took about ten minutes.

I watched Claude. His climb and bow to empty his tub were without flourish, graceful with economy. He perched on the edge of the trailer, ate some grapes, and fiddled with a radio looped to his belt. Low strains of pop music, some American tune.

"Claude?"

Claude Bonvoisin dumping grapes

He looked over, dark eyes under a fringe of black hair. Twenty or so, I guessed, and slim, with a sidelong glance at the world.

"Aren't you on the soccer team?"

He nodded.

"You won last week, didn't you?"

He nodded again. "One zero, against Montanou. Wany scored with a header off a corner. We knew we could do it, but it sure surprised them!"

"And good weather. Not like this fog."

"Oh, it'll burn off. Fog is better than rain. It's hard to work when it's hot."

He hopped off the trailer and moved back into the field. Another porter came up, a big square fellow with a strong jaw. He had to steady himself before he swung the tub over, then swing twice to empty it completely.

"Bonjour."

"Bonjour," he replied. "Enjoying yourself?"

"The vineyards are beautiful, and the grapes are sweet. And you?"

"I take my holiday every year to do this."

"What do you do the rest of the time?"

"I'm in the army."

He introduced himself, Jean-Paul Grangier. He told me his parents were Ruchelais, farmers, neighbors of the Mayor. Jean-Paul lived in Libourne, fifteen miles away, in army housing. "I miss the countryside, so I come back."

I followed him into the rows. The Mayor stood to empty his pannier and spotted me.

"Did you get tired of sitting on the tractor?"

The diminutive old woman across the row cackled. "He wanted to see if you were really working, Beber."

"And who's been cutting longer, Jeanette? Me or you?"

Jean-Paul bent for her. She cranked back, emptied her pannier with a vigorous swoop that propelled a few grapes down his collar. *"Eh alors!"* He straightened to scoop them out, and the others laughed.

"It's not Jeanette that needs help," said the Mayor, shaking his head.

Across the row, the two girls chattered, disheveled and pretty. Their panniers were only half full.

"Hey, you two, your tongues move faster than your clippers," Jean-Paul chided.

The one close to him, blond and freckled, stood and emptied her pannier. Her partner across the row continued cutting.

"Come on, Nathalie, I'm waiting for you." She ignored him. "I guess your ears don't work as well as your mouth."

She stood, brown eyes flashing. "You're not in the army here, Jean-Paul." He turned for her pannier, and as she emptied her grapes, she pinched him hard.

"Hey!" He hopped away, and all four pickers laughed. "These women are dangerous!"

The pickers made slow progress down the rows, paths marked by scattered leaves. The shake and rustle of the branches sounded like a lazy breeze. Occasionally we could hear the grumble of a harvesting machine in the distance, or Claude would turn up his radio for a favorite song. Mostly there was quiet, except for the voices and the snap of the scissors.

When one row was finished, those first done would help the laggards, then they'd count off the next six rows and start again. Claude moved the tractor down a few feet and reset the ladder against the trailer. Slowly, the trailer filled up, and I sorted out the crew.

Sebastián, a Catalan, left Spain at nineteen during the Civil War and had never returned. A mason, he worked the harvest every year. There's less dust, he said, it makes a nice change. He worked with his wife; they were very fast. Two country girls came in their own car, sisters and both out of work. They kept to themselves. The Mayor's wife shared a row with a middle-aged woman named Nicole, whose dyed blond hair and sharp tongue suggested she resented the passage of time. Marie-Do, whose husband worked in Bordeaux, was the mother of Thomas, the third porter. She teamed with a small quiet fellow who turned out to be the Mayor's son Francis.

And the two pretty girls. Babette, the blonde, said she was a seamstress, out of work, and Nathalie waited tables in nearby Saint-Émilion. This was their first *vendange;* they were tired and a little bored. But they were easy to talk to and I lingered with them, slowing their pace even more.

Sebastián reached the end of a row, tossed his grapes into the trailer, and called, *"A la sopa!"* Five till noon, the trailer full. The others finished after him, save Nathalie and Babette, still struggling half a row behind.

"Come on, Nathalie," called Nicole, hands on hips. "You're not in the bistro now. The soup's at the end of the row!"

Nathalie ducked her head and the others pitched in to finish the row. Claude drove the full trailer to the cooperative, and the rest piled into two old cars to return to the Mayor's house for lunch. I hesitated.

"Eh, Thomas," called the Mayor. "Are you hungry?"

I nodded.

"Then come along. The soup is waiting!"

The village was lively with traffic, cars parked at crazy angles to the store. Tractors headed for the cooperative. At the Bonvoisins', the pickers shed jackets and boots and trooped into a long room fragrant with food. At one end, a wood stove laden with pots faced a large freezer. At the other, a single window looked into town. A long table was covered with an oilcloth and set with big earthenware bowls, bent cutlery, and glasses that must once have been mustard jars. Loaves of bread served as centerpieces.

Sara stood by the stove. She looked very American, tall and rangy, blue-eyed and freckled, next to the stocky, black-haired woman who was stirring an enormous pot. As I entered they were laughing, and the Frenchwoman used the familiar *tu* to ask Sara to hand her a bowl of salt.

"This is Nicole, Francis's wife," Sara told me. "I met her in the store this morning. I had to ask her why she was buying fifteen loaves of bread When she figured out I was with you and you were with the Mayor, she invited me over. We've been snapping green beans and gossiping. She's great."

The Mayor sat at the head of the table, flanked by Sebastián and Francis. The other men filled in the next seats, then the women, down to the Mayor's wife at the foot. Sara and I were placed on opposite sides just at the gender division.

"I went out walking with my camera," Sara told me, "but I didn't find you. Isn't the fog beautiful? Especially in the valley, where it just settles into the vines. I took pictures of a guy on a harvesting machine, about your age. He said his name was Philippe de Larrard. He's the grandson of the old doctor who lives in the château. Then I got a little cold, so I went to the store, for lunch. That's when I met Nicole."

Nicole took a pot off the stove and set it on the table. While she ladled soup into bowls passed around the table, the Mayor served *vin de noix,* thick brown walnut wine. Sweet and spicy, it tasted of alcohol and herbs. His wife made it from the leaves of the walnut tree by the house, steeped in red wine, brandy, and sugar; he claimed it honed the appetite and aided digestion. All the men drank. Sara and old Jeanette were the only women who took some.

The soup was simple, shredded cabbage in beef broth, but strong with long simmering. Francis opened a pocketknife, cut off a wedge of bread, and passed the loaf around. Everyone dipped into the soup. The first sip triggered a general sigh, and then quiet, save for spoons scraping against the bowls. The window steamed over.

When the soup was finished, conversation broke out. The Mayor started a magnum of wine around. The men filled their glasses. The women drank water, save Jeanette, who mixed hers half and half. Francis poured half a glassful into his empty soup bowl, swirled it around, then drained it at a swallow.

The Mayor noticed me watching his son. *"Le chabrol.* It's an old custom," he said. "Only the old-fashioned still do it."

Nicole brought out a tin tray heaped with rice. It was cold, dressed with oil and mustard, studded with corn, tomatoes, egg, and tuna. Sara complimented Nicole on the tomatoes. Nicole said they came from her garden, and the eggs from their chickens.

"There's a lot of corn planted around here," I said.

"That's for the pigs," Francis said. "We never used to eat it. This comes from a can."

Then Madame Bonvoisin brought out platters of sliced roast pork, bowls of peas and noodles, and a pitcher of dark greasy drippings. The men filled their bowls with food, then poured on the gravy and sopped it up with bread. More loaves appeared on the table. The wine went around again, too.

"What's this wine?" I asked Francis.

"Ordinary red, from the *cave*. It's good, isn't it?"

Dark red with a purple tinge, it looked young and raw, and was. It tasted of ripe grapes and tart red cherries, with a sharp, slightly bitter note that reminded me of crushed leaves. It had an edge sharp enough to cut through the pork fat, and plenty of fruit to match the strong flavors of the meal. The more I drank, the better it tasted.

We finished the meat and cleaned our plates with bread. Nicole brought out a green salad, soft leaves of garden lettuce tossed with oil and a smoky wine vinegar.

"You don't get vinegar like that in America," Sara said.

"It's nothing special," Madame Bonvoisin said. "I make it from the same wine you're drinking."

"Time is the secret," said the Mayor. "It's been sleeping in a keg with its mother for ten years."

"Its mother?" Sara asked.

"That's the starter that makes it work," Madame Bonvoisin explained. "Like yeast for bread."

"The mother is the key," said blond Nicole. "A good mother can turn the ordinary into something special."

"Don't forget the holy spirit, Nicole." The Mayor paused. "That's where the men come in!"

Then came the cheeses, a whole Camembert and a large wedge of red-rimmed Edam. More wine; the seven and a half of us who were drinking were on our second magnum now. Francis turned his bowl over and cut cheese onto its bottom. "That's another thing the old men do," said the Mayor. "He's more old-fashioned than I am."

The women cleared the bowls and the cutlery; then Madame Bonvoisin poured small cups of strong filter coffee and passed them around with demitasse spoons. The sugar bowl followed close behind. Most people took two or three cubes. Sebastián took four. The Mayor offered brandy, but no one wanted any.

It was a quarter to two. Nathalie and Babette got up and went outside to smoke. Jean-Paul joined them. Slowly, we followed, to find the fog gone and the sun warming a languid afternoon. Thomas fell on the ground spread-eagled. Sebastián leaned up against a wall and tipped his cap over his eyes. The women struggled into their boots. For a few minutes, all was tranquil. Then the tractors fired up. *"À la vigne!"* the Mayor called, and we made our way down the steps, back to work. Sara grabbed her camera and jumped in, too.

We rumbled through town and into the vines. The spires of the church and the *mairie* rose above the compact mass of houses. The plateau was an emerald river of vines, running between the light green of the soccer field and the black green of the forest. The rolling rows flowed in and out of harmony; they were rigidly regular in the small parcels, then crazily random as the parcels jostled each other, but melted back into unity as distance smoothed broken patterns into continuous texture. The picture was simple as a child's drawing: soft hills under a blue dome, with green lines etched on a brown ground.

The wholeness held to the closest focus. The vines played with half a dozen colors from a single palette: the grayish brown of the splintery trunk wood, the nut brown of the branches, rusty edges on yellowing leaves, golden grapes flecked with copper. Even the moldy grapes, deep purple and soft black, married the colors of fruit and wood and earth.

"What are these grapes?" I asked the Mayor.

"Sémillon. We used to make sweet wine with them, but that's out of fashion now. These are some of the oldest vines I have. I planted them right after the war."

The pickers finished the parcel. The Mayor and Francis consulted and decided to move to a field of red grapes across town. The trailer was less than half full, but the Mayor climbed on the tractor to drive it down to the cooperative. Sara wandered toward town. The rest of us piled into cars or the trailer behind the other tractor. We bumped and rolled down narrow roads, no barriers between us and sun and wind. The patterns of the vine rows shifted like a kaleidoscope.

The new site was the Mayor's oldest parcel of Merlot—"These we planted after the freeze in '56," Francis said—rows of thick, gnarled vines trained close to the ground. They sloped gently down a southwest-facing field, open to the sun; the soil was the gravel-studded clay the variety likes best. Full clusters of fat dark fruit nestled against the rough vines. They were ripe and sweet, and it seemed a shame to lose them in the mass of grapes at the cooperative. But perhaps they would help balance the failings of the rotten grapes I had seen arrive the day before.

The pickers ranged themselves in the rows. With the Mayor missing, Jeanette was left alone. I asked Francis if the Mayor would return soon. He shrugged.

"What about Jeanette?" I asked.

"She's a fast worker. We'll help her at the end of the row."

"Would you mind if I cut for a while?"

He shrugged again. "Why not?"

I picked up the tools and moved down the row where Jeanette was working. She was on her knees, clipping furiously at the small branches that hid the grapes, squinting under the hat that shaded her face.

"Jeanette?"

No answer.

"Do you mind if I work with you for a while?"

"Eh?" She rocked back on her heels, squinted at me. *"Pourquoi pas?"*

I watched her for a minute, to get the hang of it. In 1979, when I had worked the harvest, I had been a porter, not a picker. Jeanette wasted no motion. The pannier was tucked right under the vine, against the trunk. She glared at the fruit, stripping leaves or cutting small branches to get access. Then she reached in with both hands, one cupping a bunch, twisting it to expose the short woody stem attached to the vine, the other darting in to snip with the scissors. The holding hand guided the falling bunch into the basket. She took the six bunches on the vine in just over a minute, never moving her feet or the pannier, just her scissors flashing in the sun.

The Mayor's clippers fit snugly in my hand, sticky with juice. A strong spring forced the blades wide; their edges had been filed sharp, the points blunted. I squatted, pushed the pannier under the vine, and looked for the grapes. A vine has two sides: the farmer trains the leaves to grow mostly on one, the bunches mostly on the other. Naturally, Jeanette was on the fruit-laden side, leaving me to face a small forest. I tried stripping a few leaves, but the movement threw me off balance. The branches were too thick to clip, so I pushed them aside and burrowed in for the grapes. This left my visibility limited, however, and my hands working mostly by feel.

The bunches rarely hung free but wrapped themselves in creepers and clung to branches and wires. The coiled necks were hard to find. The searching scissors often buried themselves in grape pulp, and sticky juice drained down my fingers. The bunches seldom dropped straight into the pannier but bounced through the branches like a pinball, as often as not ending on the ground.

We picked a dozen vines. Jeanette took four bunches to every one of mine, and seemed to be moving slower than before. My back began to hurt, and the joints in my knees. Jean-Paul came for our panniers. It was a relief to stand, but his little smile made me blush. I shifted to a stooped standing position for a dozen vines. My knees were better, but my neck began to ache. I decided to work on my knees.

"It's hard on the back," said Jeanette. She wasn't sympathizing, simply noting a fact. "But you get used to it."

"How long does that take?"

"Well, I've picked grapes for more than forty years, and sometimes my back still hurts."

"I can't wait that long," I said, trying the work with one knee on the ground.

Jeanette cackled. "Oh, you learn to wait if you have to."

I looked up and caught her glance, eyes blue stones bright in the sun. She hardly had back to hurt, standing even with the vines, scarcely over four feet tall. She wasn't a dwarf, though; she had grown old in the shape of a child. Her skin was dark and wrinkled, but her grin was mischievous and young. Under a round-brimmed hat, she looked like a mushroom brought to life by elves.

"Forty years. That's a lot of grapes." We snipped along. "Do you remember any harvests in particular?"

"Nineteen fifty-six," she said. "That year the winter frosts killed so many vines we finished picking in a week. All those dead vines were terrible to see." She shook her head. "Terrible."

"How about a good year?"

"This year's not bad. A very big crop."

"Have you always worked in the vineyards?"

"And not only that." She chuckled. "Mostly I was inside the house, but when there was work to do in the vines, they called me out. I worked for the doctor, you see."

"The doctor?"

"Yes, at Vaure. I started when I was a girl. My mother was there, too. Oh, he worked us hard, but he worked hard himself. He birthed nearly every person in this town. And I washed all the linen afterward!"

She began a low, tuneless hum. We worked our way through the rows, and the various pains settled into a general dull ache that became part of the background, like the sun warm on my neck or the juice sticky on my hands. Twice I cut myself with the scissors, drawing blood. Then the juice became an enemy, a stinging trickle that confirmed my clumsiness.

I lost track of the other pickers. My field of vision narrowed to the green thicket and the purple wedges woven inside it. Even Jeanette blurred out of focus as I crawled through the vines. I studied the delicate veining in the leaves, the differences in depth and glossiness from one vine to the next. There were greens from yellow to black, and yellows from gold to green. Every vine was different, young or old, sick or sturdy. I began to see patterns, how the bunches grew from the branch, one under, hanging straight and easy to cut, the next over the top, twisted and hard to free. I admired the abundant vines, the shapely clusters, the sweet, healthy fruit.

There were sounds of rustling leaves and snapping branches. People sighed and spat. Occasionally there was the scratch and hiss of a match lighting a cigarette. Bees explored the bunches of grapes, careful and slow as tipsy old men. Magpies made jumpy shadows, always a few rows away. Snails clung to the trunks of the vines, and gossamer-winged bugs shot off when I brushed the branches.

Nathalie, Jean-Paul Grangier, and Madame Bonvoisin

Our scuffing and scraping released the loamy aroma of the heavy earth, and occasionally the scent of mint. Along one row I became aware of a strong smell of onions, and suspected Jeanette before I discovered wild scallions crushed under my feet. My grape consumption climbed with the time and temperature. Jeanette never ate even one. Stickiness from the juice climbed my arms. A grape dropped into my boot. My thoughts fell into a dreamy blur.

Francis called a break. Nicole had brought a jug of weak lemonade spiked with white wine. I complimented her on the lunch, and she grumbled about the effort of fixing it. "I hope we get a harvesting machine one day. It would make my life a lot easier."

"I like your cooking, too," said Jean-Paul. "And I like the work out here in the vines. Don't get a machine too soon."

"Then there would only be Bordas," blond Nicole said. "We'd have to work with his Spaniards."

"I miss the Spaniards," Nicole replied. "They ate anything. And you could trust them, mostly. Not like the Gypsies."

"I heard the Gypsies were stealing babies around Castillon," said Nathalie. "One of the girls in the restaurant knows someone who lost one."

"I can spare a few of mine," blond Nicole sighed.

"If you needed help to replace them, you could call on me," volunteered Sebastián.

"If you could remember how." Nicole Bonvoisin laughed.

"You're never too old to try!"

"No, thank you, I've had quite enough of that," the blond woman said. "Let Babette do it." Everyone looked at the girl. "Oh, don't blush. You'll find out. You may decide the Gypsies aren't so bad, after all!"

With that we straggled back to our rows. The light turned golden as we worked, until we had filled the trailer and had to stop because the Mayor still hadn't returned. Was it near enough to six to call it quits for the day? We gathered around the trailer to await Francis's decision.

Jean-Paul said it was too bad everyone didn't work at Nathalie's speed, because then the trailer would still have room. Nathalie made a face and a sharp remark, and he threw a grape at her. She shot one back, and Claude joined the battle.

The older women edged a little into the vines. I sat next to Sebastián, who pitched a few grapes into the melee with no particular target. At first Babette tossed a few bunches from behind the trailer, and Nathalie held her own. Then the blonde caught a bunch on her ear and retreated.

Nathalie's color was high; her mood mingled playfulness and anger. The men kept laughing, but their eyes were heated. They moved to close quarters and began crushing bunches of grapes against her skin and clothes. She wriggled and swore. She clipped Claude on the temple. It looked accidental, but drove him from the field.

The big man and the lithe girl struggled on, panting. Sebastián leaned forward, panting a little too. Nathalie seemed to lose force, her movements became languid. Jean-Paul gripped her from behind. As he squeezed the grapes into her cotton T-shirt, it clung to her breasts, clearly defined and free, her nipples erect. There were grapes in her hair, stuck to her arms, juice glistened on her neck. Suddenly he let go, and she slipped to the ground, leaned against his legs. She stayed there a moment, then they separated, without a word.

Sebastián relaxed. The women's voices rose a little. Babette helped her friend clean up. Francis decided the day was over. He would drive the trailer down to the cooperative. We were close to the village and could walk back home.

My way led past the Bonvoisins' house, so I walked along with Claude. We picked through the parcels, straight-line mazes. The gossamer bugs swarmed into the air as we passed and swallows wheeled above us. The sun was slipping toward the horizon and a few clouds in the western sky were pink.

The Mayor was sitting on his tractor in the driveway, talking with the hoarse fellow from the soccer dinner.

"I know you," the fellow rasped.

"Sure, he's our new American," said the Mayor. "This is Jean-Pierre Viandon. You should pick with his crew one day, Thomas. That'll tell you why people buy machines." He looked at me, frowned. "But what happened to you?"

I became aware of the dirt stains on my trousers, the twigs in my hair, the juice that looked like black tar on my hand.

"He picked with Jeanette," said Claude.

"With Jeanette?" the Mayor examined me again. "She's a bit old for you."

"Nathalie was busy with Jean-Paul," I said. Claude laughed, and the Mayor looked at him.

"How did it go?" he asked me.

"Oh, fine. I'll be glad to clean up, though."

"Wait here a minute." He climbed down off his tractor and plunged into the garage. When he returned, he had two bottles of wine. "Thanks for helping," he said, offering them to me.

I halfheartedly tried to refuse them, but he insisted. "Thank you for the lunch," I said.

"Any time. We do our best for our visitors here in Ruch."

4

An Englishman's Story

We drank the Mayor's gift that night at dinner, while I exaggerated my efforts among the vines.

The label said 1982 Château de Vaure, Bordeaux Supérieur. The vintage was the best of the decade so far, and according to the Mayor, the Château de Vaure label was given only to a small blend of the cooperative's best red wine. "Supérieur" is a legal term which refers purely to alcoholic strength, requiring a minimum of 12.5 percent. It was the most expensive wine the cooperative made, too: 23 francs. If that was high, you could take your own jug down to the cooperative and fill it with basic red table wine at 11 percent alcohol for 6 francs a liter. No wonder France was a wine-drinking nation. Wine was cheaper than fruit juice.

"Look at this color," I said. "It's browning at the edges, but there's still plenty of purple in the center. Not bad for a simple Bordeaux."

Sara swirled the wine in her glass and sniffed. We drank wine most nights, and played this game of analysis every time. Sometimes without thinking we swirled our water glasses, too. "It's aging—you can smell it," Sara said. "It's more complicated than fresh fruit now. There's an earthy scent, like fallen leaves in the forest. That always reminds me of Bordeaux."

We had searched for a town that epitomized the region; at least we had found one whose wine fit the bill. Sara had simmered a beef stew in some of the 6-franc red. As we sat at the table eating and talking, soaking up sauce with bread, the bottle slowly emptied and the wine became a partner in the conversation. It spoke of the weather, a round richness recalling the hot growing season of 1982, and made the current autumn sharp in contrast. It complemented the meal, drawing out the sweetness of the carrots with its fruitiness, balancing the rich meat with the slight austerity of tannin.

Wine is the most articulate of beverages. To an attentive and practiced palate, a glass of wine speaks of the grapes that comprise it, the soil that nourished the grapes, and the weather that shaped the year of its making. The greatest wines are the most complex; the elaborate language tasters use to describe them is farfetched, abstruse, and often comic, but technicians are just as hard-pressed to isolate all of wine's chemical components. It has been claimed that differences in *terroir* can be discerned more exactly by tasting the wine than by analyzing it.

In America, most winemakers are trained like scientists. They are determined to prove that technical skill can teach any grape grown anywhere to speak any language; it's a kind of vinous corollary to our national belief in human equality and freedom of opportunity. In France, an older and wearier nation, vintners long ago concluded that given certain geological and climatic conditions, specific grapes were most likely to succeed in producing the balanced, elegant wines they desired, in articulating *terroir* in the clearest possible terms.

In the nineteenth century, after a millennium or more of experimentation, the Bordeaux region settled on three main red grapes: Cabernet Sauvignon, Cabernet Franc, and Merlot. The composition of the soil and the local microclimate determine, for the most part, their proportions in the vineyards. As they respond to the weather of a given growing season and the decisions of particular winemakers, these grapes express the fundamental unities of earth and sky that make Bordeaux a coherent whole, in culture, in cuisine, in architecture, and in wine.

Maybe the *terroir* of Ruch wasn't noble enough to speak with the kind of distinction that allows enophiles to identify a Château Latour simply by tasting it. Perhaps we would never be able to distinguish a bottle of Château de Vaure from the wine of the Rauzan cooperative a dozen kilometers away. But we wanted to understand as much as it could tell. At any rate, we were taking pleasure in listening.

The next morning we lingered over coffee while the sun burned away the fog. We opened the kitchen window to the moist air. The grass glistened with dew. Small pink roses were blooming beside the gravel walk. More leaves had fallen from the chestnut trees, green and yellow, thick on the ground.

There was a squeaking noise, and a scratching, and then a gray-haired man in a blue sweater came raking up leaves and piling them into a wooden wheelbarrow. He was medium-height, stocky, with a large head and large hands. He moved deliberately, almost mechanically. When the barrow was full, he disappeared.

We continued to watch, but now we were waiting, too, to see if he returned. After a while, we heard the squeaking and scratching again. Curious, we finished our coffee and stepped outside. He let us come close before he raised his eyes to us.

"*Bonjour,*" said Sara. "*Il fait beau, n'est-ce pas?*"

"*Bonjour.*" The man nodded. "Yes indeed, it's lovely today. But then, it's generally lovely round here in the autumn."

His English-accented English startled us. Could we really be in deepest France if an Englishman was raking leaves in our back yard?

"Are you English?" asked Sara.

"In a way. Name's Hall. George Hall. Please call me Mr. Hall round the village. You're American, aren't you?"

We nodded and introduced ourselves. Our surprise amused him. Once we saw past our expectations, we noticed his ruddy cheeks and watery blue eyes like scraps of sky. Nothing French about him. His boots were crusted with dry mud and his sweater studded with straw. There was steadiness about him, and a rough dignity.

"Shame about these chestnuts." He gestured with his rake. "It's a blight. No one knows how to stop it. The leaves just curl up and die early in the autumn. Every year it's earlier. One day they simply won't leaf out in the spring, and then they'll have to be cut down. Lovely firewood. Not for me, though. I get the leaves, but the Mayor's friends will get the wood. You've met the Mayor?"

We nodded, ready to praise his helpfulness.

"He's a foxy one. So long as he can get a vote or a penny from you, he's your best friend. But if he can't use you, well . . . Of course, there are others worse. They're a bad lot." He glanced around darkly, shaking his head. "I'm only warning you because you're here for some time. Ask anyone from Blasimon or Castillon. Oh, Ruch has a reputation all right!"

He swung his gaze back to us. "So you're renting by the month. And how long do you plan to stay?"

We said we weren't sure, through the winter and then we'd see.

"Oh, they'll have you out before the summer. It's a nice enough place then, and plenty of renters. Some of them come back year after year. There's an old major been here four years running now. He always takes me and Anice—that's my wife—out to dinner on her birthday. Over to the Auberge Gascon near Saint-Pey. Have you been there?"

We shook our heads.

"They put on a lovely meal. First the soup, then the pâté, the whole crock straight on the table, with a knife to help yourself. A steak or chicken, and always a lovely dessert. And not too dear. Oh, we enjoy that. We've become regular friends with some of the visitors. Most of them can't speak French, you see. They don't know where to get a loaf of bread. I send them to Blasimon. Do you know the bakery in Blasimon?"

We shook our heads.

"Best around. I buy a week's supply on Saturday and freeze it. Organization is so important, isn't it? Or else nothing ever gets done. There's always more to do." He gestured with his rake again.

"So you work for the town?" Sara asked him.

"Yes." He gazed down the valley. "Then again, it's not what I expected."

The garden wall was warm in the sun. Sparrows clucked and rustled in the chestnut branches. Sheep grazing on the hillside bleated and their bells rang. Somewhere a harvesting machine rumbled. The church hid the village. There wasn't another soul in sight.

"Five years I've been at it," he said. "We've been seven in France. This time. I was born here, you see, my mother was French. But my father was English, and took us home. During the war I came back, in the army. They shipped me to England when it was over. So I started to make my plans." He shook his head heavily. "Ah, the plans I've made."

Among what seemed many jobs, including a stint at Rolls-Royce, he bought two ruined houses in Wales and rebuilt them. Being handy and meticulous, he made them attractive. He planned to sell them and use the money to buy property near Bordeaux. His search brought him to Ruch.

France hasn't made it easy for foreigners to buy property. Access to land ownership was one of the underlying goals of the Revolution and has been built into the spirit and law of the nation. Foreign ownership is seen in the same light as the old aristocratic estates, a threat to the rights of the citizens. Hall was bound to a strict contract and a large down payment. Once the agreement was entered into, there was no turning back.

Meanwhile, nationalist extremists were burning houses in Wales. They aimed to stem the influx of English buying second homes in the country. They calculated that if they destroyed a few of the absentee manors, foreigners would become less interested in buying others. They were right. Hall's houses were spared, but their value plummeted. He couldn't afford to break the contract in France, or to conclude it.

In the end, he did manage to complete the sale and the move, but the effort stretched the Halls to the limit. For two years, the couple lived as peasants. They had no running water, no heat other than the fireplace. They cooked over the open fire, because the feeble power line wouldn't run the electric stove they had brought from England. But the property had a habit of fruitfulness. Plum trees, apples and walnuts, berry bushes and wild mushrooms, all survived on the property. The Halls raised sheep and dug a vegetable garden. They worked the grape harvest for cash and tried to live off the land.

There was no bitterness in George's voice as he recounted the hard work, the inexorable depletion of energy and resources. We could smell the stewpot bubbling on the hearth, feel the comforting warmth of the fire; as he spoke, the winter nights when the earth was hard as iron and the water buckets were filled with ice only enhanced the beauty of the dancing flames.

But some supplement became increasingly urgent. Hall swallowed his pride and went to the *mairie*. There was money in the town budget for a *cantonnier* to sweep the village streets, mow the soccer field, rake the leaves. Ruch had contracted with an English travel agent to rent the presbytère as a *gîte,* and visitors needed access to an English speaker to smooth their stay. The municipal council decided that he could answer both needs. They gave him the job.

"So there you have it," he said. "From Rolls-Royce to roadman of Ruch."

The sun, the warm stone, his rolling voice, had worked a kind of hypnosis. I could see our own lives following down the same path as Hall's. What guarantee were American passports and college degrees against an old age sweeping streets in some forgotten village? What store had we laid up in the fat times against the lean times that could so easily come?

The *mairie* clock struck the hour, twelve tinny strokes. Hall looked at his watch.

"That's enough for now," he said, casting an unrepentant glance at the leaves that still lay thick on the path. "Anice will be expecting me. I'll mow your lawn this week or early next. Don't eat these chestnuts; they're not the sweet kind. If you need help with anything, let me know. A pleasure to meet you." And he trundled the barrow away.

Sara sent me to the store for milk and cheese. It was crowded and lively. The milk was stacked next to the laundry detergent. I picked up a plasticized paper container of milk so neutralized by ultra-high-temperature sterilization that it could sit on the shelf unopened for months without spoiling.

"Is there any fresh milk?" I asked Breton, as he cut me a wedge of Gruyère.

He shook his head. "It spoils too quickly."

"Don't the Grangiers still have cows?" asked a short fellow with a wrinkled face and a hand-rolled cigarette in his mouth.

Breton considered. "I think they do. You could get fresh milk from them," he told me. "Go in the evening. Take an empty bottle."

Jean-Paul's family, I thought, and asked where they lived.

"*Par là*," said the short man, waving his arm. "Reglade."

Reglade? I shook my head.

"Near Boudingue."

Boudingue? I had never heard these words before.

"Boudingue," he said impatiently. "The Destrieux house. Past the Mayor's place. Go past their house to Reglade. That's where the Grangiers live."

We had advanced through the line to the cashier. Marie-Jo said, "Grangier? Are you sending our customers to a competitor? That's not very nice, Roger."

Then I recognized him: Roger Bordas, with the handpicked Merlot.

Roger, Pierrette, and Bernard Bordas

"He wants fresh milk," grumbled Bordas. "I was trying to tell him where they live, but he doesn't understand."

"He probably doesn't know every place in town," she said gently. "He hasn't lived here all his life." She turned to me. "Reglade is the Grangiers' *lieudit,* the name of the place where they live. If you turn right at the Mayor's and follow the road around, it's on your left. You can't miss it. You'll smell the cows."

"I haven't lived here all my life, either," Bordas said gently. "It takes a while to learn your way around. Don't take too long to find the Grangiers', though. They're trying to sell their cows."

We left the store together. As he climbed onto his tractor, I asked him if I could come around to pick grapes one day.

"Sure. Why not today? At least the sun is shining."

Bordas's house was easy to find. One whole wall of his barn had been painted over as a sign. It read DOMAINE DE PHILIPPON VENTE DIRECTE VINS DE BORDEAUX ROUGE ROSÉ BLANC. Over the years, the colors had faded, softening its stridency. I wondered how many cars it stopped on the narrow road that snaked across the plateau of vines, a detour from the main highway, a back door into town.

Behind the house, the pickers waited to return to work. A car radio played, women lounged on the grass. Steel balls flashed through the air, a game of *boules* on the dirt driveway. Four people play, two on a team, each trying to toss his three steel balls closest to a small wooden target ball while knocking opponents' balls away. Expressive sounds reported the game—the scud of metal on earth, gunshots when one ball hit another. Across the driveway, another group sat together in the shade of the barn, seven men, the Spanish pickers. Black-haired, dressed in black and grays, all wearing hats, they looked like an alien tribe. They spoke in low voices and watched the French with dark eyes.

Bordas was the only grower in town who still hired Spanish pickers. After the Spanish Civil War, tens of thousands had come to Bordeaux every year, the same poor towns from Andalusia and Castile sending troops to the same vineyards vintage after vintage. They were the final wave of harvest-time immigrants that had included French from the remote

Massif Central early in the century, from nearby Périgord and the Dordogne region since the Middle Ages, and always Gypsies, students, and vagabonds. In the 1980s the harvesting machine put an end to all that.

At 2:15, Bordas picked up his *boules* and waved to the Spaniards. The pickers straggled to their feet and moved down the road. I fell in beside Bernard, Bordas's son.

"What are you picking today?"

"Bouchet."

"Bouchet?"

I repeated the unfamiliar name softly to myself. Bernard glanced sharply at me, as if perhaps I was mocking him.

"Yes. They call it Cabernet Franc, too."

"Ah. Old vines?"

Bernard shrugged. "Older than me."

Our route followed the narrow road to a stone house whose long decay had been slowed by concrete block and plastic. Though decrepit, it showed signs of habitation.

"Who lives here?"

"My grandparents' parents lived there once. My father was fixing it up for us, until my mother died. The Spaniards stay there now."

Leeks and cabbage struggled in a ragged kitchen garden, and then the vineyard began. The plowed earth had dried to hard clods that threw up a fine golden dust. We skirted a small wooded gully; at the bottom, half concealed by the undergrowth, lay a rusty car.

"That's a shame," I said. "Who would use a vineyard as a junkyard?"

"My father pushed it there," Bernard replied. "After my accident. It put me in the hospital for a while. He blamed the car."

The workers took their places in the rows. The French and older Spanish were cutters, and three young Spaniards carried the tubs, called *hottes*. They chattered across the rows, and the two languages mingled in the air, Spanish low and liquid, French high and bright and sharp. Bordas wandered quietly through the rows stripping leaves ahead of the pickers, or cutting a bunch of grapes left behind. He kept an eye on the crew, but left its direction to the Spanish leader, Antonio, who spoke both languages.

I mentioned the sign on his barn. "Do you make your own wine?"

He nodded. "That's the only way to get ahead. Look at the figures. The *cave* sells a *tonneau* of wine to the trade for 6,000 francs. If you bottle it yourself, that's 1,200 bottles. At 15 francs a bottle, that's three times as much money. Sure, your expenses are higher. Bottles, corks, labels, tax stamps, gas for the truck when you're on the road selling it. That's damned hard work, selling it. But you'd have to be foolish or lazy not to try."

"How many growers in Ruch bottle their own wine now?"

He considered. "Oh, two. Three, maybe."

"But didn't I see you taking grapes to the cooperative?"

He nodded again. "I bought some land that was under contract to the *cave* and have to give them the grapes for three more years. But I don't have room to make any more wine, anyway. This year the vines are pissing with grapes. I've never seen anything like it."

I strolled through the parcel, picking up cigarette packets thrown down by the crew. Red Marlboro, blue Gaulois, gold Celta, crushed and glittering in the sun. EL USO DEL TABACO ES PERJUDICIAL PARA SU SALUD, one said. The sun picked out a castle on a distant ridge, turning old stones to gold. Somewhere a harvester grumbled and whirred. A small dog came barking, and then Nathalie and Babette arrived on a motorbike. Babette carried a baby in her arms.

"Eh, Babette!" a woman called out. "Why aren't you working?"

"The *cave* is full, Maman. They aren't taking any more grapes."

Bordas jumped into his car and drove away. The Frenchwomen clustered around the baby.

"Did you hear?" asked Nathalie. "Duclos is dead. Killed in a fight!"

The Frenchmen dropped their panniers and gathered around her.

"That must be the young one, Robert; his father lives by Grand Bernard," someone said.

"Didn't he live in Bordeaux?"

"No, Cérons. He was a mason there. Kind of a drifter. Lived in a boardinghouse. What happened, Nathalie?"

"There was a problem over rent money, they said, and then a fight. Another fellow who lived in the house hit him with an iron bar. Killed him."

"*Oh la,*" a woman said, shaking her head. "These days young men just won't be good. They drink, they fight, they're just no good at all."

The Spaniards worked slowly, straining to understand. "*Un hombre muerto,*" muttered Antonio. Francisco and Juan, porters, hovered round the French group, but the conversation wore down. No one had details, no one knew the victim very well. The women turned back to the baby. The men picked up their panniers.

Babette and Nathalie wanted to hunt for chestnuts in the woods. "We'll get some *bourru* from the *cave* and have a party," they said.

"It's still too early for chestnuts," scoffed Serge. We had recognized each other from the soccer dinner; he told me he was a postman in nearby Branne who took his holiday to work the harvest. "Picking is fun, but a vineyard like this is too much work. I own five rows. Each row has a hundred vines and each vine gives two liters of wine. That's just enough to last me through the year."

"There are too chestnuts. Claude found some," replied Nathalie.

"You need a dog or a pig." Serge looked around. "Oh! Juanito!"

Juan was about eighteen, a buffoon with a huge gut, a wide smile, and

Ruch from the south

beady anxious eyes. He sang and laughed and danced as though he were drunk. He jigged over. *"Carga, hombre?"*

"You're always looking for women, Juanito. Here are some." Serge spoke slowly and loudly in French. He pointed at the girls.

Juan glanced at them. A sly smile.

"Women!" said Serge. "But you have to find chestnuts for them. Do you know chestnuts?"

Judging from his blank look, Juan didn't know chestnuts, at least not in French. But he knew women. He broke into a hopping dance. He jigged on one foot, then the other. The girls laughed. He clutched his belly, rolled his eyes, yelped, slung the *hotte* to his chest like a partner and began waltzing it. He twirled, lost his balance, crashed into the vines, and fell to the ground.

"Oh, bravo," said Serge. "But I don't think he'll find any chestnuts that way. Come on, Juanito. *Carga. Carga!"*

Juan stumbled to his feet. He sighed and leaned for Serge to empty his pannier.

Nathalie drifted down a row of vines. Francisco emptied his *hotte* into the trailer, then joined her. Serge noticed them. "Hey! It's fine to talk, but who's going to empty our panniers?"

Antonio looked around. *"Paco, carga,"* he shouted. Francisco blushed and moved back to the pickers. Nathalie tossed a few grapes at his back. They bounced off his *hotte,* and he smiled.

Bordas returned. "The vats are nearly full for tonight, but they're still taking hand-picked grapes," he told Bernard. "Let's finish this parcel. Antonio! Four more rows, then *la sopa!"*

The pickers worked faster. Grapes were piled high over the edges of the trailer, so Antonio sent Juan to climb on top and tread them down. He staggered to one end of the trailer and back again, knee-deep in grapes, smoking placidly. Suddenly he bent down and brought some-thing shiny out of the vat.

"It's a watch," he called to Antonio in Spanish.

Antonio glanced around. "Don't say anything. Paco! Look and see who lost a watch."

Paco picked up panniers, craning to look at the pickers' hands. "I think it's the big-nosed one," he called. The French paid no attention.

"Serge!" called Antonio. The Frenchman looked around. "Aren't we ever going to finish? What time is it, anyway?"

Serge pulled back his sleeve. "My watch! Where's my watch?"

Antonio pointed to the trailer of grapes, and everyone turned to look. Juan was holding it so it glittered in the failing light. "Chestnuts?" he cried in French. The whole group collapsed in laughter. Juan smiled broadly as he handed the watch to Serge. "Chestnuts!"

5

Fermentation

The fine weather held, morning fog sooner or later yielding to the persistent sun. It was the anticyclone, they said, a high-pressure system that normally sits above the Azores, southwest in the Atlantic. In autumn it can drift close to Bordeaux and give just enough Indian summer to ripen the grapes. The growers gamble it will stay long enough to finish the harvest, before low pressure brings chill rain from the north. In an average decade, they win three times, lose three times, and muddle through the rest. So far, 1986 looked to be a winner.

I came on two men in a field behind the Mayor's house. White-haired Sorbier, who had brought in the rotten Merlot my first day at the cooperative, was talking with Guy Petit, a thin-lipped fellow I had seen around the garage; they were watching a harvesting machine trundle along the narrow rows of vines.

"Does the machine do a better job than people?" I asked.

"Not if people worked as well as they ought," said Petit. "But since they never do, the machine keeps us calm."

Big as a tank, it rumbled through the field spraying a mist of grape juice over everything in its path. Straddling the rows, shivering the vines, it spit leaves and twigs in a roar of wind, lumbered to turn, so wide it had

Philippe de Larrard with his harvesting machine

to skip a row to reverse direction. Deep inside, plastic rods beat the vines, shaking the grapes from the stems. The berries fell to a conveyor belt, which carried the fruit to small holding bins by the driver. When the bins were full, the machine rumbled over to the tractor to dump them in the trailer. The short swing looked like a porter emptying the *hotte;* it was the machine's only graceful motion.

The job is noisy and jarring. The driver can't even see the grapes he harvests. There's no contact with plants or people, just a slow steering through a green maze. When the trailer filled, one of the others would drive it to the cooperative. In the meantime, they were smoking.

"Most of Ruch is harvested by machine now, isn't it?" I asked.

"Most of Bordeaux, in fact," Petit replied. "Only the fancy châteaux still pick by hand. For the image. And a few hopeless laggards like our Mayor."

"The wages today make it too expensive to hire pickers," said Sorbier. "And the government subsidies make it easy to buy the machine. The three of us own this one. Some people rent time from an entrepreneur, but that can be risky."

Petit gave a dry chuckle. "Last year a fellow in Mérignas canceled his machine time because the cooperative was full and wasn't taking grapes. When the *cave* was free, the machine was due somewhere else. He lost a whole parcel."

"My pickers used to come from everywhere," said Sorbier, squinting at the machine. "England, Denmark. I even had an agricultural student from Vietnam once. One fellow from Calvados came three years running, then married a girl from Castillon and settled down. Most of them were wilder than that. They did things they couldn't do at home. Ah, it was folklore.

"But I don't miss those days. Not much, anyway. They made plenty of problems, too. I think the women are the most relieved. They thought the Gypsies would steal their babies. They didn't like all the cooking, either. Though some might miss those strong young men, eh, Guy?"

There's a rigidity to a vineyard—the taut gleaming wires, the vines trained to identical heights, the endless parallel rows—that seems suited to an industrial age. When a machine is roaring, a radio blaring pop tunes, a tractor grinding down the road, the rustle and snip of the scissors seems archaic—gratuitous from the laborer's perspective, inefficient from the farmer's. Once, harvest time was the year's culmination, bringing the whole community together. But it had become just another chore. Only old people and the young pick grapes now, enjoy playing parts from the past. The Mayor, stooped and sore, seemed to enjoy the harvest days more than these men who watched as machines worked.

I made my way to the cooperative as evening came on. Claude came in with a load that registered 11 degrees, 3,950 kilograms, a normal afternoon's work for the pickers, an hour for the machine. Everyone was drinking *bourru;* it was dryer now, less fizzy, becoming wine.

Tractors were lined up waiting, all filled with Cabernet Sauvignon. The small blue-black berries weren't as ripe as the Merlots had been, many only 9 or 10 degrees. I asked Petit why the growers didn't hold off a few days. "Oh, once one starts, everybody follows. Nobody wants to get caught in the rain."

Inside, the heady, sweet smell of new wine was almost overpowering. Fermentation gives off heat; the steel walls of the full vats were warm to the touch.

Breton was wrestling with a hose; his blond hair was plastered to his forehead, his blue jumpsuit stained with sweat and juice. He paused to shout at two youths who were shoveling pomace out of a vat that had been drained of juice; the wet cake of skins and seeds would be pressed to make darker, harder wine. They were inside the vat, wearing bathing briefs and rubber boots; a single bulb dangling above them threw angular shadows across the round metal walls. They worked in pairs for safety: alcohol fumes and carbon dioxide, fermentation byproducts, overcome a few workers every year, despite the fans that pump fresh air down into the vats. Some pass out. Some die.

Red wine ferments along with the grapeskins and seeds, which provide color and tannic structure. The alcoholic fermentation finishes in a week, but the juice macerates longer in the vats, until the winemaker decides it has extracted enough. At some wineries, this maceration period can last a month. I asked Breton how long he was leaving the wine on the skins.

"Eight days." He grimaced. "Not enough. Not with the grapes we're getting this year." He picked up some of the pomace from the pile outside the vat. "See how rich it is still?" It was warm, greasy to the touch, left purple stains on the fingers. "We should be taking another week's extraction, at least."

"Why not, then?"

"There's no room. Too many grapes this year. Too much wine last year, and too much of it still in storage. We have to empty the vats as soon as we can. The pomace takes up about a third of the space in there. We need to drain the juice off to storage vats to make space for the next loads of grapes. Once they're picked, they can't wait around."

"But why don't the growers just wait longer to pick them? The sugar levels are low, anyway."

Breton banged the hose against the spout of the vat. He pulled a steel hook from his belt and tightened the screws. "We refused to take any Cabernet until the eleventh. But by then the Merlot was finished, and we couldn't hold them back. They look at the calendar, the sky. The rain could come any day. They figure the grapes are ripe enough. Better light wine than none at all." He pulled at the hook. "This is a cooperative. They're in charge."

Breton had twenty years' experience behind his words. He had followed his father as chief *caviste,* and old Breton had begun when the cooperative was founded. Neither had formal training as winemakers, but they had helped guide Ruch's vineyards through the greatest social and economic transformation since the Revolution.

In the nineteenth century, the landscape was more varied than today. There were fewer vineyards, more pastures, fields of flax, wheat, and oats, and deep woods for hunting. The town's vineyards were mostly owned by the aristocrats from the two châteaux, Vaure and Courteillac, the turreted pile on the bluff west of the village. Most of the townspeople were smallholders or laborers. They raised sheep for slaughter and cattle for milk. They grew grapes, too, and vinified their own wine for sale to the merchants in Libourne and Bordeaux. At the turn of the century the village counted nine coopers, to make the barrels in which the wine was made, sold, and transported. There were carters, blacksmiths, bakers, butchers, and carpenters. There were three small stores and two cafés.

In the hard times after World War I, costs rose and small farmers found it difficult to invest in both vine growing and winemaking. The struggling merchants offered prices that threatened the farmers with ruin. Cooperative wineries had sprung up in socialist Provence early in the century. The merchants resisted them at first, fearing they would lose control over prices. But once they realized the cooperatives provided better quality wine in economically sensible quantities, they became faithful customers. Even the government supported the movement. The left saw cooperatives as a way to encourage socialism, the right as a means of preserving property ownership.

Bordeaux's first cooperative was set up in Saint-Émilion in 1932. Ruch followed in 1936, beginning with 60 growers and 350 hectares of vines, about 900 acres. The Baron of Courteillac held aloof, but Vaure was in the hands of the town doctor and mayor, Delom-Sorbé. He could see political advantage in helping so many voters and was busy enough with his practice to welcome some relief from the property. The winemaking *chai* at Vaure had been built in 1890, big enough to handle Vaure's 250 hectares of vines. Delom-Sorbé sold it to the cooperative. By the 1950s, the cooperative accounted for nearly 80 percent of the town's production. In 1985, the society counted 110 members and 550 hectares of vines, and grossed nearly 13 million francs. Founded as a remedy against ruin, it has become big business.

The cooperative sold most of its production in bulk to Bordeaux merchants. The Baronnie of Baron Philippe de Rothschild was a loyal customer; Mouton-Cadet owes some of its flavor to Ruch. Nearly 15 percent of sales were wines bottled at the cooperative and sold directly to the public. The winery labeled most of its production "Vieux Vaure," but saved its best vats for two "château" labels, Vaure and Blaignac. They accounted for nearly 9,000 cases, 2 percent of total production.

But since 1983 about 15 percent of the wine remained unsold each year, stored in cement vats in the oldest part of the *chai*. Insofar as wine improves with age, these stocks could be seen as investments. But at Ruch's level, Bordeaux is appreciated more for its freshness than any complexity that comes with evolution. Though the cooperative would consider it a catastrophe to receive a big order it was unable to fill (producers have been driven to fraud by such circumstances, and disgraced), by 1986 the quantity of unsold wine had become an embarrassment of riches.

"Our inventory has risen as a result of healthy harvests," Monsieur Colette told me. "Acreage isn't increasing, but the yields per acre are better. I would say they've just about doubled. The market has grown, too, but not so quickly."

Colette, an enologist and administrator, had been hired by the town in 1980 to direct the expanding cooperative. I watched him pull up in his Renault 16, the car successful salesmen drive, jump out in his spotless blue lab coat, dash around the winery for half an hour, then disappear. We were talking in his office, and he seemed out of place behind the battered desk.

But isn't quality generally considered to come from reducing yields? I asked.

"Not necessarily. If the vines are healthy, and the year abundant, you can have quality along with quantity. 1982 is a perfect example. And the sanitary state of Ruch's vines is excellent. Oh, more could treat against rot," he conceded, "but we're on the right path."

But would the wine improve if these healthy vines reduced their yields?

"Perhaps. And perhaps if everyone in Bordeaux reduced yields, prices would rise along with quality. But how could Ruch do such a thing alone? The only result is that we would have less wine to sell and the growers would make less money."

Colette's solution had been to increase the winery's storage capacity. His tenure had been marked by a rapid expansion of high-tech equipment, from huge stainless-steel vats to the control booth equipped with an electronic scale and digital readout. Breton complained that the farmers spent all their money on harvesting machines and had little left over to equip the winery to handle the increased flow of grapes. But he was working under much different conditions than his father.

The newest vats, set up outside the winery along the entry drive, were the most intrusive. They marred the composition formed by the magnificent oak tree and the low-browed receiving platform. They broke with the human scale of the old *chai*. But Colette insisted they were necessary, and managed to cover most of their cost through government subsidies and the rest with loans.

A bell rang in the control booth. Sylvie threw a switch that shut down the presses and picked up the phone.

"Oui?"

The last available vat was full. Were the new ones hooked up to the system yet?

"Attends."

She turned off the crusher and sent her assistant to check. A worker perched on top of the 20-foot tank shouted. Sylvie's assistant returned to say that all was ready. She picked up the phone and relayed the news. Another bell rang. She threw the switch to restart the presses.

With audible bangs and gurgles, the new wine was pumped from deep in the winery up the long pipe to the top of the new vats. A cheer went up as the purple slush came out of the pipe and rattled into the shiny container. The fellow at the top waved and smiled. The farmers went back to their tractors.

Ten minutes later, another cry went up. *"Arrêtez!"* A worker waving his arms. Sylvie threw the switch that stopped the presses again.

A purple stream was flowing along the base of the loading dock: grape juice. The farmers jumped off their tractors. The stream was quickly traced. It led directly to the new tank. Someone had neglected to close the draining valve near the bottom of the tank. Wine muddied the driveway. Breton and Chatelier took advantage of the delay to smoke cigarettes in the sunshine. The valve was closed, the press restarted, and the rumble began anew. Duly baptized, the new vats were officially in service.

·   ·   ·

Early one morning, the church bells tolled a slow, rhythmic message. At twelve, and again in the afternoon, the cadence was repeated, five long minutes of slow beats. I stopped in the store to ask what it meant.

"That's the funeral bell. Hear how there are two beats? That means a man died," explained Marie-Jo.

"A woman gets one," added her daughter.

"It's for young Duclos," continued the woman. "The mason, the one who was in the fight over the rent money. Part of his family is from Ruch, and they're burying him tomorrow." She rang up my groceries. "Still buying milk? Have you been to the Grangiers' yet?"

I shook my head.

"You better hurry. They're going to sell those cows soon."

The next morning the fog lifted early. By nine, people gathered in front of the church, sitting on the wall, strolling to the war memorial for the view. Some wore the stiff fabric and dull colors of country folk, others the jewelry and shiny shoes of the city.

I strolled the long way to the cemetery, to approach inconspicuously from the *mairie* side, and leaned against the wall. A dozen people were at the graveside. A hearse pulled up to the iron gates. A priest got out. Four men carried a ladder-like frame of black metal to the hearse and slid the coffin onto it. Then they lowered the coffin into the grave and threw dirt on top. A priest spoke, but the wind carried his words away. The ceremony was simple and plain and quiet. The people got into their cars and left.

The sun warmed the air. I stepped into the empty cemetery. It was crowded with tombs, from small markers to mausoleums the size of toolsheds. There was polished marble and cracking cement, plastic flowers and broken glass. Faded plaques bore messages: We prayed for you at Lourdes. I found family tombs for Bonvoisins, Petits, and Grangiers. In a corner hard by the church a blunt concrete slab was engraved Dufoussat de Bogeron, the family from Courteillac. The Delom-Sorbé tomb was in the far corner, just as the two châteaux were at opposite ends of the town. The newest grave was just a mound of fresh dirt, strewn with fresh flowers, with a small cross at the head.

I wandered into the store, though I didn't really need anything.

The church and the cemetery

Marie-Jo noticed my tie and asked if I had attended the funeral.

"Not really. I saw some of it from the street."

She smiled. "Too shy?"

"No one I knew was there."

"Oh, he wasn't from here, not really. They were from Mauriac."

The next day, *Sud Ouest* reported the funeral and recounted the circumstances of the young man's death. He had rented a room in his boss's house. The boss, an ill-tempered man, had a running quarrel with his neighbor, a North African. The argument turned violent and a shotgun went off. The Arab attacked with a tire iron. Duclos caught hold of him, trying to calm him. To no avail. Furious, the Arab struck the young man in the head. Both fighters were arrested. Duclos died in the hospital three days later.

How had this tale of virtue and courage degraded into rumors of shiftlessness and theft? Only the shopkeeper's offhand dismissal of the family as outsiders seemed to explain it. Besides the Ruchelais, there were only strangers.

The days repeated themselves; the harvest seemed to last forever. But slowly the parcels were picked, and finally the fields were empty. Except for a few scattered showers, the weather held. The huge crop had been gathered in sunshine. Fortune smiled on Ruch with abundance.

October was almost over. The weather turned colder. What would we do next?

We maintained close contact with our old lives. We wrote letters to editors, friends, our families. On any given day, we could project what we would have been doing in New York. But America was losing its substance for us. It appeared as a French caricature in an editorial cartoon, an unflattering comparison in a stranger's conversation, a place where a relative had moved long ago. It had become what Ruch made of it, a blurred image of abundance and greed.

Then America came to the presbytère. Mark and Chris, two friends on their honeymoon, initiated the guest room. They arrived late, in a spiffy rented car. We roasted a chicken for dinner and served it in the kitchen, warmed ourselves by the oven and plenty of wine.

In the morning, dew sparkled on the roses in the garden and the low sun sent long shadows across the fields. We tramped into the valley, where cows grazed by the Courbut, and found a swimming pool built by summer people, a blue scar on a green meadow. We zigzagged along the rows through vineyards high and low. A winding road brought us to the faded sign, DOMAINE DE PHILIPPON.

We knocked on the door. Only the grandparents were home, but the old woman recognized me and they left the wood stove to show us around the winery. They were the opposites of Jack Sprat and his wife sprung to life: her face a dried fruit, wrinkled and hairy, folding in on itself; his a sausage, swollen and jowly, his eyes closing under folds of fat.

They led us into the damp, chilly barn. The yellow glow of a Vaslin grape press was the only color amid raw concrete vats, dark wooden rafters, stained cement floor. A good year, they said, lots of wine. Did we want to taste? Thousands of bottles slept in neat stacks. The old man drew new red wine from a tap on a cement tank. He urged us on, refilling the glass; she scoffed, "Oh, don't listen to him. He'll make you drunk." The wine was purply red, cold and sharp, still cloudy, off-key but alive.

Four o'clock, the sun low, the sky deepening. A chill breeze had picked up. We made our way back to town and spotted Nicole Bonvoisin in the street. *"Eh beh!"* she cried, spotting Sara. They embraced, we introduced Mark and Chris. *"Ça va?"* Nicole smiled at the Americans. *"Oui,"* they said, smiling back.

Nicole had been at exercise class, she told us, fifteen women doing aerobics to reggae music on the linoleum floor of the town's multipurpose auditorium.

"All that grape picking makes you stiff. It feels good to stretch. Marie-Do and Colette brought their little girls. They were in hysterics the whole time. You should come next time, Sara."

"We want to go out to dinner tonight, Nicole," Sara said. "Where do you suggest?"

She thought about it for a minute. "Well, there's Château Lardier and La Canelle. That's about it for Ruch. They say Lardier is very nice. It's expensive. The Mayor used to go there with the municipal council, but then he fell out with the woman who owns it. We always go to La Canelle. My parents lived there once. Before it was a restaurant, of course. It's all right. They give you plenty of food."

La Canelle sat beside the main road from Castillon to Sauveterre. It looked like the farmhouse it once had been, with its pigpen beside it. The sign was small.

The restaurant was empty when we arrived, except for a couple of men at the bar. The room was modern in construction, rustic in detail. The Sheetrock walls had thin strips of dark-stained lathe tacked on them in half-timber patterns. Fluorescent lights hung from the raftered ceiling. There were a dozen tables, set with paper tablecloths. Our footsteps were loud on the concrete floor.

A young girl showed us to a table, told us the main courses were steak and chicken *confit,* and asked if we wanted an apéritif.

"Do you have a wine list?" I asked.

"Wine is included with this menu," she replied. "That's 45 francs."

"But that's just ordinary *vin de table,* right?"

She looked doubtful.

"Do you have other wines?"

"You mean with a cork in it?"

I nodded.

"That's 40 francs extra."

"We'll just have the regular *vin de table.*"

We decided to take the menu of the day. The steaks would be lean and gristly; steaks in French cafés always are. *Confit* is meat simmered in its own rendered fat, which makes it salty and greasy and, done right, amazingly tender and tasty. Usually it was made from duck. Chicken sounded like the poor man's alternative. Mark and Chris and I decided to pass it up. Sara was dubious of tough steak and chose the *confit.*

More men came in. I recognized some of the young workers from the *cave.* They waved. The waitress gave them a water pitcher, tall glasses, one ice cube, and a jolt of liquid that turned cloudy on the ice: the inevitable *pastis.*

She brought our wine and we ordered. The wine was crude but lively. Chris choked on her first sip, and Sara showed her how to cut it with water to make it easier on the palate. The soup came; it was greasy and dull. We guessed it was chicken.

"Real locals would finish this off with the *chabrol*," I said. "Watch this." I poured a few ounces of wine into the soup bowl, swirled it around, and drained it. There was laughter from the bar.

A cold appetizer came next: four tiny slices of pork pâté, small sour pickles, and a pile of shredded purple cabbage dressed with garlic and vinegar.

"Tasty," Mark commented. "Cheap and easy to make, too. Country cooking is best when it's simple. Balance seems somehow to be built right in."

Breton and Chatelier came in, and now there were two dozen people at the bar. They were loud, and the hard surfaces of the room magnified the noise. The harried waitress was hard-pressed to keep their glasses filled. Half an hour went by. We were still the only people seated.

Finally the main courses came. One plate held our meat, another a huge pile of French fries, golden, steaming, fragrant. We ordered another carafe of wine, then attacked the food. The fries were delicious. The *confit* was dry but tasty. The steaks were raw and chewy. We sawed away for a while, then stopped.

"Should we send the steaks back for more fire?" Mark asked.

"We can try."

A vigorous wave managed to catch the waitress. She came over and I asked to have the meat cooked a little more. She looked distraught. I insisted, so she took the plates away.

The crowd at the bar finally sat down at a long table in the back. Newcomers filled other tables, a few families, a solitary salesman. A young woman wearing costume jewelry ate with a stolid older man in total silence; both cast longing looks at the table of rowdy men.

When the steaks came back they were still raw, but colder. We finished the fries and the wine. The cheese was still to come. We hoped, in this land of hundreds of cheeses, for a miracle. Instead, we got foil-wrapped sections of La Vache Qui Rit, France's equivalent of pasteurized processed cheese food, and a shriveled, ammoniac Camembert. Dessert was the kind of ice cream that comes in paper cups with flat wooden spoons.

"This is an authentic country experience," Sara said. "This meal could have come straight from a harvest kitchen, where the vintner's wife hated to cook."

The big table had no complaints. The young men shouted and laughed.

"They're just a bunch of kids," said Mark. "What's ahead for them?"

"They don't seem too worried about it, do they? At least the harvest is finished and the grapes are in. The worst is over. That's enough for now."

We thanked our waitress, paid, and headed for the door. The hot, smoky room had taken on the intimacy of a house party. As we left, Serge jumped on the table and broke out into the Ruch fight song. *"Allez les bleus, allez les blancs . . ."*

6

Days for the Dead

The harvest over, the world turned gray. Cold northwest winds pushed the anticyclone back to the Azores, flooding the sky with low clouds and rain squalls. Damp winds drove leaves from the vines, exposing twisted gray trunks and spidery branches. Without sunshine to gild the stone, the village took on a cemetery pallor. Shutters closed early against the rain; houses huddled against a gray horizon.

The garage across from the store filled with flowers, but their colors only accentuated the melancholy: pots of chrysanthemums, caramel and cream and moss and rust, destined for the dead on Toussaint, All Saints' Day.

I learned about the custom from *Sud Ouest*. The paper carried only two pages of international news but rarely missed an item of local interest. The sports coverage reached even Ruch's level, reporting the scores of the local soccer matches. When the national government planned a new highway through Entre-Deux-Mers, every mayor along the route was interviewed to complain about losing vineyards to concrete. A weekly wine column reported the shifting prices for bulk wines and the occasional multimillion-dollar sale of a famous château to an insurance company or a Japanese syndicate. The United States was rarely mentioned.

The paper said that 11 million French households, one in two, placed 30 million pots of chrysanthemums on their family graves each year, spending an average of 100 francs on grief and respect. The tradition began in 1789, when the flower was first imported from China, where it was called "glory of autumn." According to polls, 80 percent of youths between fifteen and twenty-four couldn't care less about the holiday. Nevertheless, the florists sold more chrysanthemums every year.

A hundred francs would buy the biggest pot on sale in Ruch. The prudent could find one for 40 francs. Women finished their shopping in the store, then wandered across the street to examine the flowers. They pointed and compared, then settled on a pot or two. The old women stayed a long time talking, and sometimes came back to change their minds.

On Halloween, at the cemetery, people cleaned graves with scrub brushes and buckets of soapy water, or just wandered around chatting. The flowers glowed warm, earthy tones, the clean wet stones glittered and shone.

George was raking chestnut leaves from the path outside. "Look at those hypocrites," he muttered. "So many of them live around the corner, yet they set foot inside just this once a year. It's nothing but a social occasion for them. And a competitive one at that. Who has the biggest bouquet? Who has more flowers?"

Toussaint dawned heavy with fog. The streetlights stayed on, dim spots in the gray air. No shutters opened. The only light on the street spilled from the store. Fog hid the far side of the cemetery from view. It seemed huge, each tomb a house wreathed in cloud. The colors of the chrysanthemums were muted and dull. A crowd gathered slowly, wandering the pathways or standing in groups by the tombs, stiff and awkward with formality. Children scuffed the gravel, hanging their heads.

Just after eleven, the mayor led a crowd through the gates. They moved together to a tomb and paused. Gray-haired Sorbier placed a pot of flowers on the grave, said a name, then, "Let us offer a moment of silence to the dead." After a pause, the ragged procession moved to another grave. They made a dozen stops in twenty minutes, then dispersed.

Toussaint

The people who remained in the cemetery relaxed and began to chat. I spoke with old Lacosse, a Ruchelais by birth whose work as a *menuisier,* a kind of handyman in wood and metal, had included building coffins. He was a dapper dresser, with suspenders, slicked hair, and a couple of gold teeth, and spoke with a flat twangy accent I could barely understand.

"Pine always was the cheapest," he said. "But almost everyone could find the money for brass handles or a silk lining. I never made the really fancy ones, though. Those who could afford oak and silver went to Petit in Castillon. Ah, he was a real artist. But he's joined his customers now. They might as well have buried his tools with him. No one can do that sort of work anymore. No one at the funeral parlors, that's for sure."

I asked him how old the cemetery was. Did it go back to the construction of the church?

"Oh no. The oldest burying ground in Ruch is at Gleziat, out toward the *cave.* Old Viandon dug up a Roman sarcophagus there once, plowing. His wife used it as a washing tub for years. No, the church is *bien ancien,* but this cemetery's not so old. I remember when there were vineyards just there where the garage is now. The priest got the wine they made. This was probably all vineyard in the old days. Or a garden. Except maybe for the corner nearest the church. That's where the children have been buried, as long as anyone can remember."

Another group gathered outside the cemetery. This time they filed into the church, and we went, too. Except for tiny Jeanette and a woman who worked in the cooperative office, there was no overlap with the Mayor's crowd. It was colder inside than out, and people shuffled their feet on the stone floor to keep warm.

The church was small but solid, in the rugged Romanesque style typical of those built and rebuilt all over Entre-Deux-Mers in the twelfth and thirteenth centuries. The squat forms, the thick walls and tiny windows made a fortress, recalling the long wars between English and French, Protestant and Catholic. The gray stone walls matched the rest of the village. A slender, neo-Gothic spire was the only architectural false note, built by an overweening bishop in the nineteenth century. But over time, as the stone weathered and owls built nests in the tower, even the spire had mellowed into a kind of rough harmony.

Inside, the church was ageless. Not ancient, but out of time, a mix of styles and ornaments and attitudes that defied classification.

Heavy nail-studded doors under the spire led to a small vestibule built like a bank teller's cage, cheap wood and frosted glass. Through that, the church offered a single long volume visible at a glance, startlingly bright because the stone walls and ceiling had been whitewashed not too long before. The floor was flagstone, the chairs were straight-backed wood and cane. The place was simple and well kept, but musty and cold, as if the owner had gone away, leaving only the caretakers at home.

With long sitting on the hard chairs, the white space came into focus. The single small chapel showed fine stone carving on its columns and barrel vault, but the blunt geometry of the column capitals had been given a coat of bright modern paint. A florid wooden sculpture of the Madonna and Child standing in a niche in the nave could have been rococo. The Infant Jesus snapped his fingers in a gesture that bordered on the impertinent. Ceramic statues of St. George and Joan of Arc guarded the door, but, cast in kitsch, were listless and fey. A painting of St. Stephen stoned was a surrealist dream, an underwater ballet.

Plainly, the church decor had never been finished, never quite satisfied the needs of parishioners or preservationists, but had continued to be pushed and pulled into a more suitable shape right up to the present. Questions of authenticity or originality lost their point. Each piece of the puzzle seemed a temporary response to some forgotten need, but as the provisional was trapped into permanence, the ensemble gained the harmony of inevitability.

Fifteen minutes late, the priest hurried into the chancel, straightening his vestments as he came. A short, sturdy man, he had a round pink face which gave little impression of his character. He didn't so much lead the service as play one role among many, with the woman who coaxed music from an old harmonium and the children who struggled to light the altar candles.

There was a Scripture reading, a ragged hymn, and then the homily. The priest was barely audible, rushing to make up for lost time. He began with references to a pagan Gallic ritual for the dead which had taken place in the same season and had been slowly preempted by the Christians. He noted that Toussaint had been declared an official Church holy day in 835. Then he recited the message from Rome. The congregation nodded and dozed. The priest looked at his watch, cut off the last two hymns, and led his acolytes down the center aisle and out the front door.

We had never seen him leave that way before. Usually he slipped out through the sacristy to the parking lot behind the church. He always parked his battered blue Citroën *deux chevaux* there and drove away before the last of the faithful were out the door on the other side, neatly avoiding any secular contact with the congregation. But today, everyone rose and followed him into the cemetery.

The fog had lifted, the sun fell bright on the flowers and lit gold threads in the priest's cassock. The acolytes carried the incense and the cross behind him. He halted in the middle of the graveyard. After a moment of silence, he offered a prayer to the dead. Then he resumed his tour and marched the acolytes back into church. We heard his engine fire up behind the walls, but people lingered among the graves or paused outside the gates to chat. Then the last of them slipped away, too, leaving the flowers to the birds and the stones to the sun.

We met the Grangiers in the cemetery. Monsieur was short and energetic, with gray hair and steel teeth. Madame was larger, rounder, with frizzy brown hair wild about her head. Smiling, they asked us why we hadn't been around for milk. It must have become a town joke: the city folks who want real milk but can't find their way to the farm. We said we'd stop by soon.

They asked us to come in the evening, and it was dark when we set out from the presbytère. We wandered down the country lane until we saw cows, puddles of light in the moonlit fields, and turned up the next drive.

The building was typically Bordelais, a long rectangle with the house at one end and the barn at the other, blank walls on the north and west sides, with the doors and windows facing south. A small door led into the house part, and a large one to the barn. The only light shone from a window between them. We knocked on the house door, but Grangier came out through the barn.

"*Allo?*" A dog barked behind him.

"Bonsoir. It's the Americans, come for milk."

"Come inside, then."

A single naked bulb hung from old rafters. The open room held bales of hay, watchful cats, and the sweet smell of milk. There was a pile of russet apples in one corner, a pile of green tomatoes in another. In the middle of the floor stood a stainless-steel cylinder the size of a refrigerator, beaded with condensation, humming with power.

"Did you bring a bottle?"

"No."

"This isn't a store, you know." He found a plastic liter jug. "Here. Bring this back next time, with one of your own."

He opened the cylinder's lid and picked up a long dipper. Inside, a metal handle stirred creamy liquid. He dipped a little and rinsed out the jug, then carefully filled it. It foamed up; he let it subside, then poured more in till the milk trembled at the top.

"There. That's two francs fifty."

The sterilized long-conservation liters in the store cost nearly four francs a liter.

"It smells good," Sara said.

"And it is good. My cows are certified healthy. They eat only hay from my fields, and some oats in the winter."

"But why are you going to sell them?"

"Nobody wants the milk anymore. Ten years ago I sold fifty liters a day at the store. Last year, it was only ten. Now I have to sell it to a dairy. There's no money in it, believe me. And for no money, it's too much work. We're slaves to those cows. Morning and night, every day of the year. My wife and I haven't taken a vacation together in our lives.

"Before, you had to have cows if you wanted milk or butter. Chickens, too, and rabbits. Everybody did. Now you can make a living from grapes. That's hard work, too, but at least you can leave them alone from time to time. So everyone's giving up the animals. That's the way it goes."

"How much longer do we have?"

"We'd like to sell them before the New Year. It would be better for taxes that way."

"Well, we'll be back before then. This is one of the reasons we came to the country. Now it seems the country is leaving us."

Grangier laughed. "It's the right direction for me." He gave us a bag of apples, too, and we found our way back to the village by moonlight and the glow of the streetlight on the *mairie*.

One afternoon I saw Frédéric, a mechanic at the garage, working in the ruined building across from the garage.

"Is this really going to be a restaurant?" I asked.

"That's what they say."

He was wrestling with a cement mixer. Steel beams were going up over a large space which must once have been a barn.

"Every town needs a café."

"There's always La Canelle."

"I hope this one will be better than that."

From the *mairie,* Madame Tallon took a dim view of the venture. She grumbled that the proper construction permits hadn't been completed, that the café would only draw hooligans and drunkards, that Jourdan, the garage owner building the place, was a poor influence on the town.

"You know the house behind the presbytère, the new one next to the garage?"

I was in the *mairie* making photocopies. I had become a regular customer, kept an account on a scrap of paper tacked to the wall.

"That used to be vineyards for the priest. The *garagiste* built it and rents it out to dreadful people. Last summer the tenants went away and simply left their young boy behind. Someone called the social workers. They put him in camp for a month, until the parents returned. No one ever knew where they went. The café won't be any better, you'll see."

Madame Tallon had hard words for many of the Ruchelais. The Mayor was her chief target: alcoholic, illiterate, indolent. *"Et en plus il est communiste!"* she would hiss. Once, in the fields, Bonvoisin warned me about her.

"She says terrible things about me, doesn't she?"

I shrugged.

"It's because I defeated her husband in the last election for mayor.

Actually, he's not her husband, but let's not go into that. I keep her on because in France today it's impossible to fire anybody. It's a cross I have to bear."

George said both were right: the Mayor was functionally illiterate, his secretary a viper in an impregnable nest. He suggested their enmity had its real roots in a failed love affair.

George had taken to finding work near the presbytère in the mornings, and we had taken to inviting him in for coffee. An English streak of decorum held him back on the details, but his judgment was firm: Ruch was a rabbit hutch. He told us about the Mayor's affairs, pitied Madame Bonvoisin trapped in her house by shame. One day he confided that Madame Tallon had made overtures to him.

"After the council gave me the job as *cantonnier,* she thought I might be useful," he said. His eyes were bright with disgust. "She tried to poison me against the Mayor by telling me of his affairs. Then she moved right close to me."

He dropped his voice to a whisper. "She looked right into my eyes. 'George,' she said. She touched my arm! She said, 'People have desires, you know.' Bloody hell! I cleared right out. She's hated me ever since."

France devotes two November days to the memory of the dead. The second is Armistice Day, commemorating the end of World War I.

Every town in France lost sons in the Great War, and even the smallest have built monuments to the dead. *Monuments aux Morts* are a leitmotif of French town topography. Most are set in the principal *place* or at an important crossroads, embedded in everyday life. Generally, they take the form of a stone plinth engraved with the names of the dead. A heavy chain, held at the corners by cannon balls or shells, protects it; crowning it, a simple Gallic cock, a helmeted Victory, or an advancing soldier. When the monument is inside a church, the statuary group is often more complex, men dying in the arms of angels.

When the Great War ended, Ruch already had a monument. It had been built twenty years before to honor their casualties from the battles when France took North Africa from the Spanish. In 1918, the town was

The monument on Armistice Day

poor. The survivors made do by moving the marble plaque honoring their fathers' heroes to the back of the old monument and engraving the names of the newly fallen on the front. Later, the few casualties from the Second World War joined the colonial war dead on the back.

So Ruch's monument was different. On a small tapering base a slender obelisk rose twenty feet tall. It was formal and pure; it lacked the trappings of soldiers or shells. A low chain ran around it, setting it off from the path. It stood in front of the presbytère on the edge of the bluff. This must have been one of the oldest defined spaces in town, serving as a lookout over the Courbut valley for those defending a settlement which dated at least to Gallo-Roman times. The tightly built, T-shaped village lacked a central *place,* but this was a space at the heart of its history.

By the time we arrived in Ruch the chestnuts were dying. With the presbytère inhabited by strangers, the path became a private promenade rather than a public procession. The monument was a magnet for the few tourists who stumbled on the village but had become peripheral to the daily rounds of its citizens. Its only regular visitor was an old man who walked his small white dog every day up and down the path.

Armistice Day dawned to the clatter of guns. Hunting is an obsession with the Bordelais, and a fine holiday morning brought out maximum firepower. Dogs bayed, birds screamed through the trees. At 8:30, a bleary, unshaven Mayor trudged to the monument, carrying three French flags.

"I've got to go home and shave," he said, "then go to Castillon to pick up the wreath. It's not all glory being mayor." He told me the ceremony would take place at noon. Would there be a church service as well? He didn't know, shaking his head as he trudged away again.

At 11:00 the dog walker made his way down the path. The dog noticed the flags and slipped under the chain to sniff the cloth. The man stepped close to straighten the biggest one. He took his time, almost caressing it, then stepped quickly off the platform, back to earth. He gave the arrangement an appraising glance. The dog was sniffing a corner of the wall. The fellow whistled once, and they left.

Half an hour later, another couple strolled down the chestnut path, an older man and woman. Dressed up, they still had the look of farmers, lined skin and worn shoes. They gazed at the view. He put his foot up on the wall; she nestled close, then kissed him on the cheek.

At a quarter to twelve I went out the back door and around the cemetery to find a crowd in front of the *mairie*. The Mayor had changed into a suit and was holding forth in a knot of his cronies. A dozen old women huddled in the sunny shelter of the cemetery wall. Old men stood talking in the street.

Grangier waved. He and Petit were talking about the *taille à mort,* the death pruning. The vignerons' first winter task, after a hard frost had shaken the leaves loose, was to grub up old, unproductive vines in order to prepare the parcels for replanting in the spring. They talked about how important it was, and how difficult, to get all the old roots out, so as not to leave diseases in the soil. They discussed different techniques: plow, chemicals, fire.

The crowd grew to fifty or so. Most of the people were old. Grangier said the town offered a free meal to all those from the *Troisième Age,* over sixty, and if it wasn't for that no one would come. A clutch of scrubbed schoolchildren fidgeted beneath a teacher's gaze. An old man sat in a black Peugeot with the door open. He had a fierce gaze and a firm jaw, and I asked Grangier who he was.

"That's the doctor, Dr. Delom-Sorbé. He's ninety-six years old. He was in the war himself, and there's not many left. See that woman next to him? That's his daughter, Nanette. They live at Vaure. He used to run the town, the doctor did; he was mayor for forty years. We don't see him much anymore. But I don't suppose he'd miss this."

The church bells tolled noon, with their triple-note cadence, then the tinny *mairie* bell chimed in. The crowd moved slowly down the path. The old doctor climbed out of his car, took up two metal canes, and made his slow way. At the monument, most of us hung back or leaned against the wall to the presbytère garden. The children arranged themselves near the chain.

The Mayor read a proclamation about the depth of sacrifice, the power of glory, the virtues of peace. He spoke with feeling; it concluded with an exhortation from de Gaulle and a fervent *Vive la France!*

Vive la France! echoed the crowd.

The Mayor caught his breath, then read a list of the dead. After each name, he paused, and the children chanted, *"Mort pour la France."* The doctor and a few old women joined the mournful response. The list was long, the repetition dolorous, and by its end the cost of the war was almost palpable in the air.

The Mayor paused. Stepping over the chain, he laid the wreath, worked from blue, white, and red flowers, at the base of the monument.

"May we have a moment of silence, please."

Heads bowed. Wind rustled the dying chestnut leaves, a dog barked. The doctor's daughter muttered something unintelligible. The sun warmed the back of my neck.

"Merci."

Silently the group moved away from the monument. When it reached the street, people broke into conversation again. Grangier and the Mayor turned to wave to me. *"Bon appétit,"* they called. The *mairie* clock read quarter past twelve.

Three days later, the flags disappeared. But the monument wasn't completely ignored. The wreath remained, and a pot of chrysanthemums laid after Toussaint. Every few days, an old woman brought a jug of water to them.

The hard frost finally came, whitening the fields, echoed by plumes of smoke from the village's chimneys. In the store, people stamped their feet and blew on their hands and predicted a long winter to come.

I found Grangier in the vineyard behind the new café. He was pulling up vines with a tractor, a chain, and an ax. The twisted black trunks and skeletal branches were piled high in a corner of the field. The stakes were stacked neatly in another corner alongside bales of wire. He said he was pulling up Merlot Blanc and Muscadet, two white varieties no longer in fashion, to plant red Merlot. That would complete the parcel in red grapes and make it easier to work. His vineyard would be 70 percent red grapes overall then, just about reversed from when he bought his farm, thirty years before.

"I found a buyer for the cows," he reported. "Only a few more weeks now until we get all the papers straightened out."

Autumn fell into winter like a person aging. Brilliant gold leaves showered from a tall poplar outside my office window, leaving a scratchy silhouette against the sky. The sunset point swung from north to south of it, as the days shortened and the light thinned.

I spent more time in my office, worked bundled in a hat and scarf at the desk, spent hours gazing out the window. It was a kind of in-between space—no longer in New York, not quite in France. Writing for Americans kept me rooted there, but every day we planted new, French habits and hopes. The first check came for an article written from France, and I decided to balance my accounts. I figured we were three months in the country, settled now and working again, for a total investment of about $3,000. Not so much for a new life, I thought. I wondered if we would find ourselves in Ruch for a second harvest.

7

Château de Vaure

November slipped by in the rain. Sometimes low, angry clouds would flood the sky, only to dissipate in damp breezes and trembling dew. Then cold clear days warmed to a radiant stillness that lured cats to sunny stones in sheltered corners. Winter crept in at night, though, leaving delicate trails of frost along the windowpanes.

The presbytère's stone walls drew in the cold and damp of night and held them all day long. A portable heater—an oversized toaster with a small fan—began to follow us around the house. We'd reach out for it from bed, then drag it to the bathroom. We were leery of mixing electricity and water, but the metal shower stall was colder than flesh could bear. In the kitchen, its small heat helped the teakettle fog the frost from the windows. Sara kept it under her table like a pet in the main room, where she worked bundled in sweaters and fingerless gloves. At night, preparing for bed, we danced around it, not so much undressing as changing one set of clothes for another.

One frosty morning I found a dead mole in the garden. George had already deciphered the small piles of earth that dotted the lawn, but he wasn't optimistic about halting them. Moles are cunning brutes, he said, and he's more determined to stay than you are to get rid of him. Now some predator had done the job for us.

I scooped up the small corpse with a shovel and tossed it over the wall. Sara opened the kitchen window and scattered the breakfast crumbs on the lawn. It had become a habit, and the birds had caught on. Sparrows and finches pushed and chattered around the small bounty. Suddenly a cat streaked from the shadows, scattering them into the air.

"You know what?" I called. "You and I killed that mole."

"How did we do that?"

"We drew the birds with our crumbs. The birds drew the cat, and the cat killed the mole. We may even have sacrificed a sparrow or two as bait."

We looked at each other for a moment. "Does that make you feel smart or guilty?"

"What would George or Grangier say?" she said, and shut the window.

The Bretons began to expect me in the mornings and saved a paper if I was late. Sara joined Nicole's exercise class, gasping and gossiping with the town's young mothers and restless girls. She started attending church, too. Madame Barde complimented her on her singing. Sara said she had often sung in choirs. Madame Veder, who lived behind the *mairie,* said that the ladies of the church managed a small choir at Christmas and Easter. Would Sara like to join?

Rehearsals were held at Madame Le Barazer's house. A short woman with iron hair and steely eyes, she was the real leader of the church. She took charge of cleaning the building, conscripting the acolytes, cajoling the support of an indifferent municipal council. Her husband owned one of the town's largest vineyards, and their house had all the comforts and conventions of the rural middle class: dark furniture and somber wallpaper, an old armoire of burnished wood, a souvenir of Lourdes propped on a color television, steam-heat radiators.

"We sang for about an hour," Sara told me. "No accompaniment, just a pitch pipe to start. No music, either, just the words. I knew some of the hymns, but not in French. We struggled a little, but it was sweet. After, we sat in the kitchen and talked. Mostly they complained about their health."

"Did you ask them about Ruch, their backgrounds?"

"This was a choir rehearsal, not an interview. I did find out one thing, though. They know more about us than we thought."

"Like what?"

"I asked if they ever sang for other occasions. Madame Barde said they'd be happy to sing at our wedding!"

"I wonder how she knew. Maybe Denise saw our passports and told her we weren't married."

"They all laughed and laughed at that. So much for worrying about living in sin in a Catholic community. They couldn't care less. But maybe we ought to."

"Ought to what?"

"Get married. I'd love to have them sing at our wedding."

Not everyone was so hospitable, though. At the Grangiers' for milk one evening, we could see lights burning, hear the television, but no one answered our knock. We called out halfheartedly, spent a minute looking around the flower beds, then went home empty-handed.

The next evening, Grangier greeted us more warmly than usual. When we joked about the irregular supply, he grew apologetic.

"*La mère* was at home," he said. "She told us you had come. But she didn't want to get the milk for you. She's old and she's like that." We wondered if she had watched us poke through the flowers. He pressed a bag of apples on us as we left.

We tried to pull the village into our lives, too. One morning as George was finishing his coffee, we invited him for dinner.

"You've been a real help, and we want to get to know Anice. Nothing too fancy. Just a casual dinner."

"Well, it can't be Wednesday, because I take eggs round to my customers after work. And Thursday there's a program on the telly Anice fancies."

"How about Friday? Is seven all right?"

"I might be a little late, because the chores take a while after I leave the village, you see."

"Why don't you come on Friday, as soon after seven as you can."

"Well, all right. If you're sure. It's very kind of you."

Friday we cleaned the presbytère, put some of Sara's drawings on the walls, went to the cooperative for wine, laid a fire.

"What do you think they like to eat?" Sara wondered.

"They're English. Anything we fix will taste good."

"We should do something American. Something nobody doesn't like. How about spaghetti?"

"Spaghetti is American?"

"You know what I mean. With a big salad, garlic bread, and maybe I'll make a cake for dessert. And George likes pâté, so let's have that as an appetizer."

They arrived just after seven. George had put on a coat and tie and Anice wore a woolen dress. We had on turtlenecks and sweaters, and wondered how they would have dressed if we had said formal. George knew the presbytère better than we did, but Anice acted as if it was her first visit. People said she was reclusive, but she certainly wasn't reserved. We went through two bottles of white Entre-Deux-Mers with the pâté and opened a bottle of Château de Vaure 1985 while Sara boiled the pasta.

"What do you think of Ruch's wine, George?"

"Not too bad, this. I prefer Yon's wine, myself. He lives over in Mauriac. Do you know him?"

"No."

"Pity. I'll take you over there one day. Quite a chap, Yon. Does everything himself."

Sara brought in big steaming bowls of spaghetti and sauce. "I'll serve," she said. "Anice, how much would you like?"

"Oh, heap it on," she said. "I do love pasta, and we never have it."

"Why not?" Sara asked. "It's simple to make."

"Oh, George doesn't like pasta. Never has. Have you, George?"

George looked down at his plate. Sara blushed. Anice sniffed the sauce. "Smells lovely," she said.

"This is American spaghetti," I said. "Entirely different. More wine, Anice?"

"Don't mind if I do," she said.

. . .

The autumn colors were gold on gray. The sun fell molten on the stone walls. The vineyards rose from a carpet of copper leaves. The plantations of poplars in their checkerboard patterns were brushes dipped in yellow paint, the wild asparagus by the roadside were lacy gold braid, a ginkgo gleamed with buttery brilliance.

When winter finally came to stay in December, the palette changed to red and black. As always, the vines set the dominant note. The bare wood glowed like coals in the sunset, crimson branches on deep purple trunks. All harum-scarum, they shook their arms in a witches' dance, stiff, twisted, and menacing. But in number, unity emerged. The infinite rows swept over the hills like waves, rosy and luminous under the low, raking light.

The poplars and chestnuts, bare now, gave the stage to the oaks, rusty red leaves thinning to reveal majestic black trunks and gnarled branches. The red sun lit the tile roofs early and late and scarlet shutters gleamed in the waning light. Night hurried down, and distant taillights echoed the cigarettes glowing outside the store.

The cold triggered the next phase in the vineyard year, the *taille,* the pruning of the vines. The vignerons wait until the leaves have fallen to begin the task, to be sure the sap has retreated deep into the plant. The wait also gives them a month or so after the harvest to cut wood, repair machinery, slaughter a pig. Or simply to hunt and holiday.

Because, once begun, the *taille* is a long road. Around Ruch, the vineyard density is about 1,500 plants per acre. Each farm family prunes its own vineyards; most have at least ten acres, and some have three or four times as much. The *taille* must be finished before the sap rises again in the spring, sometime in March There are long hours during the short days, hard work in heavy weather.

The work itself hasn't changed for centuries; it's the last major vineyard task done by hand. The worker focuses on each *pied de vigne* in turn, searching for the most fruitful branch to let grow, shaping the trunk so it matures straight and centered, watching for any sign of disease or damage. It's an old maxim that for wine grapes quantity and quality vary in inverse ratio, and laws regulate the maximum yields vineyards are permitted. But while the winemaker may be willing to trade grapes for extra taste in the bottle, sacrificing fruit goes against a farmer's deepest nature. During the *taille,* he has three months to come to grips with this contradiction.

It's a meditative task, rewarding steadiness and concentration, and some of the vignerons enjoy the work. Others took long breaks in the store, coming in for a shoelace or a pack of cigarettes and staying for an hour to talk. They decided it was too wet or too cold or the moon was wrong and took the day off. They invented errands in Castillon or Sauveterre, consulted with the mechanic, called the doctor. Three months is a long time to spend kneeling in cold mud with clippers in your hand and branches in your face.

One drizzly morning I came across a knot of dark-clad figures talking in the road. The Mayor, Claude, Grangier, Petit, and Madame Jourdan were standing between the cemetery and the emerging café. Behind

Francis Bonvoisin pruning his vines

them, a man was chiseling away at the cemetery gate. His blue jumpsuit was covered with stone dust streaking in the rain.

I shook hands all round. The conversation lapsed. Claude and Grangier left. "The vines are calling," Grangier said. Petit and Madame drifted back to the garage. The Mayor walked me to the store. I wondered if I had dissolved the group, and what they were discussing before I arrived.

"Who's that? What's he doing?"

"That's Madame Lunardelli's brother," replied the Mayor. "We're rebuilding the gates."

"What's wrong with them?"

"They're too big."

The rusty wrought-iron gates were the height of the stone wall that surrounded the cemetery, about six feet, and creaked open about seven feet wide.

"Too big for what?"

"The Jourdans are building a café in the old building across the street," the Mayor explained. "That's a good thing for the town. It'll keep the young ones at home. But the law says you can't have the door of a café within fifteen meters of the main entrance to a cemetery. Why? I don't know. Our cemetery has two entrances. The law considers the bigger one the main one, and it's too close to the café. The Jourdans can't move their building. So we have to make the big entrance smaller than the small entrance. That way it's no longer the main one."

I tried to frame a question about the letter and the spirit of the law. Bonvoisin shook his head.

"Fifty years ago there wasn't a gate at all on this side of the cemetery. It was only opened to allow bulldozers to get in and dig the crypts. They're all built now. If we really wanted to be faithful to tradition, we'd just close the gate up entirely. Some people wanted to. But I argued against it. It's convenient for people who might be too old and tired to go all the way around to the other gate. This way we satisfy the law, tradition, and the needs of the people all at once. Not bad, eh?"

We paused in front of the store. Bonvoisin squinted at me.

"Et en plus, there are subsidies for this kind of thing. France is a generous nation. And the mason needs the work. Well, Claude will be wondering where I am. No one escapes the *taille,* not even the Mayor."

By going to church, Sara led us to Vaure. Nanette Delom-Sorbé always sat in the front row and kept a keen eye on the acolytes as they fidgeted and squirmed behind the priest. Sara fell into conversation with her one Sunday, and as they parted, she invited us to stop by for afternoon tea.

The château sat off the road, just above the cooperative, hidden by a stand of trees. A weathered stone cross marked the dirt driveway.

Seen from the road that ran through the valley below it, Vaure was a fortress rearing above the ridge, but our approach from above and behind made it look almost cozy. The house formed a U around a graveled court. Its three sections were all two stories high, but they differed in length and the disposition of their windows, suggesting they had been built at different times, even different centuries. The center and eastern sections were covered with the same gray concrete and patches of orange lichen that skinned most of the town's houses. On the large western arm, though, the stone had been scraped bare and the joints repointed, according to the latest fashion of refurbishment. The ensemble resembled three family members who had gone separate ways in life until old age led them home again.

We crossed a small stone bridge over what must once have been a moat. There was a large arched doorway in the central side and we made for that. After the noise of the car, our voices, our feet crunching the gravel, knocking seemed redundant, but we knocked and waited and knocked again before Nanette came to the door.

"Bonjour," we said.

"Bonjour."

"Thank you for inviting us to tea. Is this a good time?"

Her black eyes were hooded. I wondered if Sara had misunderstood her. Then she turned inside and motioned for us to follow.

The room we entered was large by any standards, and huge for Ruch. It was as wide as the building, almost as long as the whole central section, and the ceiling was at least eighteen feet high. Yet it shared the essential elements of every *séjour* in town. A big table dominated one end, set with a dozen chairs. The inevitable armoire had become three, old and massive. There were family portraits, armchairs, and a television on a spindly stand. No lights were lit, and the windows couldn't coax enough of the waning afternoon sun inside to dispel the gloom. We didn't notice the doctor until he began to stir in his chair.

"Bonjour," he said.

We turned. *"Ah, bonjour, Monsieur. Comment allez-vous?"*

He was struggling with aluminum canes. His jaw was set and the tendons in his hands were rigid as he gripped the arm of the chair, half rose. *"Ah, moi, je suis foutu."* I'm shot to hell.

"These are the Americans," Nanette said. "They've come for tea."

"How kind," murmured the doctor. "So Americans drink tea, do they?"

"Not with the ceremony of the British, but yes, we do," said Sara. "In the South we drink it iced."

"Iced? But of course. It must be very hot there. We're quite partial to English ceremonies here in the Gironde." He shook his head. "Quite affected of us. They've been gone five hundred years. Are you sure you wouldn't prefer a glass of wine? Or a whiskey, perhaps?"

"No, thank you. Tea will be fine."

"Well, Nanette will make us some." The small black-haired figure scurried off. "Do sit down."

The old man lowered himself slowly back into his chair. The setting was at once the most foreign and the most familiar we had encountered in the village. It was rooted in the crafts of French culture—the massive beams, the red-tiled floor, the richly carved armoires spoke in the dialect of the region. The artifacts, too, were utterly French, from a collection of old plates decorated with the châteaux of the Loire to bottles of gentian liqueur and Armagnac on the sideboard. Objects that would have been collector's treasures in America, restored, displayed, and untouchable, were simply part of everyday life, battered and showing their age.

Yet the decor didn't have the simplicity that marked the other rooms we had visited in Ruch. Glossy cocktail-table books described the churches of Paris and the cave paintings at nearby Lascaux. A glass case held tailor's dummies wearing clothes from the last century. The family photographs weren't random survivors but a studied historical record. The objects suggested that the family saw themselves in a distinct relation to their culture, privileged and perhaps threatened. They had a perspective on Ruch that set them apart from it.

Nanette brought the tea and bustled about pouring. We'd been told the doctor was ninety-six, so she must have been sixty or so, and a tremor betrayed her age. But she poured with the fixed intensity of a child practicing a hard-won skill. After distributing the cups and passing a bowl of savory biscuits around once, she pulled back into her chair like a shell.

The doctor paid her little attention. We avoided her bright hard glances. Her voice was cracked and harsh, her accent difficult to understand, and she finished every sentence with a mirthless laugh that left no response. We directed our questions about Ruch to her father. They seemed to amuse the old man. After all, he said, what did he know about it?

"I'm not from Ruch, you know."

"But you've been here for . . . how long?"

"Came here in 1922. I brought these good Ruchelais into the world, most of them, and many that are now gone from it. But I wasn't born here myself. I'm from Béarn, near the Pyrénées."

"How did you come, then, in the beginning?"

"I studied medicine in Bordeaux. This was before the war, of course. Vaure was owned by a distant cousin of my father then, M. Carrère. He had married a daughter of Vaure, a Mlle Follardeau, and had two daughters of his own. I used to come to visit and reached an understanding with the younger daughter. Then the war came. I went to Alsace. When it was over, I finished my studies, married, and moved here. That was in 1921. The property was twice as big then. Half a dozen families lived and worked here."

"You said 1922, Papa."

"Did I?"

"Yes, 1922. Hahahahaha."

Nanette and Dr. Delom-Sorbé

"I've been here ever since. And I suppose I'll be here a little longer."

Delom-Sorbé had been the town's only doctor, major landholder, and from 1935 to 1971 its mayor. He had the first telephone in town, in the twenties, and the first harvesting machine, in 1980.

"By the 1930s, my practice kept me too busy to keep up with the vineyards," he reflected, "and the town was happy to buy my *chai* instead of building a new one for a cooperative. At that time, the white wine sold much better than the red, and the members planned not to make any red at all, to save on the vats and barrels and so forth. But I wanted red wine for myself, and I insisted they equip themselves to make it. Now it sells for twice as much as the white, and the growers are pulling up their white vines as fast as they can." He chuckled.

Had Ruch changed much over the years?

"People are still being born," the doctor said. "They work and they die. Life is easier now, I suppose. We have running water and tractors and television. The cities seem closer, and more people go and live in them. There used to be seven hundred people in Ruch. Now there's only five hundred, and we'll be lucky if we don't lose more. But there will always be vineyards, as long as people drink wine."

The light had faded, the room was dim and soft. The doctor leaned back in his chair. Nanette looked at him with shining black eyes, dark pools whose meanings were impossible to read. The big room overshadowed these two pale sparks, yet at the same time it seemed to embody the lives they had lived, as if each act had become an object and all the objects had remained to recall them. Now there was no energy for new efforts, and no new objects would be added. The sparks would flicker until the room was left in darkness.

We wished we could simply vanish without disturbing the silence, but finally stood. Nanette's glance flashed at us.

"Thank you so much for tea," Sara said. "It's been wonderful meeting you at last."

The doctor struggled to his feet. "It's been a pleasure to have you. You must come back when more of the family is here. Have you met Philippe, my grandson? He's about your age, and used to live in Paris. He works the Vaure vineyards now."

We promised to return and crunched across the gravel. Night was falling; the château was a blocky silhouette against the darkening sky. Our headlights glittered off its windows as we turned the car around toward the village.

Two days later I stopped into the *mairie*.

"The doctor is in fine shape for ninety-six, isn't he?" Madame Tallon asked.

I agreed.

"I suppose you talked about politics," she continued. "Did he speak of my Guy? He was deputy mayor for many years and naturally took over as mayor when the doctor retired, after his wife died, poor thing. He was devastated.

"But every sorrow brings some good. The doctor had been mayor for a long time. He refused to spend a centime and many things needed doing. Guy built the schoolmaster's house, repaired the church, and created the *gîte* where you live." She glanced toward the door, sighed heavily. "But the French are suspicious of success. We're a petty nation and we dislike those who stand out. People became jealous of poor Guy. Our new mayor is the result."

The phone rang and her voice changed. She solved someone's problem, then left her desk to fiddle with the controls of the old gas heater blasting away in a corner.

"This morning it was 45 degrees in here," she complained. "The only way to warm up the room is to turn the heater up to the maximum, and then it leaks gas fumes and I get a headache. But this whole office is a mess, isn't it?"

It was simple enough. The narrow plank flooring was bare and splintery in spots; the green plaster walls were marred by scars and water stains. The files were stacked in an old armoire. The photocopier sat on a child's school desk.

"I suffer in here," she was saying, "while the council meets next door with every comfort. Have you seen the council room?"

She led me through the base of the tower, around a spiral stone staircase, and into a large room. It had been recently restored, shiny as new, plaster stripped from the walls and the rough stone scrubbed golden. The windows had been replaced and now had a vaguely Gothic air, with heavy wooden mullions and small panes. A huge beam running the length of the ceiling had been varnished, then disfigured by the addition of a track-lighting strip.

"The people from the National Historical Monuments said they would put the building on their list. We hoped they would reimburse some of the cost. But when they came out to look at it, they said that the interior hadn't been properly studied and some of the changes were wrong. The windows, especially. I think they were being a bit small-minded, don't you? Anyway, we didn't get the money."

The weather stayed cold and the conversation in the store turned to warmth. Old people in old houses lived mostly in their kitchens in winter, by fireplaces where they burned stumps of vine. Many of the farmers had installed wood stoves in their fireplaces for more efficiency. Central heating, fired by diesel oil, was only for the newest houses and the well-to-do. Those who had it compared the dates when they finally turned it on, and those who didn't mused about its costs and dangers.

One family pushed a portable heater too far. Fire broke out and destroyed the house where Philippe Sartran lived with his wife and infant son. Fortunately, no one was hurt. In the store, no one talked about insurance or compensation, only about the heater that had started the fire and how to avoid a similar fate. The family moved to the town's second *gîte,* on the main street.

We knew Sartran, a stocky fellow in his twenties who played on the soccer team. Madame Tallon told me that he worked at the cooperative winery in nearby Rauzan and his parents were Ruchelais but had divorced. His father lived next door to the Bonvoisins. His mother had married a plumber and moved to a new house on the edge of the village.

One night after the fire Philippe came to visit. He was the first Ruchelais to knock at our door. He wanted to invite us to tour his winery. He smelled of *pastis*. He told us that he and his mother had lived in the presbytère for a few months after the divorce. He visibly regretted the visit the moment he stepped inside. He wouldn't come farther than the hallway. Later, we did go to the winery. The director showed us around and we spotted Philippe driving a forklift. We never returned his house call, but always exchanged words in passing.

The Mayor told us it was the first fire in Ruch in twenty years. We had stopped by his house after a walk. By four in the afternoon, the vines were stumpy twisted silhouettes against a deepening sky. By five, they had been woven into a black carpet under the stars. The only light in the Bonvoisins' house came from a room in the back, where we found Nicole knitting a sweater for Claude's girlfriend, Isabel, and Madame sitting in a rocker. A wood stove warmed the room and the television filled it with sound.

They acted as if they had been expecting us. Madame brought out *vin de noix* and a box of salted peanuts. Claude appeared, riffled through a few magazines, and left again. The Mayor came in and talked about the Sartran fire, about a French businessman who had been gunned down by extremists in Paris, about a striptease show coming to the Scorpion. Francis returned from feeding his cows, stamping the cold out of his feet.

After another glass, the men drifted out of the room. We decided to take our leave, too. It was hard to quit the stove for the chilly presbytère, but the cold air quickened our steps. We looked forward to dinner, and bed.

8

Christmas

Ruch withdrew into dark December days. Our walks were shorter; we spent more time by ourselves. People were unfailingly pleasant, but they lost their curiosity about us. *"Bonjour,"* they smiled. "Still here? So your vacation is going well?"

One cold morning men clustered around a sleek Citroën at the garage. It was a late-model BX, and they were discussing its merits compared with the bigger, more traditional CX. Grangier was in the thick of it.

"Hey!" he called as I passed. "This goes faster than a cow, eh?"

I stopped to admire the car.

"You haven't been around for milk in a while," he said.

"It's true. Maybe we'll come by this evening."

"Too late!" He smiled. "The cows are gone. Now this will sleep in the barn." He patted the car.

"You sold the cows?"

"Last week. The fellow got a better deal than he deserved, but the timing was right. Madame Silva wanted to sell her car."

"Well, we'll miss the milk," I said. "That's something special gone."

"It turns a page in life," Grangier agreed. "Now the evenings will be a little more restful. I can read the paper or look at television. I'm a free man. Maybe we'll even go on vacation. This will take us anywhere."

He patted the car again. Antoine asked him a question and he turned to answer. I went on to the store. Old cows for a new car. Who could blame him?

I never missed my morning walk for fresh bread and the newspaper. I needed to look at the sky, chat with Marie-Jo at the register. But we stopped buying much food at the Galeries. What had seemed abundance when we arrived—overflowing baskets of leeks and lettuces, plump sausages, fresh-killed rabbits and birds—became monotonous, and the prices looked higher and higher. Then Sara discovered the Monday market in Castillon, and her weekly trip there became another of the small routines that made France home.

France's *hypermarchés* may be the world's largest grocery stores, but they haven't put the farmers' markets out of business. The French, who take their food seriously, have an unshakable bias in favor of local produce. Castillon lay across the Dordogne River, 10 kilometers north of Ruch. It wasn't the only nearby market town, or even the closest, but the weekly fair drew the Ruchelais and had for generations. It was an easy ride, down the hill past the cooperative and across the fertile river plain. A stone bridge arched over placid water and the town of 3,000 rose on the high banks beyond.

The silvery winter light played over stone houses reflected in gray water, knitting river and town and sky into a single tone. The high-bluffed bank was a building site favored by both beauty and logic. Archaeological remnants attested to Paleolithic settlements, and the Magdalenians who painted the cave walls at Lascaux some 15,000 years ago left chisels and awls in Castillon. The Romans arrived in the first century and improved a natural ford just east of town which became part of the medieval pilgrims' route from Paris and the north to Santiago de Compostela in Spain. According to old maps, the road ran right by Ruch.

Castillon had probably always been a trading center. Its archives held a document from 1440 discussing the local fair, called an ancient custom even then. As the market grew, the ford gave way to ferries, and for centuries regular service connected the town with Entre-Deux-Mers. Castillon's first bridge was built in 1835, a second in 1905. Both were

The market at Castillon-la-Bataille

destroyed in 1940 to hinder German troop movements. Then ferries again carried the commerce, and when old people told us of walking to market and back, we were listening to the habits of the Middle Ages.

"Fresh lettuce, fresh lettuce, just picked this morning!" cried a woman behind crates of romaine, red leaf, *mâche,* and bibb, all spangled with dew and smelling of earth. "Best prunes from Armagnac! Walnuts from Périgord! Olives from Provence!" brayed a fellow whose face resembled a walnut, and his beret a silky black olive. It was a cook's paradise, and plump women with string bags and straw baskets joked and jostled to get the freshest of it for a few francs less.

The market overran Castillon every Monday. The town squares were jammed with stalls. Cars crowded every inch of sidewalk, traffic island, and open field within walking distance of town. Each kind of merchandise had its own location. Cheap clothes and serious hardware set up in the long *place* by the church. One street bloomed with flowers, another with fruit. The covered market, a cast-iron structure built in 1912, held all the rest; the butchers and bakers, the cheese merchants and fishmongers, whatever was in season and tempting to eat.

Sara made most of the marketing trips, and soon made friends. A young man who sold cheeses recognized her from the market in Cadillac and caught her custom; an old woman gave her a taste of warm walnut bread and it became our Monday-afternoon snack. She met Ruchelais there, too, and in Castillon's new grocery store, where meat and staples were cheaper. On her way home, she treated herself at the *chi-chi* stand, where a woman squeezed ropes of dough into a cauldron of hot fat and cooked them into sweet crispy crullers.

Some days, when a check had come in, I went, too, and we celebrated with lunch at Le Centre, a café-restaurant on the main street. Daniel, the owner, had once raced a car in the rally from Paris to Dakar. He had a sideline business as a small *négociant,* buying and selling the fresh, fruity red wines from vineyards in the hills outside of town. There was a man-sized fireplace in back where he cooked lamb chops and steaks, and sometimes a whole haunch hung from a chain and spun slowly over the flames.

We got there early, to get a table near the fire, and ordered lamb and a liter of his latest discovery from the Côtes de Castillon. Daniel knocked a shower of coals free from the burning logs, oak and vinewood, and raked them into a pile on the skirt of the hearth. He set a long-handled grill over the coals, brushed it with oil, and when it was hot threw on the meat. A few sizzling minutes later the chops were done, and he served them with French fries and a green salad. By then, the room had filled with beefy men and their wives and their bundles; they drank and laughed and steamed the windows. We left a hundred francs poorer, but ready to face another cold week in the presbytère.

Just before Christmas, our friends Dan and Anne came to visit from New York. We took them to Castillon and to the Mayor's for *vin de noix.* The winter skies hung gray and low, and every day got colder. The presbytère felt like a walk-in refrigerator. They couldn't sleep in the unheated guest room no matter how many blankets we piled on the beds, so they moved close to the fire. We spent a lot of time in the kitchen. Christmas Eve day was the color of iron. We went for a walk, but the village was deserted. We put up a small tree and decorated it with paper ornaments, strings of popcorn, pinecones, and a tinfoil star.

Midnight Mass in Ruch was scheduled for eleven. At 10:30 we went to pick up Madame Veder. The streets were quiet, mist rising orange in the streetlights. She let us in while she put on her coat. On television dancers dressed like sexy Santas were kicking their long legs high.

"It's American," she said, turning it off. "Amusing, isn't it?"

We walked back to the church. Now cars were parked by the *mairie* and groups of people drifted down the chestnut path. Inside, the air was as cold and damp as the winter night, despite the feeble efforts of a few gas heaters perched on chairs. Fluorescent lights brightened the church with a hard, blue-edged glow, given a lurid tinge by the orange flames of the burning gas.

Sara and Madame Veder took their places with the choir. The church filled. When the Delom-Sorbé family entered, nearly twenty strong, they brought the congregation close to a hundred.

There was no music, but the church was full of sound. Heels clicked on the stone floors, chairs scraped, programs rustled, sibilant whispers echoed from the walls. In the back, children stirred and tittered. Madame Le Barazer glared at them from her front-row command post. She signaled to Mademoiselle Grelety at the harmonium, who adjusted her glasses and her music, gave a few preliminary pumps with her feet to fill the bellows, and began to play. People fell quiet as the ancient instrument sighed into life. Its warm, breathy voice was almost human. A carol filled the air with hope and reassurance.

The priest was late again, squat and squinting but resplendent in white robe with gold embroidery. Half a dozen costumed children followed him from the sacristy, culled from the catechism class and the choir families to act out the Nativity. Nanette Delom-Sorbé kept them in line.

The flagstones numbed our feet, we puffed into stiff fingers. The priest read the Nativity story, while Nanette pushed the children into place. There were prayers and carols. The congregation was rusty. We faltered on the hymns, staggered a little standing and sitting down. At the altar, the priest concentrated on the sacred words and solemn gestures. In between lay a chasm, a note of sadness like an empty place at the dinner table. Then he closed his book.

"My friends," he said, gazing at the vaulted ceiling, "tonight is a night for gifts. God gave us the greatest gift of all in the birth of His Son, and we in our ways repeat that act of love. Even the humblest can be graced. Tonight I arrived at Clairac to find a dozen bundles half hidden in the darkness beside the church door. What can they be? I thought. Sheep waiting for the Infant's birth?"

He paused an instant, as if waiting for laughter. "Then a crowd of people came out from the church to say, Open them, Father! And I did, and they were new chairs for the church, a gift from the town. The Mayor himself made a speech. My friends, the spirit of Christmas is strong!"

Was it a salutary message for benighted Ruch? He paused, an air of rapture about him, nothing of the accusing prophet. Then he finished the service and vanished through the sacristy. We shuffled out to the cold and laughter of the night. Clear sky as midnight struck, the chestnut path was dark, then suddenly lit like day as headlights went on. Exhausts steaming, engines lowing, the cars were like animals at the manger, and we the shepherds, calling our farewells.

Some were going on to a *Réveillon,* the traditional Christmas midnight feast. But we waited for morning to settle into the kitchen.

We had spent a week assembling the ingredients. We collected fresh Arcachon oysters from the bay south of Bordeaux and the truffled pork sausages spiderwebbed in caul fat called *crépinettes* that are always eaten with them at Christmas. We filled our bags with carrots and celery and onions damp with earth. We bought a capon still costumed in tailfeathers and crest from the ample woman who had castrated, fed, and slaughtered it in Armagnac country to the south. We picked up local chestnuts and walnuts and cheeses and the famous prunes from Agen. We splurged 250 francs for a four-ounce block of foie gras. We stood in line with harried laughing women snaking out the door of a bakery famous for its *bûche de Noël,* a sponge cake shaped and iced like a fireplace log, adorned with meringue mushrooms and spun-sugar holly.

Our meal began at the traditional beginning, with foie gras and a bottle of Sauternes. The marriage of the unctuous liver and the honeyed wine amplified the richness of each. The foie gras melted in my mouth; the sweet white wine was thick enough to eat with a spoon. When it was gone, we woke as if from a dream.

Then Dan shucked oysters and I opened a bottle of Entre-Deux-Mers from the cooperative. The crisp, citrus-scented white wine and the briny oysters revived us like a sea breeze. The spicy sausages, given a wild earthy note by the truffles, sent us back thirsty to the wine.

"This is what regional cuisine is all about," Sara said. "The local wine evolves until it's a perfect match for the local food."

"Do you drink wine like this with every meal?" Anne asked. "I'm a little tipsy already."

"We almost always have a glass or two," I said. "It's like the bread; it becomes a habit and you don't understand how you got along without it."

"Is alcoholism a big problem in France?" Dan wondered.

"People drink a lot. Look at the old men with the crinkly red lines in their face. But I don't think it's a plague, at least not here in the south, in wine country. Drunken driving is a problem, though. Don't plan on traveling after lunchtime on a holiday."

"Americans could never eat and drink like this on a regular basis," Anne said. "It takes too much concentration."

"It's almost become a reflex here. They've been doing it for centuries."

I carved the roast in the drafty high-ceilinged room roaring with fire and fragrant with pine, a feudal lord. We drank two bottles of Vieux Vaure, a fleshy, fruity '83, with the capon, and then a '79, thin and elegant as twilight, with the cheeses. The *bûche de Noël* brought the meal full circle back to sweet. We washed it down with strong coffee and then staggered to the fireside to nurse small glasses of Armagnac. Was this gluttony? We couldn't feel sinful. We had abandoned ourselves to the goodness of the earth and been amply rewarded for our faith.

In the evening, Claude Bonvoisin and Isabel stopped by to wish us *Joyeux Noël*. They had gone to La Canelle for *Réveillon* on Christmas Eve. The menu was much like ours, from the foie gras to the Armagnac. They were twenty friends, Claude said; it finished at 2:30 A.M. The visit was our first since Philippe Sartran's brief stop. It felt like a present from the whole village. They wouldn't come in, but we held them on the threshold for a moment to savor it.

We spent New Year's Eve in Paris with Dan and Anne and a crew of American friends. We met in a crowded café near the Place de la République, lively with revelers, some smart in dinner jackets and long dresses, many scruffy and soused. We drank some wine and warmed up, and I threw my jacket over a chair. Some thief noticed my wallet in a pocket, and when we left it was gone.

At midnight I was in a police station filling out forms. In another corner of the waiting room a fellow consoled a friend with a bloody gash on his forehead. Policemen came in and out with cases of wine. The one who talked with me was bored but kind. He offered no hope of retrieving the wallet.

So much for New York street smarts. The weather was crisp and clear over the next few days, and Paris was Paris, but my heart wasn't in it. Sara and I said goodbye to our friends and headed back to Ruch with relief.

Our first morning back, the temperature in the bedroom was 43 degrees. The pipes had frozen: no water in the sink, the shower, the toilet. In the store people were talking about a Siberian cold wave; half the village was without water. Marie-Jo shrugged. "At least it kills the mosquitoes." The temperature stayed below freezing all day, and at night with the fire roaring and the heater at its maximum we were still cold. We put on as many clothes as would fit. At ten o'clock it began to snow.

The next morning it was colder and still snowing, fine and dry and swirling. We holed up in the kitchen with hot tea. Around noon, we smelled smoke and rushed outdoors to find the plumber thawing our pipes with a blowtorch. He said Marie-Jo Breton had told the Mayor about our frozen pipes, and the Mayor had sent him round. He restored the water, but the freeze had broken the toilet: it would drain but not fill. As we struggled to fix it, the power went out in the windowless bathroom. We retreated to the fireside to watch the snow. In the living room, it was 51 degrees.

The snow fell all day. In the village, an old man died; a wedding was postponed. The crowd in the store debated whether the baker would make it through the snowy roads next day. People tried to remember how long it had been since the town was snowbound. They weren't sure: a long time.

The next day snow lay six inches deep on the ground. The only tracks betrayed a dog who had come through the gate and circled the apple tree by the church. Our sink wouldn't drain; I discovered the drainpipe had frozen. So we used the dishwater to flush the toilet. No mail from Castillon. No school. No *Sud Ouest*. But the bread did arrive, to the great relief of the store crowd, who turned the talk to the great freeze of 1956, which killed a third of the vineyards in Bordeaux.

The snow continued through the next day. No snowplows came through, and the baker failed us. Panic emptied the shelves of the store. No milk, no meat, no vegetables, no cheese. About the only things left were laundry detergent and ammunition. Suddenly everyone was wearing moon boots, thick puffy tubes like rubber sausages. They all looked like Michelin Men. Madame Duprat, who lived opposite the store, slipped and fell on her way over and broke her wrist. Was the store responsible? The debate was lively. Gérard decided to salt his sidewalk. A few of us stood by, watching.

"Like New York, eh?" Petit asked me.

"In New York, they clean it up faster," I said.

"In France, we're not in much of a hurry to clean things up."

Someone suggested the municipal counselors should clear the roads with shovels and brooms. After all, they were responsible for the town. Petit, himself a counselor, protested they weren't paid enough for that.

"Then how about the Mayor? He gets paid."

The idea elicited general laughter.

"Or the *cantonnier*. After all, that's his job, isn't it?"

The laughter increased.

"Ah well, he's English. What can you expect from him?" Gérard packed up the salt bag and the subject was tabled.

The cold and snow halted life for a week and people began to grumble. The mail finally got through from Castillon, but Ithier would ride only his bicycle because the back roads were still too slippery for the motorbike. So he delivered mail to the village and skipped the 32 kilometers of rural route. He got angry phone calls in return. The garbagemen failed to come for the second week. In the *mairie,* Madame Tallon blamed it all on the Mayor. "He's a do-nothing, that's all. He's fine when it comes to opening a bottle of wine or asking someone to vote for him, but when something needs to be done, he's a do-nothing."

The cold snap reduced the Sunday faithful to a shivering half dozen. But the priest let nothing stop his catechism classes, and one snowy Wednesday I helped him wrestle a chalkboard from his car into the church.

"Thank you," he said.

I waved a hand. "How many children do you have for catechism?"

"Here, in Ruch? Of course, it varies from year to year. Now, I'm afraid, there are only two. But they're eager students of the Church."

"It must be cold in there. Would you like to stop in for tea when it's over?"

He reflected. Perhaps he'd rather just go home and put his feet in a tub of hot water. But then he nodded. "That is kind of you." He went into the church, and I went to tell Sara and straighten up the house.

An hour later he knocked on the door. We ushered him into the living room and gave him a seat by the fire. Sara poured him a cup of tea and he nibbled on a cookie.

"This is a wonderful house," she said. "Did you ever live here?"

"No. My predecessor did. He served this church for nearly fifty years. But by the time his strength failed him and I was called to the flock, I was already settled in Blasimon. And then, of course, the townspeople decided to rent this house to visitors. It's quite comfortable, isn't it?"

He seemed at ease but distracted. His gaze drifted constantly upward, his chin tilting to follow, as if he were straining to hear something in the distance, some call that might come at any moment and compel him to leave. Even close up, his age and appearance were difficult to determine. His short hair wavered between blond and gray; his eyes were watery and indistinct.

The priest

Madame Barde had told us that he was an amateur archaeologist who had assembled a collection of artifacts in the *mairie* of Blasimon. She said he saw animals in old stones and had gathered so many the floors were sagging. I asked about the distant past.

"You know, this region has been a center of spirituality for many, many years," he said. "Have you visited the abbey at Blasimon?"

Blasimon was built on a hill five kilometers south of Ruch. The abbey nestled by a stream at its feet. Only a small thirteenth-century church remained standing. But its west portal was embellished with sculpture of an elegance astonishing for its rural site, and ruined walls and partially excavated foundations testified to the grandeur of the medieval establishment. The abbey was on many tourist maps and the town had put up picnic tables by the entrance.

"Well, the Benedictines were not the first Christians to build on that site. Nor were the Christians the first to worship there."

He described the coins and carved stones he had found there, along with nearby votaries, tomb relics, and menhirs, large oblong stones set upright in the ground, for unknown reasons, presumably by Gauls. He believed the early Christians had chosen the spot because the Romans had already established its divinity, that the Romans had only replaced more primitive cults, that before there was history Neolithic man had sacrificed to the gods of water and fertility on the marshy ground where three springs converged.

"The abbey church has been sanctified by the prayers of millennia," he said. "But there was a holiness in the place before there were people to worship it. God's message is clear. It doesn't need our ears to hear it. But when our tongues repeat it, He is pleased. Christianity is the most pleasing form of the message because it is the truest. But that message has been ours to know since there were men to know it."

His voice seemed disembodied, solely a medium to repeat this message from another realm. We felt no closer to him than when he was behind the altar. I wanted to ask about the town, its church, their relations with each other and his with them.

"You must find it difficult to care for so many churches," I said.

"Especially in this age when churchgoing seems less important than it once was."

He nibbled another cookie. His gaze roamed the ceiling and his face flushed a little. "I can't speak for other parishes. But I consider myself the most fortunate priest in the world. Do you know why?" He paused rhetorically. Then, with a small smile: "Because I have the good among my parishioners!"

Sara and I glanced at each other.

"I beg your pardon? Our French . . ."

He turned to us, smile still echoing. "There is a family in Blasimon called Good—Dominique and Marie-Claire Bon. They come to church faithfully. So if the Bon family is in my parish, I have the Good around me. How can I help being a happy priest?"

He finished his cup and took his leave.

After ten days, the snow melted from the roads. The garbagemen came, the store was restocked, the vines were saved. Our drainpipe unfroze, the plumber fixed our toilet, the roads were clear to Castillon. The world slowly woke up again. But January was almost over, wasted. The pruning which had gone so well in sunny December was now behind schedule. It was time to get to work.

9

Pruning in Winter

Melting snow dripped like diamonds from trees and splashed through the streets. Plumes of smoke rose from the fields where farmers were burning branches pruned from the vines. It was warmer outside the presbytère than in, so we took a long walk and wound up at the Bonvoisins' house as the sun set. Nicole was knitting her fifth sweater of the winter, two ahead of schedule, because the cold had slowed the vineyard work.

"Yesterday the priest said the Mass was for Jean Barde," Sara said. "Was that Jeanette's husband?"

"Eh oui," sighed Madame Bonvoisin. "He died just a year ago."

"They ran a shop together," Nicole added, "in the house where she lives now. Did a good business, too."

"She doesn't seem like a shopkeeper somehow," Sara said. "She's so quiet."

"Oh, she was a hard worker," Madame Bonvoisin replied.

"And Jean was, too," added Nicole. "He came from the north with his brother. There were some fine vineyards in his dowry! He and Jeanette opened a store in her house, while the brother set up a garage in the Grangiers' old barn." The knitting needles pointed. "Where Jourdan is building the café for Nathalie." The needles wagged. "People will try anything in this world!"

"Then the brother built the new garage," said Madame Bonvoisin.

"The old priest wasn't happy about it, either," said Nicole. "But more people had cars after the war. The doctor even had a tractor. Yes, they were workers, the Bardes."

She refilled our glasses with thick sweet *vin de noix*. Sara tried to refuse, but Nicole insisted it was good against winter chills. "The *garagiste* moved away, to Lesparre in the Médoc. Parisians were going there for the beach spas. He thought he could make more money from them. He sold his place to Jourdan. Then Jean got the cancer. Jeanette was always with him. They closed the store. After he died, she stayed alone. She just lost the habit of people."

Francis came in from feeding his cows. We shook hands and he sat down. Nicole poured him some *vin de noix*. "Did you win anything last night?" he asked.

"No. But your father won two magnums."

"He always wins the wine!"

"Philippe Sartran won a ham, a bottle of Scotch, and a crate of oysters. Ever since his house burned down, he's been lucky."

· "What were you playing?" I asked.

"Quine," Nicole said.

"What's that?"

"You don't know *quine?* You have a card with numbers on it and they call out the numbers and the first to fill a row calls 'Keen!' and wins a prize."

"We call that bingo. When you get all the numbers you say Bingo."

"Bean goh." Nicole laughed. "It's easier to say *quine*. We have them during the winter, every Saturday night. They're for charity. Next Saturday it's for the football club."

"For the best prizes, though, you want the Delom-Sorbé Foundation," Francis said. "Then you can win a television."

He got up to leave. We did, too.

"Thanks, Nicole. See you at Bingo."

She waved her needles. "You'll never win if you call it that. No one will know what you're talking about."

The next Saturday we slipped into the Salle des Fêtes just after eight.

Overcoats were piled on long tables set in rows. Children crowded the stage, fingering the prizes lined up for display: crates of oysters, half cases of wine, a tea set, a cured ham, bottles of liquor. In the back of the room, men stood in loose groups near a table where Madame Lunardelli's brother and fat Dupuy, the president of the soccer association, were selling soft drinks and beer. There were homemade sweets on the table, too, cold sugared crêpes and ginger cake. Dupuy had a ring of powdered sugar around his mouth. We joined Grangier and hoarse-voiced Viandon. We all shook hands. "How's the pruning going?"

Grangier shook his head. "I'm not pruning this week."

"But the weather's been warmer."

"The moon is wrong. Never prune the last few days of the moon. The vines have no force. Oh, maybe you can cut a young vine then, once. But if you do it three years running you kill the plant."

"Not everyone believes those old tales," Roger Bordas said. He was sitting at a small table strewn with number-covered cards.

"Are you pruning now?" asked Grangier.

"No. But the Portuguese are."

"The Portuguese!" Grangier snorted. "They use pneumatic clippers!"

Viandon let out his wheezy chuckle. But Bordas shook his head. "They laughed at the harvesting machine, too. Now everybody uses them." He turned to us. "How many cards would you like?"

The cards were 15 francs apiece, 30 francs for three. People studied them, looking for lucky numbers. The money mounted up on his table, and the chairs began to fill. Loud laughter rang from tables in the back where the soccer players sat with their girls. We bought one card and sat near Nicole. She had half a dozen cards and a heap of dried corn kernels in front of her and pointed to another pile at the end of the table.

"Take enough to cover your card," she said. "You just never know —you might get lucky!" She shuffled her cards and laid them out carefully in front of her.

A dapper man climbed onto the stage and took a seat at a small table that held a box and a microphone. He tapped the mike, cleared his throat. *"Mesdames et messieurs! Bonsoir!* Welcome to the *quine* to benefit the football club of Ruch, a worthy organization deserving of your support." Cheers and laughter. "Will you please take your seats. The game is about to begin."

"We play for a magnum of Vieux Vaure 1985." He drew a token from the box. "Number 20. Twenty. That's number 20."

Around the room, corn kernels rustled onto the paper cards, loud in the sudden silence. The fellow onstage drew number after number out of the box. Finally, from one of the tables of soccer players, came the cry:

"Quine!"

Laughter and applause, loud groans, and an excited buzz. Philippe Sartran was the winner. He took his card to the front for verification and came back smiling with the bottle in his hands. The rest of us slid our kernels back onto the table.

"I think I'll burn down my house," Nicole muttered.

"The next game is for a bushel of oysters, courtesy of the Galeries Ruchelaises. And we begin with number 46. Forty-six. Number 46."

Each game took ten or fifteen minutes. After each quarter-hour of quiet the crowd cheered, scolded the children, or descended on Dupuy for refreshments. The room temperature climbed and the air filled with smoke. Someone broke a beer bottle on the concrete floor. The prizes thinned on the stage. Nicole won a loin of pork. Sara and I never even came close.

The last game ended at eleven. We raked our kernels into heaps at the ends of the tables and tossed our cards into a box. Mothers roused sleeping children from piles of coats. Someone opened the door onto the cold, still night, and suddenly the room seemed small and cozy. The crowd flowed into the *mairie* courtyard, then home.

Sara and I crunched the gravel of the chestnut path past the cemetery wall and under the dark porch of the church. Even a quiet place has degrees of stillness. The bulky silhouette and the moonlit cemetery felt far away from the empty Salle des Fêtes and the sleeping town. On our evolving map of Ruch, the presbytère lay somewhere in between.

Compared to the machine-driven harvest, the small teams at the *taille* made little impression against the dull horizon. But we saw the results of their slow progress everywhere. Before pruning, the bushy vines gave a red feathery cast to the landscape, delicate but voluminous. After the excess wood had been cut away, the *pieds* that remained were stumps, naked and black.

Wandering one day, I came across Bordas smoking a cigarette at the end of a row. He was working with Bernard and his daughter, Pierrette, and a middle-aged woman I didn't know. All wore hats, layers of sweaters, and calf-high rubber boots caked with mud.

"Do you mind if I watch for a while?"

Bordas shook his head, dropped his cigarette, and stamped on it. He approached a vine. The thick black stump rose straight up from the ground about three feet, then twisted to the right. A long branch grew parallel to the ground, bound to the lowest of three wires that ran along the row. A dozen smaller branches rose from the long one and climbed the other two wires. It looked like a comb or a fan.

"The long branch and its shoots gave the fruit last fall," he explained. "It's exhausted, so we cut it away." He nestled heavy clippers close to the main trunk and squeezed. The blades sunk in, stopped. He squeezed again, grunting a little. "Cabernet Sauvignon vines have the hardest wood of all." The blades met, the branch sprang away from the *pied,* quivering, hanging on the wires.

"The women will pull these away," he said, making a few additional cuts to ease their task. "Now we make the important decision. We have to decide which will be the fruiting branch for next year and how much fruit we should ask it for."

Opposite the cutaway growth, a shorter branch carried only two vertical shoots. He looked them over. Cutting quickly, he left one long branch studded with buds and one short one with only two buds.

"The long one is called the *aste.* Each of those buds will become a fruiting branch next year. The more buds we leave, the more fruit. In theory, anyway."

"How many buds do you leave?"

"Generally eight or ten. It depends. On how healthy they look, how sturdy the branch is, how old the vine is, how generously it gave the year before. Oh, a lot of things." He spat, then lit another cigarette. "The government gets its say, too. The law regulates the number of vines and the final yield per acre, and you can pretty much work out from that how many buds to leave."

"I've heard that you get better fruit when you prune short. Is that true? If the crop was smaller, would you make better wine?"

"Maybe. So much depends on the year, on the vine. But once you prune, you've set your maximum crop. And a thousand things can happen between now and next fall—frost, hail, disease, rain. You have to give yourself some room for error. There's a lot you can do in the winemaking if you have too much wine. But if you have too little, maybe you'll shiver next winter!"

He pointed to the short stump with two buds. "Now this branch is the farmer's friend. This one is the future. It's called the *cot*. Next winter, I'll cut that long one away, as I just did with this year's dead wood. But this one will give the wood for the year after. If the vine stays healthy and I've chosen well, the outside bud will become next year's *aste,* and the one closest to the branch will become next year's *cot.''*

"How do you choose which branch will play which part?"

"That's the whole question of the pruning. That's the question you ask yourself a thousand times a day every day of the winter. The answers separate the good workers from the bad—and, as the years go by, the rich vineyards from the poor."

He pulled some of the cut wood away to reveal the trunk. "See? You want a strong, straight vine. Close to the wire, in line with its neighbors. When you prune it, you have to keep it on the good path. I normally choose the sturdiest branch to leave as the *aste,* and the closest to serve as the *cot.* But there's no rule. The vine decides. You have to pay attention to what it wants, then teach it to do what you want."

"It sounds like a cross between sculpture and parenthood."

He laughed. "I don't know about sculpture." He pulled a saw from his belt and scraped heavy mud away from his boots. "But it's like raising children in one way—you're always deep in shit!"

He cut away a few more vines. His gestures seemed both intimate and mechanical.

"Do you like the job?"

"At first. At first it's quiet, and the air is clean, and you get reacquainted with all your vines. Each one is different. But soon you've looked at thousands of vines. You hardly even see them, you work like a machine. Then the weather gets bad. And your wrists get sore and then your elbows get sore and then your back and your legs. If you're old like me, you still hurt in the morning, especially when it's cold and wet. And in Bordeaux, it's cold and wet all winter long."

He pulled on his cigarette. "Do I like the job?" He threw it on the ground. "It's a job you have to do. It comes around in life. Like winter. Do you like winter? What can you do? It comes when it comes, and you get through it."

Pruning is quiet work, and the tools are simple. The clippers are like those used for harvesting but heavier, with a powerful counterspring to magnify the force of the hands. The men also carry short saws to cut the thick wood, a sharpening stone for the clippers, and pliers to wrestle with the wires and ties.

"Say, Roger," called the woman working in the next row, pulling cut wood from the vines, "did you hear what happened at Jourdan's *bordel?* A fight, some guys from Pujols."

"Anybody hurt?"

"Who knows? But someday."

They worked on by and I followed her.

"A fight in the café?" I asked. "But it's not open yet."

"You'd be surprised." She grunted as she tore the cut branches loose. Chips flew through the air and the wires sang. "That's what happens. But it'll do plenty of business. Madame Jourdan's got an eye for that. Look at Guy Petit and his friends. Oh, they'll do fine."

Bordas's mother-in-law came with coffee, and everyone took a break. Bernard sharpened his blade. The women chatted about the weather, and whether the mildness would hold.

"How do you learn how to do this?" I asked Bordas.

"By watching," he replied. "When Bernard was young, he would come out with me and watch where I cut. After he understood, I could go ahead and make the main cuts and let him finish. Now he knows."

"What if your father isn't a vigneron?"

"There are schools," he said doubtfully. "Like the one over in Fargues. But that's only two years. It takes longer than that to learn. You have to watch how the vine responds to your training."

He waved the little crew back to work. The grandmother stayed on, too, going through the rows to cut away some of the small branches. She piled them up separately.

"What are those for?"

"They're *sarments,*" she told me. "Haven't you ever had steaks grilled over *sarments?*" She patted her stomach. "Once we cooked everything with wood. They're a bother to bundle up, and you have to dry them for a year before they'll burn hot. But I still keep a few."

She moved on, a small stooped woman with long gray whiskers on her chin. The task hadn't changed for centuries; Thomas Jefferson's description of pruning during his visit to Bordeaux in 1787 described exactly what I saw, from tools and techniques to the division of tasks between the sexes. I moved on, too, and found a tractor hitched to a large metal tank and a chugging motor. Black hoses ran from the tank into the vines, and I followed them until I found the men known in the village as "the Portuguese," an older man and his nephew. The hoses were attached to their clippers.

We nodded to each other. I introduced myself.

"Oh, you're the husband of the American woman," said the younger man. "She took our pictures during harvest. How's your vacation going?"

"Fine. What have you got there?"

"Pneumatic clippers. Aren't they great?" He squeezed them. The blades closed with sharp clicks and puffs of air. He explained that they increased his pruning speed by a third. One tank of air lasted about two hours, and then he recharged it.

"Recharging takes just long enough for a cigarette," he said. "Once you've pruned with these, you'll never go back."

"Do many others in Ruch use them?"

"Here? *Merde.* They're behind the times. But you'll see. One day,

they'll all have them. They hate to spend the money, but when they see
how much easier it makes the work, then they'll jump. The only vice
they have worse than greed is laziness."

The old man shook his head. "Don't exaggerate. Maybe they started
with enough to eat, so they never had to push for more."

The younger man recounted how they had come to Ruch in the
fifties, and the only land they could afford was planted with weeds. They
started a vineyard and added more till they had nearly 50 acres.

"I put it all in white grapes," he said. "That's all anybody wanted—
sweet white wine. Then the fashion changed. The price for the red went
higher and higher. So I started ripping out the white vines. Now I have
35 acres of red. You have to work hard, you have to change with the
times."

I asked if I could try the clippers. They were about twice as heavy as
Bordas's manual ones and the hoses felt awkward. I squeezed, barely: the
blades snapped shut and hissed. I made a few cuts. The clippers seemed
eager to attack the wood, forcing themselves open with the hiss of air,
ready to cut again.

"It'll cut the vine just like thinking of it," said the older man. "But if
you're not thinking, it'll cut off your finger like a twig."

A warm spell opened shutters all over town. Young boys flooded the
soccer field, their shouts floating on the breezes. The ground was soft and
fragrant.

Antoine and Frédéric went back to work on the café, and Nathalie
worked most days with them. They put on a new tin roof, corrugated
to mimic the tiles that cap the region's houses. Inside, they scrubbed the
stone walls clean and golden, stained the rough-hewn beams mahogany
brown. They salvaged a secondhand bar in Arcachon, a resort down the
coast. It was hardly a New York designer's vision of old France. With
a plastic laminate wood-grain top and phony fieldstone embedded in the
sides, its fake rusticity mocked the dilapidation of the old building. But
it had admirers in Ruch. An old woman wandered in to stroke its
polyurethaned finish.

"I suppose you'll put in a ceiling next," she said, gazing up at the exposed underside of the tin roof.

Nathalie followed her gaze. "Oh no."

"Well, then will you paint those beams?"

"No, no. They give the place charm. Don't you think?"

"Well, yes, but they do look like a barn, don't they?"

The building had been a barn, then a garage, then abandoned. But attitudes had changed since the sixties, when the primary school had been built in a thrifty modern style. The overenthusiastic restoration of the *mairie* was an example. The past had taken on aesthetic value, even though the veneration was rarely grounded in knowledge. The beams gave the café an authentic past. The pseudo-rustic bar was a machine-age echo of the same style. To the Jourdans, it fit the room better than the industrial stainless steel that now covered old zinc bars in Paris and Bordeaux.

The café wasn't officially open, but Antoine rigged up a beer tap and a cooler and people stopped by in the evening. Guy Petit was often there, and the men who worked with him. Soccer players came after practice, and the Mayor always seemed to show up when there was a crowd. But it felt somehow detached from the village. The store gossip seemed almost indifferent to its fate. The *garagistes* had come from the north and no one knew their families. Jourdan worked hard and kept to himself. Rumor had it his wife didn't. Some people disapproved. They weren't sure they would patronize the café. They weren't sure who would.

A French town needs a café. Without one, it's a house without a hearth; its inhabitants grow irritable or dull. Cafés soothe early-morning grumbles with hot coffee and pastry, sate noontime appetites with sturdy food and a *coup de rouge,* provide bragging ground for the old men and videogames for the youngsters.

Viandon told us that after the war Ruch had two cafés. The conservatives gathered in old Madame Joxe's place. There were dances there, and once a month she showed a movie. Up the street, the Chateliers drew a younger, more radical crowd, including the left-leaning farmer who would become mayor.

The conservatives dwindled, and when Madame Joxe died her café closed. Guy Chatelier took over the other café from his father. He married a woman from Libourne who knew how to cook for crowds and opened a restaurant, too. Business was good. Then one day she found Guy in bed with a local carpenter's son. She took their children and returned to her parents. The café foundered, then failed.

Chatelier was forced to sell the building to the town to pay his debts. But though the incident was embedded in town gossip, neither man moved from Ruch. The council rented the upstairs living quarters back to Chatelier and gave him a job at the cooperative. They remodeled part of the building into the town's second *gîte*.

The remaining space, a large ground-floor room with a plate-glass window that had been the café itself, became a kind of café again, the Salle des Jeunes. The construction was done by donated labor when hands were free, and the work had been so desultory the project was almost a secret. But in February it was ready, and a dedication was scheduled to follow a soccer game.

The warm weather held, and a big crowd turned out. Ruch's opponent was a bigger team from Lormont, a Bordeaux suburb. The field was a mud bath. The players skidded and slid, tore great divots out of the soft ground, missed kicks, tackles, and goals in sloppy, frustrating play.

Ruch scored early and the fans exulted. The team was jaunty and confident. But Lormont equaled the score on a short kick with a smothering attack that left Ruch ragged. In the second half the local men were disorganized and tense. Their scrappiness soured into aggression. There were two Arabs and an African black on the visiting team, and the crowd saw infractions and savagery in every move they made. *"Le noir . . . c'était le noir, encore le noir , , , oh, ce noir-la, c'est pas possible . . ."* The rancor spread to the referee. "You're for the blacks," they called. "Your mother is a Gabonnaise."

The match ended in a tie. It wasn't a bad result for Ruch, but the teams parted in sullen silence. Madame Lunardelli was frantic. "Oh, wasn't it terrible?" she moaned. "But you will come to the inauguration, won't you, to show your support. They're still our boys."

Madame Lunardelli applauded at the dedication of the Salle des Jeunes

By the time we got there, the room was crowded and smoky. The players and their supporters were all there, and so were old Jeanette and Ithier the postman and Madame Veder. Ithier said he had come for the free drinks.

The room measured about 30 by 15 feet. A small bar took up one corner, and a door led to a back-yard toilet. Old team photos hung on a wall. The windows faced onto the street, and low afternoon light filled every corner of the room. Empty bottles littered the bar and children crumbled cookies under the scattered chairs. Then someone clinked a bottle and the crowd turned its attention to the Mayor and fat Dupuy.

"Mesdames, messieurs, mes amis," began the Mayor, reading from a small square of paper. "We're here today to dedicate this space we all know well to a new purpose, as the Salle des Jeunes. Many of your neighbors have given freely of their time and talents to make this dream a reality, and today we see the happy result. A town that loses its youth dies like a tree that loses its leaves. With this Salle des Jeunes, we

demonstrate once again that Ruch is determined to keep her sons and daughters near. Enjoy yourself today, continue to support the soccer teams, and thank you for coming."

There was applause, and then Dupuy stepped forward, groping through his pockets. "Welcome, my friends. I only have a few words to say today." He paused.

"Well, what are they?" Serge called out. "We're thirsty." People laughed.

"I wanted to thank everyone who helped, who worked, worked to help make this possible." He shifted his weight from foot to foot as he went through his pockets again.

"Oh, you're welcome," someone said. There was a chorus of approval and the sound of a beer bottle opening.

"No, but I, I just wanted to say," Dupuy stammered. The Mayor leaned over and murmured something. Dupuy shook his head. *"Merde.* I've lost it. Now where . . ." He looked squarely at the crowd, then his gaze bounced away. "I've lost my speech, but if you'll just be pa-tient . . ." The crowd quieted. He spotted Madame Lunardelli moving across the back of the room. "There! There's the reason for our suc-cess. Marie-France! A round of thanks for Marie-France!"

The crowd turned to her with applause. She reddened and looked down, twisting her hands. "Oh, but . . ." she said.

The applause died, and Dupuy raised his voice again. "And to all of those . . ."

But the crowd had tired of him. Even the Mayor leaned over toward the bar for a beer. A baby began to cry, and Dupuy trailed off. Jeanette and Madame Veder left. By twilight the crowd had sorted itself out into the usual configuration. The women moved chairs to the walls, talking about their neighbors and calling to stray children. The players crowded the bar and boasted. The old men moved slowly from one group to the next.

At eight, the women set folding tables with paper plates and plastic cups. Magnums of red wine appeared, alternating with long loaves of bread. Dupuy sat at the head in a knot of older men, then the players and their girls, and the older women and children. There was a cold rice salad studded with corn and peas, then slices of boiled ham with buttered noodles, a salad of avocados and tomatoes, and rounds of Camembert. The wine bottles were emptied and replaced; the sound level rose. There was fruit on the table when the young men burst into song. *Allez les bleus, allez les blancs,* they roared.

We went home to bed. It was just after ten and the village was closed tight, silent and dark. The butcher's dog barked as we passed the *mairie,* and dry leaves rustled along the chestnut path.

10

Giboulées de Mars

We ran low on money. Our diet dwindled to roast chicken and root vegetables; we ate meat at the beginning of the week and soup at the end. I didn't see how we could pay for both heat and the telephone.

Then a job offer came for Sara. An English fellow we knew from New York wanted her to sell advertising space in a new restaurant magazine he planned for Paris. She would earn commissions, and he would publish her photographs of the restaurants.

"I could stay with Regan," she said. Dinner was over and we were sipping red wine. "She has room, now that Philippe is off in Africa. I'd like to take the pictures."

"How long do you think you'd be gone?"

"Three weeks?"

"At least Regan's apartment will be warm."

The Bordeaux-Paris train stopped in Libourne, about 30 kilometers west of Ruch, past Saint-Émilion on the Dordogne. The big engine pulled into the small station; the loudspeaker crackled *"Libourne, Libourne. Deux minutes d'arrêt."* The platform cleared and she was gone.

I didn't want to go back to the presbytère so I called Ed from the station. He was a diplomat we had met at a dinner party. He lived in

Bordeaux, in a big house with a bodyguard, a cook, and a dog. A visit there was a little vacation. Ed was free and invited me to stay. We drank good wine at dinner, then a bottle of very old cognac in front of the fire. When I crawled into bed, loneliness was not the problem.

Ruch was a different place the next day, small and muddy. Tractors rumbled through the streets, old women scratched in gardens, children rode bikes home from school. I felt like a castaway.

The mild weather drifted on, under a thin cloud cover that gave the light a bleak, grayish tone. I was moping through the village and saw Madame Veder knitting in the feeble sunshine outside her house. Her hands worked mechanically, but her gaze drifted down the street.

"Bonjour, Madame Veder."

"Bonjour, Monsieur."

"It's a nice afternoon to sit outside."

"Yes, it is."

"May I?" I waved at the gate, her garden, the two dogs sniffing at my legs.

"Bien sûr."

I opened the gate. The dogs barked. She called sharply and they retreated to her side. From inside the garden, the village seemed far away. The open lawn was unusual in a French town, where buildings normally form unbroken walls along the street, hiding private space from public view. The Veders' green grass and vegetable garden were sheltered by two magnificent trees, an immense cherry and a cedar that rivaled the nearby *mairie* tower.

"What are you working on?" I asked.

"It's a sweater for my son."

"How old is he?"

"Twenty-two. He's at university in Bordeaux. He never comes home. I knit and think, Well, at least he'll be warm."

I nodded. "Sara's in Paris. It's cold in the presbytère without her."

She glanced up at me. "What do you eat?"

"Oh, you know. Men aren't as helpless as that."

She shook her head. "Would you like to come to dinner tonight?"

"Well . . ."

"So it's settled. Come at seven."

When I knocked at the door, the television was on, tuned to *Dallas,* dubbed in French.

"Isn't this curious?" Madame Veder clucked. "It's the most popular show in France right now."

"It's a shame what television has done to social life," said her husband. "People used to visit each other to talk. Now everyone stays home to watch."

We sat in the kitchen, warmed by the stove. Madame served cold steamed leeks with red-wine vinegar, an omelet with mushrooms, and a salad. Veder served the wine, a jug of red from the cooperative. His wife drank water.

"This salad is good. What are the greens?"

"Dandelions," Madame said. "My husband hunts them in the fields."

"Don't eat too many, though," Veder warned. "There's a reason they call them piss-in-the-bed."

They asked about New York and why we came to Ruch, then I asked them about their families and why they came to Ruch. Madame told me her father had run a general store in a room of the house that faced the road. But the shop had been gone for years.

"And so will the room, if the Mayor has his way." She turned to her husband. "There was another letter today. The departmental council voted to widen the road. They say it's too narrow for regulations."

The street did narrow and swerve where her house bulged into it. There was no sidewalk, and Madame Pagant's garden wall gave no space on the other side. I liked the kink. It suggested that the town's builders cared less for rationality than for convenience. But I could see the hazard, too. The T-junction just beyond it was practically blind. If two cars met turning, there was no room for error.

"But what will they do?"

"Tear down our house," she said grimly. "Oh, not all of it. Just one room. My father's room. And what will they get? Sidewalks and an extra 60 centimeters of roadway. It's a bedroom now, and afterward no bed will fit in it. And that's a solid stone wall. They want to replace it with brick. Oh, I'm not against improvement and safety. But this is unfair." She shrugged her shoulders. "It's all the Mayor's idea. It's a sad thing when they can take your property just like that. A sad thing."

The next week the wind changed, and another spate of snow set the Ruchelais grumbling. An old woman in the store said, "Late snow is winter's fertilizer." The young men laughed at her. They said she must never have been fertilized if she didn't know the difference between snow and manure. The old men talked again about the freeze of 1956, which killed nearly half the town's vines in a week. Everyone agreed that the fifteen white days of January had been quite enough.

It was snowing when I walked by the Bordas house and saw silhouettes through the window. I knocked, and Bernard let me in.

"Still the bachelor, eh? Well, come in and join the rest of us."

Roger and Ithier sat at a round table in the middle of the room. Roger smoked and shuffled cards.

"Monsieur Ithier's no bachelor," I said.

"No, that's true," said Roger. "He only wishes he could be."

The room was bright, hot and heavy with smoke. It was crammed with furniture—a sofa, easy chairs, low tables, the inevitable armoire. Every flat surface was covered with trophies, all showing the same small figure balanced on one leg, with one arm extended, palm down. It's a gesture repeated in any French town, any evening, men tossing steel balls in a game of *boules*.

"Who's the champion?" I pointed at the trophies.

"Roger," said Ithier. "He's played with the best, all over France. You didn't know we had such fame in Ruch, eh?"

The stubby, laconic fellow dealing cards lacked both glamour and physique, but then *boules* mostly wanted calmness and coordination. "Oh, I used to spend a lot of time at it," he said. "It was fun while it lasted."

The card game flowed swiftly and quietly. I couldn't decipher the rules, and even the cards were strangers. Two young men came in, and one took Bordas's place at the table. Roger got up, lit another cigarette, and pointed out trophies from Bordeaux, Toulouse, and Pau.

He told me he wasn't from Ruch but from Brie, in the north. His father owned a small lumberyard there, but a jealous older brother had forced him out of the business, so he wandered south in search of work. He started at Philippon as a handyman, then married the owner's daughter. There were only 5 acres of vines then. That's when he had time for *boules*. He had expanded to 25 acres of vines and began bottling the wine himself. Did I know the stone house where his pickers stayed? He had intended to renovate that for his family. We have dreams when we're young, he said. But when his wife died, he lost interest. So he built this room instead, for card games with his friends when the weather was bad.

A couple of warm afternoons later, the snow was only a memory. I stopped by the *mairie*. "I hear Marie-France had you for dinner," Denise said. "She said you looked so lonely."

"Dinner was delicious. But I don't understand about the expropriation. Why is a meter of road more important than their house?"

"Four hundred thousand francs will be wasted! But my Mayor has a grudge against the Veders. He hated Marie-France's father. The poor fellow died five years ago, but no matter." She shrugged. "He ran a store, you know. Perhaps he made the Mayor pay his bills!"

Jeanette Barde came in and Denise embraced her. "So! Back from Paris! Thomas wishes Sara would come back from Paris, too. But we take care of our own in Ruch." She told how the Veders had invited me to dinner. "But how was your trip?"

"Oh, it was cold," said Jeanette. "And there was the trial of that awful terrorist going on. People were expecting more bombs every minute. Between the snow and the commotion, I didn't go out at all, except for bread. I'm glad to be back."

Rain settled in for the last days of February. The fog never quite lifted, the sky stayed low, the air was damp and heavy. I put on boots and raincoat and set off into the fields. The tinny sound of a radio led me to the Bonvoisins'. They wore boots and heavy sweaters with the sleeves pushed up to their elbows. Elastic belts with canvas slings held sheaves of bright orange willow branches. They carried small crescent-curved knives.

"What are you doing now?"

"It's called the *acanage*," Francis said. "We have to attach the branches to the wires."

The operation was quick and deceptively simple. They grasped the end of the *aste,* the long pruned branch that would bear the next season's fruit, bent it up over the middle wire of the three on the trellis, and pulled it down to the bottom wire. Holding it there with one hand, they yanked a length of willow wand from the sling, looped it around the branch and the wire, twisted it into a knot, and cut the wand free. If the branch was stubborn, they would repeat the tie where it passed over the middle wire. Then on to the next vine.

"It's amazing to find a plant supple enough to twist but sturdy enough to hold," I said, fingering the willow branches.

"And then the next winter when you're pruning, they're so brittle they break easily when you want to pull the dead wood away, after the

Acanage, *and bud break in the vines*

pruning," Francis said. He showed me the brown knots still hanging on the wires, snapped one off with his fingers. "People use plastic ties now. But they're harder to get off afterward. And these are free—we grow the willows at the ends of the rows, in spots where the land is wet. All it takes is a little work to harvest them and strip the leaves."

"There's no pollution, either. The willow just rots back into the soil. Maybe they should make the plastic ties illegal."

Francis wouldn't go that far.

"Stand up for your beliefs," Nicole teased him. "Tell old Petit he can't use plastic anymore or you'll put him in jail."

"How long does this take?"

"Oh, most of March," said Nicole. "It's not bad work—quiet and clean, except for the mud. But you want wet weather—it makes the branches easier to bend. You have to be careful, though. They can snap like whips and cut your face."

"Where's the Mayor?"

"He had a meeting in Castillon," said Madame. Nicole rolled her eyes. They turned back to work and I set off. All around me, the bright orange knots glowed in the mist.

A few days later I saw the Grangiers working in the vineyard behind the new café. The setting sun tipped the willow wands holstered at their hips fiery red.

"Is this your vineyard?"

"Yes," said Grangier. "That is, it's her mother's."

"But we're trying to sell it," added Madame.

"Why?"

"Look at us," she said. "We're getting old. We have too much land to work by ourselves. And we'd like to fix up the house some—put in a toilet, for example."

"First the cows, then the fields? What's next?"

"This parcel never gave the best grapes, anyway," said Grangier. "With the roads on three sides, every time a departmental crew oiled them, the vines would get sick."

"Have you found a buyer?"

"Jourdan would like it," he said. "He'd probably make a parking lot for the café. We've got it listed in Castillon, but no interest there so far. Maybe in the summer. It'll go for building, no doubt—it's listed that way on the town plan."

"Why bother working it, then, if you might sell it before the harvest?"

"Well, you never know. No sense letting it go to waste."

I called Sara that night. The magazine project wasn't going that well but she had found some work translating and was a little ahead financially. "The Grangiers were working side by side," I told her. "Even though they didn't know whether they would harvest the vineyard or not. Why don't you come back?"

Spring was only waiting for her return. The sun shone hard for a few days, and one early March morning the presbytère lawn turned into a carpet of flowers. There were tiny daisies, with petals tipped pink like lipstick smudges, small striped blues like cat's-eye cuff links, extravagant purples, and tight-furled reds. The grass came greener, the forsythia swelled with buds.

George reappeared. We heard the mower roaring after breakfast and took him a mug of coffee. He cut the motor, and silence rushed back like cool water.

"I knew the weather would change," he said. "The cranes flew by last week. It's a sure sign spring's on the way. By the way, would you be interested in truly fresh eggs?"

"Crane eggs?"

"My chickens lay more in the spring. Mostly we have them all sold in advance—people know how good my eggs are. But just now we have a surplus, and I can let you have a dozen a week. Ten francs a dozen."

"Sure, George. That sounds good."

"I just happen to have a dozen in my truck. I'll bring them by before lunch. And I'll prune those rosebushes this week. Can't let that wait too long, you know."

"Did Monsieur Hall cut your lawn today?" Denise asked when I stopped into the *mairie*.

"Why, yes, he did."

"Good," she snorted. "I told the Mayor it was a disgrace. And did he prune the roses?"

"No, not yet."

"That doesn't surprise me," she said, shaking her head.

There were footsteps on the gravel outside, and the Mayor entered.

"You really must speak to Monsieur Hall," Denise said. "The roses still aren't pruned at the presbytère. I can't imagine what he does all day."

Bonvoisin shuffled papers at his desk.

"I visited the Veders," I said. "Are you really going to widen the road there?"

"Nothing too important, I see." He looked up. "I have to go over to the café. Do you want to come?" He headed for the door. "Goodbye, Madame Tallon. If anything comes up, I'll be by tomorrow."

Outside, he took my arm. "Discretion is an important part of a mayor's job. Now, what did you want to know?"

"Is it true that the Veders will lose a room to widen the road?"

"Well, yes, part of a room."

"But is it really worth it?"

"If one day a truck driver doesn't see some child playing around that corner, you won't be asking that question. The departmental engineer says the curve is very dangerous. We've already straightened the main road through town, you know. Many people lost property."

We were standing at the entrance to the café. Inside, Nathalie was polishing the bar and Guy Petit beckoned. The Mayor went in, and I went home.

Up in my office, I found it hard to keep my concentration at the desk. The earliest green of the leaves is infinitely gentle, and I rested my eyes on the valley below.

A boy of about thirteen darted into view. He ran down the path toward the monument, jumped over the chain, and huddled up to its stone base. He was mostly hidden from the path, but I had a full view. He spread his legs and fumbled at his trouser. His hands went to his crotch, began a rapid, jerky movement, and I realized he was masturbating. He proceeded in fits and starts, peering around the monument, and it took him a long time. Finally he wiped his hand on his leg, then strolled away.

Sap rising, I thought. The priest's old blue car stopped in front of the church. Wednesday, catechism class: one last sin before confession.

Downstairs, the door banged. It was Cadapeaud, the plumber, come to fix the toilet that had been running since the January freezes.

Chatting while he worked, he told us that Ruch's first indoor toilet was at Vaure, but by 1970 almost everyone had one. There was still no town sewage system—most people had septic tanks, while some just pumped the runoff into streams or woods. There was town water, though. There had to be. All the wells were contaminated. The fountain below the *mairie* went bad around 1980. He blamed the septic systems, along with pesticides and fertilizer from the vines. Now the town bought water from a consortium based in Rauzan. He didn't much like the idea that no one really knew where it came from.

Cadapeaud lived in one of half a dozen new houses clustered on the northern edge of the village. Just ten years ago the land had been a vineyard, he said, and vines still sprouted in the yards like weeds. Lunardelli bought the acreage and built all the houses. Each was set in its own little lot, at odd angles to the road, like a little suburb. Cadapeaud would have preferred an older house—even tried to buy one near Grangier. But the owner wanted too much money and eventually sold it as a second home to someone from Bordeaux. Still, the new house was nice, too. There was central heating, and the pipes were sound.

"Well, that ought to do it. It probably won't get cold enough to freeze this thing again. The cranes flew north last week."

By mid-March, the forsythia was in full bloom and red field anemones bloomed everywhere. But winter resisted the new season's advance, and the weather turned wild in what the villagers called the *giboulées de mars*.

One afternoon, a fierce northwest wind rolled clouds down the valley and in fifteen minutes night fell and wild rain raged through the trees. The clouds passed, giving way to pure, brilliant sunlight; then another wave came on blackening. Suddenly hail rattled against the windows and the long view was curtained as if by lace. The thermometer on the windowsill, packed in ice pellets the size of shot, plunged from fifty to freezing. Five minutes later, the storm was over, and a rainbow arced over the steeple, as if wrung from the combat. The forsythia shone like a pot of gold.

We spent a week in Bordeaux, reporting on a festival of architectural films. As a *journaliste étranger,* I got free admission to the films and invitations to various fêtes and soirées, and we stayed with Ed in his big house. We felt as if we, too, were blooming with spring.

A brisk wind tossed high clouds through the sky the day we returned. I strolled to the store, wondering what the newspaper would say about the film festival. I entered with a bigger *bonjour* than usual, but the store was empty, except for Marie-Jo.

"*Ça va, Madame Breton?*"

"*Pas trop.*" Her voice was dull. "You've been away?"

"In Bordeaux for a week, working. We had a good time. What's new? Is something the matter?"

"The young Marcou is dead."

Marcou. Wasn't he the butcher who ran the other general store in town? It was across the street from the Veders', a small shop crammed with canned goods. We never went in there; hardly anybody did. A dark-haired woman often lingered in the doorway. Marcou cut meat in a kind of garage next door and delivered it to farms nearby. Sometimes a teenager in a bloody apron smiled and waved his cleaver at passersby, and an old dog gnawed on bones in the sun.

"The boy who works as a butcher?"

"No, that's Marcel. Pierre was his older brother. Doing his military service. It's obligatory in France, you know. He celebrated his twentieth birthday Saturday night, then drove into Bordeaux to pick up his girl-friend at the train. He never made it. Yesterday morning they found his car crashed in a vineyard in Grézillac."

I bowed my head. "I don't think I ever met him."

"He was a young man of high spirits." As I was leaving, she added, "The funeral is tomorrow."

Marcel Marcou

The deep church bells tolled the death, echoing through the village streets.

"They were wild. It was bound to happen. I told him so myself."

Denise was telling Jeanette about the time Pierre Marcou had come in for a hunting license and she had made him apply for an identity card. "He said, That's for old people. But I said, What if you crash your car by the side of the road. Then who will know who you are?" Judgment, sorrow, and something of triumph mingled in her voice. "It was bound to happen."

"Were they at the Scorpion?" Jeanette asked.

"So they say." Denise shrugged. "That place is a disgrace to the town. But what can you do? That's what young people want these days. And now they can see what happens. Maybe some will learn the lesson."

There was a frost during the night, and low morning sun carpeted the lawn with diamonds. Sara and I watched our breath puff in the still air as we stood in the garden. People filled the chestnut path, crowding shoulder to shoulder near the church. We spotted Grangier and approached him, exchanging silent handshakes. The church doors were open; inside, the nave was packed tight, faces pale in the filtered light. We had never seen so many people in one place in Ruch before. There must have been three hundred—villagers, young people, soldiers, strangers.

The priest's voice drifted outside. I could catch words carried on the stale breath of the church air: "Jesus who is love," "family, community, solidarity." The harmonium wheezed mournfully. Inside, beside the bier, there was open weeping; by the church door, strained faces and red noses; out in the sunshine on the path, muttering, smoking, and feet scuffling gravel; in the trees, whispering leaves and birdsongs.

The bells rang and the doorway cleared. The priest emerged, then the coffin. The pallbearers were all young: the brother, Claude Bonvoisin, Frédéric from the garage. Their faces were solemn, their suits stiff. They placed the coffin in the hearse. It pulled away.

The crowd broke up quickly. Grangier told us the burial would be in Sainte-Ferme, across the Dordogne, where the mother's family lived. The Mayor, clean-shaven and wearing a gray suit, shook people's hands.

Soon the churchyard was empty. Only trodden flowers and scattered cigarette butts remained.

The next day a violent southeast wind brought clouds and cool air. In the store, Marie-Jo was still upset. "It's no secret—a person has to sleep. They say he had been up for three days in a row. He just fell asleep at the wheel."

I mentioned the size of the crowd at the funeral, the number of strangers. She started ticking them off on her fingers.

"Well, he was born in Ruch and lived here all his life. There was his military company, and his teammates from soccer, and his friends from Bordeaux. His father delivers meat over the whole canton. His aunt lives in Blasimon, his uncle played soccer in Rauzan, his grandfather was once a municipal counselor in Sainte-Ferme."

There was little talk of his life. I didn't hear anecdotes about his childhood or the promise of his future. Conversations kept turning to the accident. No one seemed quite satisfied with the simple hypothesis of sleepiness and loss of control. There were those who would have him drunk. Others saw more sinister causes.

For Madame Tallon, Marcou became an object lesson. "A good thing his mother had three children," she reflected to Jeanette. "She's still got two left. There are reasons for big families. Of course, that's very human —to plan for the future. Animals have the advantage of not knowing they're going to die. We can only try to forget. But now, when a young person turns twenty, they'll think of him."

"I heard they had Bayonne ham for his birthday meal," Jeanette said. "It's so salty, you know, so he just kept on drinking."

The Marcou shop stayed closed, but I passed two women standing outside it at twilight. I heard one describe his body. "There were grass stains all along his legs, as if he'd skidded along the ground. Or been dragged. There was hardly a mark on his body, no cuts or blood. Just bruises on his head and neck." And she touched her own head, to show where.

I saw Jeanette Barde scrubbing her front porch and stopped to chat. She looked around and lowered her voice.

"They have suspicions of foul play in the young Marcou's death."

"Really?"

"Apparently there was a fight at the Scorpion, before he left. With some rowdies from Daignac. Some say they came through the village looking for him."

She glanced around again, as if the gang might descend on her porch. "They say his body was found outside the car." She dropped her voice to a whisper. "But the doors and windows were all closed and the windshield wasn't broken! How could he have gotten out of the car? What if he had been forced off the road, pulled from the car, and beaten? What if someone wanted it to look like an accident?"

She leaned back on the porch and gave me a sidelong glance. "Those are the questions some people are asking."

In the store the next day the same speculation was circulating. Along with the growing conviction of murder came anger at the police for not pursuing the perpetrators. There was a sense that all Ruch had been wronged, that the town stood alone against a hostile world. Marcou's wildness was forgotten. He took on the sanctity of a victim, the town's own lamb.

March drew to a close. Slowly, the weather stabilized and the grief ebbed. Spring finally came without reserve. All over the village black-barked cherry trees exploded with dark pink flowers. The old man who walked the fluffy white dog came down the chestnut path wearing only a sweater against the mild air. With an occasional wary glance toward the presbytère, where I sat invisible at my desk, he played hide-and-seek with the dog around the war memorial.

In our yard, forsythia and daffodils glowed like the children of the sun. The lopsided old apple tree began to bloom and crimson leaves burst from the thorny branches of the roses. In one corner, though, between garden wall and church wall, hidden from the village, the iron cradle the pallbearers used to carry the coffin lay abandoned on its side. It stayed for days, an abstract sculpture of loss. Then one morning it was gone, and the daisies had free run of the lawn.

11

Life on Main Street

A few days after the Marcou funeral, Madame Tallon invited us for lunch. It was our first formal invitation in Ruch. Jeanette Barde picked us up to make the visit.

The road wound south down the steep hill to the Courbut, then climbed the opposite bank and turned west along a ridge. Big clouds raced through the sky. Behind us, the town rose above the valley. The church and the *mairie* stood like sentinels on the cliff.

"It must have been fifteen years ago that Denise came to Ruch," Jeanette said, "and it was Guy who brought her here. They met in Duras. He was managing some property there and her husband was teaching. The husband died, so they say. At any rate, Guy brought her to Ruch to work as the town secretary. He was mayor then, and at that time the mayor chose the secretary. Now, of course, there are tests and things."

A rain squall caught us, then it was sunny again.

"Well, being secretary wasn't all there was to the job. They say Guy just went home one day and told his wife Denise was moving in. He was nearly sixty at the time! Of course, that didn't work out, so after a while he gave the big house to his wife and moved into a cottage on the property with Denise."

Denise Tallon and Guy Bournerie

Jeanette shook her head. The widow reproached desire's immorality less than its inconvenience.

"The wife is dead now, but her daughter comes and stays in the house sometimes. She and Guy don't talk. Guy and Denise still live in the cottage. They've fixed it up nicely, I think. I visited once before, when Denise's daughter came from England. Now that Guy's in his seventies, he's not so active as he once was. But he keeps a sharp eye on the town."

She turned up a dirt driveway. A low building turned its back on the road, crouched into the vines. An asparagus bed ran twenty meters along the path to the door. We knocked, and Denise welcomed us into the kitchen. The air was fragrant with spices and wine. Pots simmered on a wood stove and a table was laden with vegetables; eggs and cheese stood on a sideboard. She took our coats and led us into the *séjour*.

Guy sat next to the fire, stood when we entered. He was tall and lean, his deeply wrinkled face rosy under a thick brush of white hair. He was formal, almost grave, but his blue eyes twinkled.

"Bienvenue, enfin," he said. "Denise is always talking about you, but I thought you would never come. Sit down, have an apéritif."

A tray by the fireplace held glasses, an ice bucket, and an assortment of bottles. Denise made kirs for Sara and Jeanette. Guy had Scotch neat, and so did I. She poured Suze for herself, a liqueur flavored with gentian root, bitter and strong. She passed a bowl of salted peanuts. We told Guy about our decision to leave New York and our discovery of Ruch, interrupted by clarifications from Denise. She asked questions for him, knowing all the answers; he nodded and smiled.

The room showed the same regard for the past as the *mairie,* genuine but elastic. A fleur-de-lis carved on the stone fireplace dated it before the Revolution. Rough-hewn ceiling beams had been stained dark, matching the long table and heavy armoire. Portraits of dogs in sentimental poses hung on the walls. An old oxen yoke was mounted above the mantel, two bare bulbs dangling from its arms. The table was set with silver serving dishes and pink flower-scattered china, abundant with flatware and glasses.

The meal began with a savory vegetable soup. Sara asked how it was made.

"Cook leeks, carrots, and potatoes in a heavy pot," Denise said. "Simmer them for a while. Add white wine if you like. If your garden has herbs, put some in. When it's cooked, pass it through a mill. Do you have a mill?"

Sara said no. Jeanette told her about a store in Castillon that sold the Moulis, the good kind. Then came a rich rabbit pâté, sharp with black pepper. Denise had raised the rabbit. Guy opened a 1986 Entre-Deux-Mers white from the cooperative. It tasted like fresh green apples. I was coming to recognize that flavor.

Denise cleared dishes, set a stack of wide bowls in front of Guy, and brought in a steaming cauldron, a bubbling *coq au vin*. The chicken pieces were enormous. Denise told us she named all her roosters Julius, after the emperor. She had killed it herself, hung it for nearly a week, and used its blood in the sauce. That was the only way to make real *coq au vin,* she said. No store-bought hen could give the same flavor. The bacon-studded sauce was the color of chocolate, velvety and deep-flavored. There were roasted potatoes, and the meaty wild mushrooms the Bordelais call *cèpes,* sautéed with garlic and parsley.

Guy served a 1982 Château de Vaure red with the stew. It smelled like cherries and cedar and fine tobacco, and reminded me of harvest time and Bonvoisin's gift, when I had first drunk the wine.

Then came a green salad, then a cheese board, with sweet crumbly Cantal from the mountains and soft, sharp Camembert. Guy opened a dusty 1978 Chai de Vaure. It was the oldest Ruch wine I'd had. Guy called it a miracle vintage, when a hot, sunny September redeemed a wet summer, producing thick, heady wines. Its color was fading from crimson to brick, and its age was evident in its raisin flavors and dusty astringency, but it still had character and life.

"The *cave* has made progress," Guy said, sipping the '78. "But we didn't do too badly in the old days."

"Guy founded the cooperative, you know," Denise added.

"I had been in the *cave* at Rauzan for two years—that was the first one in Entre-Deux-Mers. They invited me to join them because I had a tractor and could help the members carry their grapes to the press. But then I thought, Why not make the money for my own town? I went to see the doctor, and he sold us his *chai.*"

"How did the cooperative change the town?"

"It made things easier for the growers. And maybe it helped modern times come quicker. Like the telephone—that came in 1929. We needed to know what was happening around us. The doctor was the first to have one—no, it was the veterinarian, whose number was 1. I was 8 and the *cave* was 9. Life was simpler then."

"Better, too, when Guy was in charge. Now the *cave* just gets worse," Denise said. "The repair bills alone you wouldn't believe."

"They still need more vats," Guy said. "The harvests keep getting bigger. I'm urging the board to tear down the *caviste*'s house."

"That small red one in the driveway? Where Chiron lives?"

He nodded.

"But where would he go?" asked Jeanette.

"Why not to the small *gîte* in town? It's empty nine months of the year."

"Madame Lunardelli might have something to say about that," Jeanette said.

"She has altogether too much to say as it is." Denise sniffed. Guy leaned back in his chair with a small smile on his wintry face.

Denise had made crème caramel and a Savoy cake, and Jeanette had brought an apple tart. We sampled them all. Then Guy served *digestifs* by the fire—anisette, framboise, and Armagnac, and prunes and cherries soaked in brandy. Guy and I savored Armagnac, the fiery brandy from Gascony, while the ladies helped themselves liberally to the 80-proof fruit. Denise served strong coffee, but it couldn't quicken the close, warm air. Guy and I nodded a little in our chairs while the ladies chatted. A little after four o'clock, Jeanette rose.

"Thank you so much. It's been delightful."

We all got up. Guy clasped Sara's arm and walked her to the door. Denise said, "You must come back. Guy can tell you many things about Ruch. It would be important for your research. At least he'll tell you the truth!"

The wild weather continued, and I spent hours gazing out my office window. One afternoon, two boys careened around the church, leaped the garden wall, and tucked themselves into the angle it formed with the buttress. I recognized one, the young self-indulger. They were excited, peering around the corner for pursuers. They pulled small squares of paper from their pockets and held them to the light, squinting. They dropped a few, pulled out more, tore them to shreds. The sun turned the white scraps into a spring snowstorm. The boys leaped back over the wall and disappeared.

An hour or so later, Sara came home from a walk with her camera. She had stopped by to see Jeanette Barde.

"She was completely distraught. I've never seen her so upset."

"What's the matter?"

"The church was desecrated! She went in for something and found it vandalized. She said it was horrible. A stained-glass window in the vestibule broken. Most of the candles smashed on the floor. The head broken off a statue of Jesus. The sacristy was ransacked. And she found a turd in one of the closets. She said it reminded her of the war."

"When did it happen?"

"She doesn't know. But not too long ago, because there was catechism earlier this afternoon."

I told her what I had seen and went to visit Jeanette. She was sitting with her son and daughter-in-law.

"I saw them, too," she said. "They're wild young things. I called the priest and the Mayor and told them about this. I told them about the boys, too. But the priest can't believe it. They're his catechism students. He said they couldn't speak of the Passion with him, then act so violently against it."

"What about the Mayor?"

"Oh, he doesn't want to do anything. But I insisted he call the gendarmes."

"Well, I didn't see much. But if you want me to talk with the Mayor, I will."

The next morning, Jeanette, the Mayor, and two gendarmes came down the path to our door. They stopped to pick up some paper scraps that still littered the lawn. I let them in and told what I had seen.

"Do you know the names of these boys?" asked one of the gendarmes.

"No, but I think I could identify them."

"That probably won't be necessary," said the Mayor, anxious and unhappy. "Thank you for the information."

"The Mayor took the gendarmes to the boys' houses," Marie-Jo told me the next morning, in the store. "They questioned the boys in front of the parents. They confessed. Then everyone went to the church. The boys wept. The parents agreed to pay for the damage."

"What will happen to the boys?"

"That's up to their families. If they were mine, they'd get a good whipping. That kind of foolishness doesn't help anything, does it?" She shrugged. "The priest is going to be disappointed. It's a shame. But that's the way boys can be."

Sara and I hit a streak of work. We cobbled together a half dozen assignments for articles through a wide swath of southern France.

I took the car to the garage for a checkup before we set off. Jourdan listened as much to the motor as to me and quickly decided on spark plugs, a fan belt, transmission fluid. Then two farmers in their newest suits came in, clutching a crumpled piece of paper. It advertised a vineyard machine Jourdan had invented. He waved Antoine to take over my car and led the visitors to the prototype.

Antoine shook his head. "That machine takes all his time."

"What does it do?"

"Oh, everything—sprays pesticides, hedges the vines, pulls a harvester . . . He's been working on it for years, and every year it does something new."

He bent over the motor. Jourdan slapped the machine, pointed at the men, more animated than I had ever seen him, a lamplit silhouette in a corner of the dark garage.

Sara and I spent two weeks on the road. Ruch dwindled to a speck on the map, but the Renault never faltered. We hiked in the Pyrénées above Perpignan to explore a ruined Cathari stronghold. We ate bouillabaisse with strong garlicky *rouille* in the Mediterranean port of Bandol. We stumbled through the stone-strewn vineyards of Châteauneuf-du-Pape. In the Côte-Rôtie, we tasted perfumed young wines in cellars with beaten-earth floors. We battled a snowstorm over the peaks of the Massif Central. We slept in an creaky four-poster bed in Argentat, a foggy river town of slate and stone and silence.

There were days when no one in the world knew where we were. There were afternoons when we had no idea where we would spend the night. There were nights in musty hotels, motorcycles roaring under the window, when we longed for a lamp in a familiar window. France isn't a large country; you can drive halfway through it in a day. But the changes are sudden and sharp. In an afternoon, low rolling hills become gorge-cut mountains; vineyards give way to pasture; olive oil turns to pork fat and butter. Our small, dark lunch waitress became gray-eyed and plump at dinner, and her new accent set the menu into a foreign language.

We came back from the northeast, through Périgord and the upper Dordogne, following the migration paths of thousands of years. As we dropped from the Massif Central, the land became less wooded, more fertile; then pasture turned to corn, tobacco, and finally vines. The stone of the houses changed from hard gray granite to the soft gold of Entre-Deux-Mers limestone, and their roofs from black slate to red tile. We crossed the Dordogne at Castillon and reached Ruch on Palm Sunday.

The next day the Mayor knocked on our door.

"Well, this is an honor," I said. "What can we do for you?"

He shifted his weight; his bad eye wandered. "In France, we consider that spring begins at Easter."

"We're ready for it. The presbytère was cold in winter!"

"And when spring comes, so do the tourists." He paused. "There are certain regulations about the *gîte*. Certain agents have it listed. We have to make it available to them."

"Does that mean we have to leave?"

"Well, not exactly. But you would have to apply for it, like anyone else, for certain periods of time."

"And pay the high season rates, like anyone else."

"Yes, that, too."

"We couldn't afford that. But we're not ready to leave Ruch. Is there anywhere else we could stay?"

"Philippe Sartran has moved into Rauzan. The small *gîte* is empty now. It would be slightly irregular, but we could offer you that."

Feeling both gratitude and resentment, we accepted. Built in the old café building that now housed the Salle des Jeunes, the *gîte* had once been the café's barn. Chatelier still kept a chicken coop in the building's back corner. Town workers had whitewashed the walls, tiled the ground floor, and carpeted upstairs, built an open, wide-planked staircase. It had new appliances and a new view, east toward the Mayor's house. But the biggest change was its location. Now we lived on main street, and suddenly Ruch came to life.

We saw old women open their shutters in the morning, young men roar home from the Scorpion at night. We got to know Madame Cadapeaud, a widow who lived down the street. Her old German shepherd, Bill, put us on his rounds, after his visit to Madame Pagant on the corner. Raspy-voiced Jean-Pierre Viandon lived across the street with his old parents; he put us on his rounds, too. One day a tramp trudged by carrying a cat in a wicker basket. Another day a long-haired young artist peddled sentimental scenes of children door-to-door, fifty francs a frame.

We heard cars in the road, motorbikes spinning aimlessly around the café, tractors in the vines. These were spring noises, and they crescendoed at Easter week. All France takes a holiday in the country then, and Ruch was full of visitors. Madame Barde's sister and her husband came down from Paris. Viandon's six brothers and sisters all returned home, one from Guadeloupe. The summer houses were open, and strange children played in their yards. In the store, we learned that five English tourists were in the presbytère, and wandered down the chestnut path in curiosity. They were sitting on the lawn, enjoying the view. We called to them in English, startling them. I felt bad, afterward—as if we had shattered their illusion of being explorers deep in the heart of France.

The Delom-Sorbé family gathered twenty-six members, from Paris, Pau, Tours, and Toulouse. They packed the church on Easter Sunday. Sara asked the old doctor if she could take a family portrait, and he agreed. Around five, we went to Vaure. We were introduced to everyone, apéritifs were put in our hands.

"How are you today, Doctor?" Sara asked. When she reached for his hand, he pulled her toward him for a kiss on the cheek. She reddened, then smiled.

"*Foutu*. But if Christ can rise from the dead, I can keep going a little longer."

"There was quite a crowd in church today."

"Not bad. Not as many as when the old *curé* was alive, though. When people change, habits change."

"It's not the priest, Papa," said Hélène. The widow of the doctor's

Madame Cadapeaud

son, she divided her time between the refurbished west wing of the château and her mother's house in Biarritz. "The townspeople are all Communists now. That's why they don't come to church."

"The Easter crowd is always smaller than Palm Sunday's," added Philippe de Larrard. "On Palm Sunday, the priest blesses the boxwood and the *paysans* take it home and hang it over the mantel for good luck. That's more important than the Resurrection to them."

"Have the people changed that much?" I asked the doctor.

"Not all. Madame Sorbier's family has seven generations in Ruch. But most of the families don't go back more than two or three. Like me. They came from Périgord as domestics or sharecroppers and married Ruchelais. Some were refugees from eastern France during the war. Now we have people from Bordeaux buying old farmhouses for vacation homes. The young people who grew up here are leaving, because there aren't any jobs. Old women live in most of the houses in the village."

Vaure had changed, too. The estate had dwindled for three generations, and its future as a working farm had hung in the balance until Philippe decided to give up his career as a landscape engineer to tend the vineyards. The best times were gone, they sighed, remembering family picnics in summers past. The shadows lengthened in the big room. Nanette bustled with the tea tray. Shouts drifted in the windows, cousins playing soccer in the vines. Sara came in with her camera.

"The light is beautiful. Can we take the portrait now?"

Everyone got up. Too many tried to help the doctor, who fought them off and raised himself on his shiny canes. Mothers called their children, who nestled under skirts. The clan gathered on the north steps, the château's most formal façade. Sara urged them closer and closer together, till they were shoulder to shoulder around the doctor, who planted his canes in the center of the highest step, chin up, eyes glinting. For an instant, four generations of life came together in the shadow of hundreds of years of history, one entity with its own character and features, the achievement and embodiment of family. The shutter clicked. An instant later, a cat streaked by and a child darted after it. The silence broke, and they were free again.

· · ·

Bud break came to the vineyard in April. The first tips of new growth were deep red, like the branches, and for a few days they blazed red in the sunset, blurring the spaces between the rows. Then green took over, first in the ground cover, then like a soft mist rising through the thickening foliage as the new leaves unfurled.

The renewal was haunted by the January freezes. Many vines had died, remained stubborn black stumps. In the oldest vineyards, the losses were isolated, evidence of faulty rootstock or irreversible disease. The young vines were hit harder, especially in low-lying areas along the river—places the growers' grandfathers would never have planted grapes. Vines hate to have their feet wet, they said, and left the floodplains in meadow for grazing cattle. But for the last fifteen years, wine had paid better than meat or milk.

The farmers would plant even more, but they were blocked by the bureaucrats in Brussels, the administrators of the Common Market who were desperately trying to drain the vast European wine lake. The wine market has always been controlled; in A.D. 92, the Roman emperor Domitian ordered Gaul to uproot half its vines in an effort to increase wheat production. Juggling supply and demand in the face of declining consumption and changing tastes, the government orders one-fourth of France's wine production distilled each year, stockpiling worthless industrial alcohol in an effort to keep anachronistic and unprofitable family farms alive.

But the Bordelais weren't worried. Bordeaux wine has been an international commodity since the thirteenth century, when the English developed a taste for the light, elegant wine they called claret. The region reached its apogee of glory when Napoleon III proclaimed an International Exhibition in Paris in 1855, and commanded a presentation of the best wines of Bordeaux. Brokers drew up a ranking of the top châteaux, divided into five levels called *crus,* or growths. This hierarchy of price and prestige remains sacrosanct more than a century later.

Despite its small villages and meandering roads, Entre-Deux-Mers found its way to the international market in the sixteenth century, when the Dutch bought its thin white wines for distillation into brandy. In the first half of the nineteenth century, Bordeaux's Golden Age, vineyard acreage was greater than when we arrived. The small farms became linked not only to the world economy but to its diseases, too. Phylloxera, a plant louse native to North America that ravaged all Europe's vines in the late nineteenth century, was first spotted in Bordeaux in an experimental vineyard in Entre-Deux-Mers.

As prices rose and fell, the growers scraped up rocks to plant vines or let the forest run wild. After two wars and a depression, the wine market finally recovered. In the 1950s, the farmers bought tractors. In the sixties, they installed toilets and telephones in their houses. By 1986, they had harvesting machines and some of them took vacations in the Alps.

The second Golden Age kicked off in 1982, when a hot, dry summer led to a rich, fruity vintage. It was not only the biggest crop of red grapes in the century, but winemakers and journalists proclaimed it the best since the legendary 1961 vintage. A rising dollar triggered frenzied American demand. Prices went up, and the good times began in earnest.

The 1983 vintage was almost as good and almost as big. Demand held steady and prices increased again. In 1984, a poor flowering in late June erased much of the Merlot crop. As a result, October birthed a small, hard wine. But though quality was down, so was supply. Prices went up.

The scorching summer of 1985 produced another huge crop, and some compared it to 1982. But there were rumblings of discontent. Through the winter of '85, the dollar sagged against the European currencies, and merchants warned that they had too much wine on their shelves. The great châteaux traditionally announced prices for their new wines six months after the harvest, selling the wine *en primeur,* as futures for delivery after bottling two years later. In April 1986, the five first growths, the leaders of Bordeaux's wine aristocracy, counseled caution and kept their prices at '84 levels. But the tier of châteaux just below them—the Super Seconds, led by Léoville-Las Cases and Pichon-Longueville Lalande—weren't satisfied with stability. They had big investments to amortize and big egos to fill. One raised prices and the others followed suit. The market swallowed hard, and bought.

When 1986 provided another huge crop of reds, even the growers of

Ruch could see that the pipes were full. Their tanks were overflowing and there was nowhere to put the new wine. They tried to sell more wine directly from the little store, but the cooperative's principal markets —bulk wine to the big merchants for supermarket blends—were beyond its control.

Prices froze over the winter of '86–'87, thawed only to settle downward. The going rate for bulk red Bordeaux dropped below 5,000 francs per *tonneau,* the standard measure of 900 liters, from the fat years of 6,000 francs and more. At the cooperative, Chiron complained when the director postponed the purchase of a must chiller he wanted for the white wines. As April went on, the growers waited anxiously to learn the first-growth châteaux' opening prices for the '86 vintage.

"It's ridiculous that we should worry about Mouton-Rothschild," Chiron expostulated in his lab one day. "Those classified growths make up only 5 percent of Bordeaux's production. Their wines won't even be bottled for nearly two more years—all our wines had better be sold before then. They're competing on the world market against Burgundies and the new wines from California. We compete in French supermarkets against the Côtes du Rhone. There's no relation."

"Tell that to the merchants," said Philippe de Larrard. He was testing new wine in the laboratory, checking levels of volatile acidity, the threat of spoilage. "If Mouton-Rothschild goes down, do you think Mouton-Cadet will go up? If the Baron de Rothschild is selling his wine for less, do you think he will buy ours for more?"

The daffodils gave way to wisteria and iris. Great chestnut trees, planted in formal borders along old roads and châteaux drives, leafed and bloomed, their flowers huge cones of pink and white. On sunny garden walls the ivy was suddenly studded with small purple flowers. After windy nights, the car was covered with sticky yellow pollen.

In the valleys, wide fields of low green plants flowered into brilliant yellow carpets. Grangier told us they were rape flowers, to make oil from the seeds. "It's for land that's not suited to corn or vines," he said. He was driving his tractor, and he was smiling. All the tractors were out in the fields, and it seemed as if all the farmers were smiling under their caps on the breezy, sun-drenched days.

On a country drive, we passed a vineyard flooded with yellow and stopped to admire thousands of tulips growing thick between the rows. The Mayor told us that the whole region had once been famous for the delicate, flame-petaled flowers the Ruchelais called *étoiles*. No one knew where they came from—one botanist claimed a Roman origin. Children used to harvest them for sale in Bordeaux, he said, but now that most of the growers used herbicides on the vines instead of plowing, the tulips were almost gone.

The visitors went back to the cities and the children went back to school. There wasn't much to do in the vineyards but wait for the buds to flower. I spent a morning in our sunny doorway, watching sparrows hop through the new grass, and heard the church bells toll another death.

"An old widow," said an old widow in the store. "She lived down the hill, at Castaing. Her daughter's family lives down there, too. She didn't come up much to town."

"A real Ruchelaise," added the Mayor.

"How did she die?"

"Oh, she got tired, I guess. Her body was all used up."

In the *mairie*, Denise had the town register open. "I was just filling out the forms," she said. "Let's see. Born in Ruch in 1900. Married in Ruch in 1923. Four children, one still living in Ruch. Widowed in 1961. A life like other lives. Though longer than most. If God gives us eighty-odd years, who can complain?"

She closed the book and fanned herself with a sheaf of papers. "Isn't it heavy today? And have you noticed—the birds are very loud. It means a break in the weather. A thunderstorm is coming. You'll see."

12

Shad Roe and *Lune Rousse*

A sudden-breaking thunderstorm caught George in the street near our house, so we called him inside for a cup of coffee.

"Oh, I'm quite behind," he groaned. He pried off his high rubber boots and stood them by the door. "This weather is like fertilizer for the weeds. I've no sooner beaten them back at one end of town than it's time to begin again at the other. And yet it's, George, fix the toilet in the *mairie*, and, George, run round the presbytère, and, George, rake the gravel by the church."

He ran his hands through his wet hair and sat down. Sara offered him a brownie. "Delicious. What are they?"

"Brownies, George. An American classic."

"Make them yourself, did you?"

Sara nodded. She had made them for choir practice; everyone took turns bringing sweets. The ladies liked them, too.

"So you've been round to Madame Tallon's for dinner."

"It was delicious," Sara said. "When Americans imagine French country cooking, they have Denise in mind. She even killed the cock herself."

"I'm sure she did. Was there blood in the sauce? It gives me indigestion just to think about it."

He helped himself to another brownie, and Sara refilled his cup. "Did she talk about me?"

"Actually, she didn't. We talked mostly about the old days in Ruch."

George snorted. He was quiet for a moment. "Well, you ought to come round for dinner with us. Do you like lamb?" He stood, finishing his brownie. "Rain's stopped. I'd best get back to my weeds. I'll just check with Anice. Would next week be all right?"

A few days later, George stopped by with a dozen eggs.

"Drive out of town by the garage, and when you climb the hill, turn left. There's a monument to some foolish young man killed in a car accident; turn left again. The road ends at what looks like a house— flowers in front, curtains in the windows. Actually, they keep calves in there, grow them for veal. Completely illegal. The Mayor knows all about it, of course. Turn right there. The road swings round and you'll see us. About seven all right?"

Evening was falling soft and blue as we followed the back roads to the Halls'. The long views crossed open country, rolling hills with only patches of woods or a wandering stream to break their flow. But a crazy quilt of property lines turned the fields into a maze, as the narrow blacktop twisted and turned to swing around an abandoned shed or a tumbledown wall. We wandered through the vineyards as if the road had all the time in the world. Finally, it hooked north and dropped to the Courbut. Below us, a stone barn and a small stone house nestled against the bank of the hill. The car squeezed through a wooden gate, bumped down two ruts of a driveway, and came to rest under a tall pine.

George came out of the house. He still wore his work clothes but had changed his boots for slippers. "Find your way all right?"

"No problem. Lovely spot you have here."

"That's what it means. The name of the place. L'Estebot: *l'est est beau.* The east is beautiful. We reckon this was the eastern portion of some larger property at one point. We like it well enough."

Anice joined us, and they showed us around. The large garden was just sprouting. Fruit and nut trees stood near the barn. Inside, building materials lay piled in a corner and straw was scattered across the floor.

"They would have made the wine here," George said. "We found a few old barrels when we arrived. We burned them for heat. We didn't buy any vines with the property. The idea was to build a house for ourselves in here and use the old house as a *gîte*. Now it's for the chickens, and the sheep in winter. Oh, it's a fine barn all right. Several people have offered to buy it."

He led us into the house. It was built against the hill, with two small windows almost at ground level. Three steps led down into a dark, narrow kitchen. A shiny electric stove jostled an ancient stone sink that drained through the wall. Tiles and plasterboard were stacked by the door.

"This is our current project," George said. "We brought the cooker, an oven, and Lord knows what else from England. But the power wasn't strong enough to drive them. They sat in the barn for years. We cooked over an open fire. You can make lovely things on an open fire, you know, though it was heavy work for Anice. Then we got a wood stove. All the time I was after the electric people to upgrade our line. They kept putting me off, but after all, it was the law. Finally, last year, they ran a new line out here. So now we can finally put the whole kitchen together."

"Won't it be beautiful when it's done," Anice said.

Three more steps led down into the main room. The bedroom lay beyond it. There were small windows, a northerly view. George pointed out the pasture where the sheep grazed and the poplars along the stream below. "That's all ours."

The room was a hodgepodge of scraps and make-dos. Oriental rugs warmed the floor. An easy chair sat close to the stove, its upholstery shiny with age. The usual armoire was replaced by an ornate Victorian breakfront whose shelves were filled with knickknacks and mementos. The lighting was dim, the stove radiated heat.

George opened a bottle of white wine. It was fruity and sweet, a style that had been Entre-Deux-Mers's mainstay during the fifties but had fallen out of favor with the switch to red wines. "In England they drink that sickly sherry," George said. "We like this much better. It's from Yon, of course."

"Do you miss England, Anice?" asked Sara.

Anice shook her head. George answered for her.

"What is there to miss? Poor weather, bad food, worse snobs? Mind you, Ruch isn't much of an improvement, on some counts."

"The food and weather here are certainly better than in New York," Sara said. "Have you tried that walnut bread from the Castillon market?"

"You probably think the people are better, too," George snorted. "But you don't know them the way I do."

Anice slipped into the kitchen and brought a steaming tureen. She ladled a rich crimson soup fragrant with tomatoes.

"This is delicious, Anice," Sara exclaimed.

The older woman smiled. "We do get beautiful tomatoes here. I make the soup in the autumn and freeze it. It warms the cold nights nicely."

"It could do with a bit more garlic, though, don't you think?" asked George.

"He's always saying that. He'd put garlic in the tarts if I'd let him."

"I guess it's my French blood." He smiled at her. "It's the only thing we argue about."

"That's why I never let him in the kitchen."

We all took second helpings and fell silent, eating. Anice cleared the bowls and George opened another bottle.

"This is Yon's red." He checked the label. "1985. A marvelous year round here. It was hot all summer, and not a drop of rain till November. Big crop, too. These farmers are making good money. Did you see Grangier's new car? Some kind of barter with Madame Silva. She used to own the store. They're all in the Mayor's gang. Those people do just fine."

"George?" He joined Anice in the kitchen, then came back carrying the lamb on a platter while she balanced dishes of roast potatoes and buttered carrots. "It's a proper English Sunday dinner," she said.

George told us about the sheep and how much work they were. They may look placid and sturdy, but really they're sensitive and fragile. One year he took his lambs to Castillon for slaughter, but the butcher was too busy to get to them before closing. During the night, the sheep died—

frightened to death, George reckoned. The law forbids butchering sheep that are already dead for meat, so his whole season was lost.

"I'd just as soon give them up," he said. "But Anice does most of the work. She quite likes it."

"They are gentle creatures," she said. "As long as they're calm, they don't cause much trouble. And George likes his roast."

We went on to a bottle of cognac that George had been given by a friend of the fellow who made it, hot sharp stuff with the kick of authenticity. George's red face got redder and his laugh grew hearty; Anice giggled at his tales. He told us he had been attached to Eisenhower's command as a translator during the war, how impressive the operation had been, and how the French resented his position. He reminisced about his childhood in France, about his mother's wealthy relatives, about playing in the gardens of ancient estates.

He sounded like a rich man spending the weekend in a hunting cottage to escape an elaborate life. But when I rose to look for the toilet, he directed me outside to a wooden shed behind the barn.

George had followed a dream out of his old life and made it come true, I thought, yet the truth was far different from his imagining. Now the old life had become the dream, and there was no way back. Which life was the dream for Sara and me? New York was as far away for us as Wales was for the Halls. None of us was going to wake up and find Ruch gone.

The stars were thick; the breeze was cool; the night was silent except for the murmur of the stream and a truck rumbling up a faraway hill.

I stumbled back into the house. Sara was telling New York stories and everybody laughed, happy not to be there. I recalled soft nights on a tenement rooftop, the dreamlike landscape of black towers against an orange sky, felt a pang of longing. I signaled to Sara and we made our goodbyes. The Halls stood silhouetted outside their door waving as we turned the car toward town.

On May 1, red flags flood the streets as Europe celebrates its workers. In 1981, France elected a Socialist, François Mitterrand, President of the Republic. For five years, his May Day parades were extravagant shows of pomp and media presence. Then in 1986, the conservative parties wrested control of the legislature and installed Gaullist Jacques Chirac as Prime Minister. The political swing left the holiday adrift.

The celebrations dwindled to gestures. Boutonniers of lilies of the valley had come to symbolize solidarity with the workers, and pinning the flowers to one's lapel remained *de rigueur.* Children would buy the flowers, called *muguets,* and hawk them on the streets, a lesson in capitalism that made a curious contrast to the holiday's text of solidarity. An enterprising child might net several hundred francs for a few hours' work.

In 1987, Ruch was so drowsy with prosperity that fervor had lost its appeal, despite the left-leaning administration of Mayor Bonvoisin, who had once run for council on the Communist ticket. Children didn't bother with *muguets.* The Galeries Ruchelaises stocked the boutonniers, but there were few takers in town. In May, the Ruchelais would rather talk about shad running, and the *lune rousse.*

Shad ran up the rivers from Easter to Pentecost, according to the old woman in the Castillon market who sold me one. When they were most plentiful the sleek silver fish cost about three dollars a pound. Along the Dordogne, old men dropped lines from bridges, cast bait from boats, set up straw baskets piled with shad on ice, and sold them from cars by the side of the road.

"You shouldn't buy from them," said my fishmonger, gutting the smallish shad she had picked out for me.

"Why not?"

"They're not certified."

"Certified for what?"

"Oh, you know." She waved her knife and scales glittered through the sunbeams. "Health. The government."

She told me to save the roe and sauté it in butter and shallots, just till it was firm to the touch. Stuff the fish with sorrel—the herb would melt the myriad tiny bones that made the fish such a trial to eat. Grill or bake it, till the meat flaked with a fork, then serve it with a shallot vinaigrette.

"And a good bottle of Bordeaux *blanc.*" She kissed her fingers and smiled. "That's what shad is all about."

The bounty of the sea compensated for the threat from the moon. The first full moon cycle after Easter was called the *lune rousse,* and the old men shook their heads when they talked about it. One cool evening I saw people in the café and stopped in. I asked what it meant, *lune rousse.*

"It's because the moon takes on a brown color this time of year," said Madame Jourdan, drawing a beer for me. "It's the atmospherics."

Guy Petit and Fabrice Lunardelli were at the bar. Nathalie was hunched over a video screen, shooting aliens with a laser pistol.

"Oh, what do you know," Fabrice sputtered. "You're from the north. It's called the brown moon because the ground turns brown after the frost. The early green grass freezes and dies, burned. It turns brown."

"Hah! You're wrong, too." Petit liked to have the last word. "The word is Russian, not brown. Ask the Mayor—he's a Red himself!"

The cycle had begun late in April, and after a summery May Day a strong west wind brought squalls and sharply lower temperatures. Marie-Jo teased me when I huffed into the store for the paper.

"You thought summer was here, didn't you?" She laughed. "Bordeaux is not so easy to know, after all."

"It's the *lune rousse,* isn't it? That's what they were saying in the café."

"Oh, what they say in the café!"

"They're doing a pretty good business, and they're not even open yet."

"There are plenty in Ruch who drink when they're not thirsty."

"But what is it about the moon, then?"

"They say the *lune rousse* always brings the last chance of frost. And the three days before the full moon, well, those saints are called the Saints de Glace, the ice saints. Easter came late this year, so if it does freeze there could be real damage."

A horn sounded and we both stepped outside. The Mayor's car was stopped and tiny Madame Matou was badgering Bonvoisin through the window.

"What did I ever do to you?" challenged the old woman.

Bonvoisin looked puzzled.

"You walked right past me yesterday. And what did I ever do to you?"

"Ah, Madame! If I passed you without speaking, it was only because

I didn't see you." He smiled slyly. "Of course, if you were thirty years younger, I might not have missed you. But I trust your husband is making up for my neglect."

For a moment, her face darkened, but then she laughed. "You're terrible, Beber," she said.

"May you live long enough to vote for me again!" he said, touching her arm, and drove away.

On May 8 the nation commemorated Germany's surrender in 1945 with the month's second three-day weekend. Flags flew from the monument and the Mayor placed a wreath at its base. But only half a dozen people turned out for the ceremony, and he grumbled afterward.

"I remember 1945," he said. "We danced for three days without stopping. Now no one cares."

The Ice Saints arrived. Estelle was hazy and cool. Achille thickened the clouds and dropped the temperature into the forties. Rolande was the last. Early-morning rain brought muttered relief in the store, but then the wind picked up and the temperature plunged. At two o'clock it was dark. Suddenly the drumming on the windows changed to a rattle. Slushy hail whitened the lawn, built up on the stone sills. Ten minutes later it stopped. The wind died down and the rain resumed. The *lune rousse* was over.

A whole new wave of flowers grew in gardens and beside the roads. Poppies blazed on the road banks, wildly abundant among abandoned vines. Roses bloomed everywhere, delicate white creepers, heavy-headed pink-petaled bushes, reds at the row ends of well-tended vineyards. Masses of unfamiliar white flowers, powerfully fragrant with a spicy note like cinnamon, weighed down the boughs of slender young trees clustered in valley bottoms, along the streams, at the edge of oak forests. We finally described them well enough to learn they were acacias.

Like the willow bushes, so brilliant in autumn, acacias were a crucial partner for the vine. Because the tree was fast-growing and its wood resistant to rot, it was harvested to make the stakes that held the wires that trained the vine shoots. According to *Sud Ouest,* acacias supplied about

Run-down vineyard in springtime

35,000 cubic meters of wood annually to Bordeaux's vineyards. It was still far more popular for stakes than steel or cement. There were about 30,000 acres of acacias planted in the *departement,* more than any other tree except oaks and poplars.

We hadn't even distinguished them before, had simply read them as part of the woods. The acacia flowers filled in a blank in our local map; we saw more now that we knew what they were. So our picture of Ruch, town and fields, slowly took on detail.

"They're out!" cried the wine column in *Sud Ouest.* Château Cos d'Estournel, one of the leading estates of the Médoc, had posted a price for its 1986 wine. And once one came out, the rest soon followed. The market would fall in line and the edgy merchants who had been hesitating to buy the lesser wines would begin to make firm offers.

Cos d'Estournel offered its wine at 84 francs per bottle *en primeur,* selling now for delivery in 1989. The price was down from 92 francs for the '85. The drop was less than the growers had feared, as powerful overseas buyers had been clamoring for reductions of 15 to 20 percent.

But it was a drop nonetheless, the first of the decade. The high quality of the vintage was universally proclaimed, but there was simply too much wine for the market to absorb. Even at the lower prices, the haughty Great Growths found initial sales sluggish.

In Ruch, sluggish sales would have been an improvement. I stopped by to fill up my five-liter jug and found all three winemakers hanging around the salesroom. A couple of bottles sat open on the counter.

"Business must be good if you're all here to help."

"Business is terrible," growled Chatelier. "But there's nothing to do in the winery. The wine just sits there, waiting to be sold. But the prices they offer are insulting. 4,300 francs the *tonneau!* When last year we were turning down 6,000."

"It could be a real problem in the fall," added Chiron. "If we don't move some of this wine, we won't have room to store the next harvest. Colette has ordered more vats, but even with the subsidies we have to pay serious money. We have to sell some wine. But the growers protest if the price is too low."

"What you need is a small crop in '87," I suggested.

"Small but good," amended Breton. "Poor wine always brings bad prices."

"Don't ask the growers for help," said Chiron. "They're farmers. All they can think of is bigger harvests."

"Nature could still help us," Breton pointed out. "Remember '84, when the flowering was so bad in the Merlot? It could happen again."

A car pulled up outside and Sorbier entered. "You guys drinking up the profits again?" asked the gray-haired farmer. "No wonder we're not making any money."

"There's no money because you're greedy," Chatelier retorted. "We were just explaining it to the American. If your crops were smaller, the wine would be better and it would sell for more money."

"Better?" He poured himself a glass of red and downed it. "Couldn't be better. Not with you three in charge of making it."

"What would you think of a good hard storm during the flowering?" asked Breton.

"Why not just open the vats and claim the insurance? Or get out on the road to sell some of this stuff." He banged two 20-liter containers down on the concrete floor. "Look. Fill these up. That'll improve your balance sheets for the day."

Sorbier bought his wine from the 12-franc tank, which carried the appellation Bordeaux, as opposed to the *vin de table* at 6 francs per liter I drank. I sometimes wondered how rigorous they were in distinguishing the wine that filled the tanks, but they swore it was all documented and verified. I helped Sorbier carry the heavy plastic containers to his car and hitched a ride back to town.

"Those three guys! *Putain.*" Sorbier spat out the window.

Directly translated, *putain* means whore. But around Bordeaux the word served as a broad mood indicator, expressing changing shades of incredulity and disapproval depending on emphasis and pronunciation. *Pew-taing,* he said, meaning, Can you believe those guys?

"They work hard for three weeks a year. The rest of the time they sit around and drink. Then they call me greedy. They get paid whether the wine sells or not. I'm out on a tractor every day, and if the wine doesn't sell, the bank takes the tractor away."

It rained a lot in May. The soccer season was over; August's vacations were still far away; the vineyards demanded monotonous hours on the tractor spreading pesticides that gave the farmers raspy voices and headaches. Then one day signs appeared in the store, the post office, the garage. They said, Nathalie and Frédéric invite you to the café for an apéritif for its official opening.

We passed Jeanette Barde sitting on her porch with Madame Tallon. Marie, Jeanette's granddaughter, was playing with a beetle.

"Aren't you going to the party?" Sara called.

They shook their heads. "Why can't we go, Grandma?" asked Marie.

"That café will be no better than the Scorpion," Denise said. "You'll see. It will be full of unruly young people, and sooner or later someone will get hurt. That's not the kind of café Ruch needs."

"It might as well be a clubhouse for the Mayor," added Jeanette. "Not a place for churchgoing people."

"Who do you think arranged their permits? Dug up the cemetery? Paid for the drinks tonight?" Denise shook her head again. "No, we won't go, thank you."

But the café was packed, loud with laughter, dense with smoke. We edged in and Madame Jourdan embraced us.

"*Bonjour,*" she said. "Thank you for coming."

She opened her arms in greeting, then disappeared into the crowd. There must have been a hundred or more people. The core was the Mayor's gang, the same faces that showed up at the Salle des Jeunes after the football matches. But there were strangers, too, whom someone identified as friends from Blasimon and the army. The youths who played the videogames were there. Children wove their way through the forest of legs. And we were surprised to see Nanette Delom-Sorbé at a table in the corner.

"*Bonjour, Nanette.*" We paused by her chair. She was dressed as if for church, and sat close to tiny Jeanette, her maid for forty years, also dressed in her starched best. "How are you today? And the doctor?"

"Oh, fine. He didn't want to come out in the evening, though. When it's damp, the cold gets in his bones."

"He always did want the fire burning high," Jeanette added.

"Well, it's plenty warm in here," Sara said.

"And about as smoky as that old *séjour* when the wind came from the east." Jeanette laughed. "The biggest fireplaces don't always have the best chimneys."

Nanette laughed, too, her rapid mirthless chuckle, but her eyes were bright and hard. She looked lost in the café, an exotic bird among starlings. None of the women really looked at ease. Madame Grangier, Madame Matou, and their friends hung back against the walls. We found Nicole Bonvoisin sitting with friends from the *quine*. "*Voilà les Americains,*" she cried, and kissed our cheeks.

"Good party," Sara said.

Nicole nodded.

"What do you think of the café?"

"Oh, very nice, very nice."

"Will you come often?"

The women looked at each other, then broke into laughter. "Oh no," said Nicole. "Not us. This place is for Claude and his friends. Not us."

We made our way to the bar. Nathalie wore a gauzy white cotton dress. There were men around her, and she laughed loudly at their jokes. Frédéric was dressed in black, plump, fluttering from one thirsty guest to another.

"What would you like?"

The table was spread with the regulation bottles: Suze, cheap ruby Port, Pastis 51, cassis syrup. Plastic cups were set out in ranks already dosed with *pastis*. Scattered bowls held salted peanuts, crackers, and green olives. We asked for Port and scooped some peanuts. "Congratulations. You made fast progress at the end."

"Oh, it's still not finished, but thanks," Frédéric replied.

"It's a shame you finally decided to cover those ceiling beams." A new dropped ceiling of asbestos tile made a strange contrast with the stone walls.

"The beams were nice. But those tiles make the place safer and cheaper to heat."

"Have you given the café a name yet?"

He nodded. "Malibu. You like it?"

"Ah, California! This really will be a young person's café, won't it?"

He looked puzzled.

"Sure, Malibu. It's a famous surfing beach near Los Angeles. The Beach Boys sang about it."

Frédéric shook his head. "No, we named it after the liqueur, the one made from coconut that comes from the Caribbean. It's the hottest drink in years. The salesman said he'd give us a sign for outdoors if we'd call it that. But I like the name, anyway. Don't you?"

"It's a great name, Frédéric. And a great party. Thanks again."

The acacias dropped their flowers, more roses bloomed, and peonies opened. On the fruit trees, apples and pears took recognizable form, and cherries began to color. In the vineyards, the vines grew full and bushy, and the growers moved through the rows tying the new shoots back to the wires. Where the farmers went easy on the herbicides, flowers multiplied in the ranks: pink cones, purple clusters, yellow bells, and brilliant ruby poppies.

One sunny morning I ran into Grangier in the store. "Well, the *lune rousse* is over, isn't it?" I asked. "No more danger of frost."

"That's right." He nodded. "We had some close calls, but no real damage."

"So will things go smoothly now?"

"Well, not necessarily. In June comes the flowering. We could still have bad weather for that. If there's too much rain or wind, the flowers get knocked right off the vines, and that means fewer grapes. No, we're not safe yet. Farmers are safe only when the harvest is in."

13

Flowering

Paris called in June. A couple of article assignments were all the invitation I needed. Sara decided not to go; city life had lost its appeal for her. She dropped me at the train station, and four hours later I was in the Gare d'Austerlitz, the dove-gray light of a Paris evening filtering through the lacy, sooty train shed.

I borrowed a friend's apartment in the 11th *arrondissement,* a working-class *quartier* lively with small shops, children, and dogs. I picked up bread, cheese, and fruit and climbed three flights of creaking wooden stairs. The place had been empty for months and the air was stale, but the telephone and answering machine were working and Rick had left a note. *Don't turn on too many lights at once,* he wrote. *Come round Mathilde's for a drink if you can. Here's a book you might like.* It was called *A Short Walk Through the Hindu Kush,* and I wondered where he thought I was living. I opened a window, breathed Parisian air.

I was writing about urban renewal, wandering the streets, veering from construction to decay. I interviewed architects who talked about the difficulty of rebuilding a city whose principal treasure was its past. When the Centre Pompidou, a museum of contemporary art, had opened in the 1970s, the French were defiantly modern; the multicolored tubular metal structure jarred its medieval context. But the national mood had changed. Confidence in the future had given way to a longing for tradition. The new Musée d'Orsay celebrated nineteenth-century art with a lavish restoration of an abandoned train station heavy with the ornament and overconfidence of the Belle Époque.

The same deference to the past directed redevelopment in residential neighborhoods. Where money was tight, conflicts were evident. I explored a renewal project in the 14th *arrondissement,* where new designs respected old street patterns and prevailing building heights, but declared themselves contemporary through unusual materials and ironic ornament. The results really satisfied no one: not enough originality for the architects, not enough profit for the developers, not enough continuity for the neighborhoods.

My wine journalism drew an invitation to a press lunch at Fouquet's, a boulevardier's palace on the Champs-Elysées whose Michelin star was due more to its colorful past than its culinary present. I sat next to an American stringer who said he dabbled in wine. Paris is full of writers who use tenuous credentials to fill their calendars with lunches and long meetings in cafés. It's not a bad life, Paris being Paris. But it takes effort and ingenuity to keep it up. In the country, indigence is more dignified, and concentration on the larger goals is easier to sustain. Or so I told myself, to still my envy.

After lunch the lights went out and the pitch began. Business was wonderful, said the sales manager. Slides showed shiny fermenting vats, enormous aging cellars, sales charts with rising lines in many countries. The company was introducing a new brand of wines from Bordeaux. The labels flashed on the screen: renderings of imaginary châteaux washed in pastel colors, in flamboyant frames above Gothic type. This is what people want, he said. Market research confirms it.

The labels looked like the renderings I'd seen in the architects' offices. There was the same obligation to the past and the same desire to inject novelty while sparing expense. Like the architects, the wine merchants worked hard to create the image of fidelity to tradition. Their designs were closer to the paralyzing self-consciousness of the Paris urban planners than the blithe willingness of the Ruchelais to act on their instincts.

"It's a good thing the wine wasn't better, or they'd have carried me out," I told Rick later. We were eating dinner at a bistro in the far reaches of the 12th. The chef was from the eastern Loire, and so was his menu. The sharp clean white wine from Quincy that sparkled in our glasses cut through the pall of public relations.

Rick sliced more sausage and nodded. "Soon they'll put the same wine in every bottle and just vary the labels. To target different buyers and different occasions. You should come for the Beaujolais Nouveau frenzy in November. The signs go up in all the shops and cafés: *Il est arrivé.* For a week, no one buys anything else. The press is full of commentary about the vintage. Everyone's an expert, everyone gets drunk. Then suddenly it's over. Totally forgotten. It has nothing to do with the Gamay grape or the vineyards near Macon. It's just mass hysteria."

After pike roasted with leeks, and apple tart, and coffee came tiny glasses of marc, the perfumed bitter alcohol farmers make by distilling the lees of their wines. It was from the chef's cousin's vineyard. When we finally rolled out of the small smoky room we had missed the last métro. But the streets were quiet and the air was fresh, so we walked back toward our beds. I admired the graceful lampposts, the uneven cobblestones, the gray stone houses pearly in the streetlight, the yellow lamps in the concierges' windows. Paris seemed utterly at home with itself. I hoped the urban planners and the wine label designers wouldn't triumph too soon.

I stayed two weeks. Then Sara picked me up in Libourne and we drove home through a spitting rain. The road wandered across the flat fertile plain that hugs the north side of the Dordogne, carpeted with vines, thick with leaves as the flowering approached. The Ruchelais envy these vignerons; they enjoy bigger houses from smaller vineyards simply because a bureaucrat's boundary calls one bank Saint-Émilion and their less-favored neighbors Entre-Deux-Mers. The newly turned earth was black, glistening in the rain.

"Madame Le Barazer and her mother took me visiting," Sara said. "We went to see the old couple who live next to the Bonvoisins. They must be in their eighties. They've lived all their lives in Ruch. I don't think I'd ever seen them before, outside in the town."

"Are they happy?"

"They're tired, and they complained about the cold. The old man said we're in a new Ice Age. But they sat close together and finished each other's sentences. I would say they're happy. I hope we're like that someday."

"What did you talk about?"

"After the weather? Oh, the church, and what a shame no one goes. And Pujols. It's not going too well there, either."

We were just passing Pujols. Built on a hill midway between Ruch and Castillon, the town dominates the Dordogne Valley. The *mairie,* built during the Second Empire and since neglected, anchored its broad town square. A Romanesque church, fortified and compact, stood apart on a separate height.

"What's the matter?"

"People are abandoning the village center, building new houses in the countryside. It's not easy to get up that hill, especially if there's snow. They want good heat and plumbing. The old man said there used to be bakers, a butcher, a hardware store, all around the square. Now there are only empty buildings. Madame Le Barazer said the Mayor won't give any more building permits for new houses until the old vacant ones are reoccupied."

I told her about the trip to Paris, how the organic jumble of the 12th *arrondissement* seemed so much more alive than the planned urbanity of the 14th. "Life always triumphs over design."

Sara pulled up to the little *gîte* and we unloaded my bag and books into the house. A building from the last century, its only goal acceptable comfort at minimal cost. We ate chicken soup hearty with carrots and garlic, drank red wine, and went to bed, happy to be together again.

Spring slipped gently into summer. The sheep that grazed the field behind us had been sheared, but the ewes still sheltered their lambs from cool breezes. I worked at the desk as long as I could and then took a walk around town.

I looked through the store window, saw Gérard and Marie-Jo mur-

Gérard and Marie-Jo Breton, Galeries Ruchelaises

muring close behind the cash register and passed by. At the garage, open doors yawned into darkness and all was still. Then the Jourdans stepped into the light, low voices and strained gestures.

"What's new?" I asked.

"Pas grand-chose," Madame said. She was distracted, weary. Jourdan slipped back into the garage.

"Is the café doing well?"

"Les jeunes," she mumbled. Against the café wall, bicycles and small motorbikes, the ultimate status symbol for a fourteen-year-old boy, were gleaming in the sunshine. *"Ils s'amusent bien, quand même."*

I picked my way through the cemetery to the chestnut path. The presbytère showed life, laundry on the line and roses in bloom. George was cleaning the drain by the kitchen.

"Hello, George," I called from the gate.

"Oh, hello," he replied, straightening. "They're out." He waved his arm. "I sent them to the lake near Duras. Ever been there?" I shook my head. "Oh, you must. I send all the *gîte* people there."

"Where are these from?"

"Wales. One's a schoolteacher who's been before. She's brought some friends. Nice people, they seem. They asked us out to dinner. In return for the help."

"So what's new, George?"

"New?" He scratched his head. "Oh, nothing much." He pulled his gloves back on. "But I ought to finish this before they get back. Give my best to Sara."

The church was open after catechism class, exhaling damp stone, old age, and candle wax, but no one was inside. The *mairie* door was open, too. Denise was at her desk, studying some papers, and barely raised her head.

"Nice day," I ventured.

"Ah oui, that's summer, almost here. *Enfin."*

I had noticed a new gate across the street, and wondered if small construction like that required a building permit.

"Non." She cocked her head. "Well, maybe they should have had

one." Her eyes narrowed, then relaxed. "The Mayor's niece lives there."

The cherry tree in the Veders' garden was heavy with fruit. Veder had tools set up by the garage. When he waved, I stepped through the gate. He was sharpening a curved blade like a small scythe. His knobby hands were black with grease.

"What's that for?"

"To cut greens in the fields, for Grandmother's rabbits. Not that there's much to cut. Too cold. See, the garden is way behind."

"The cherry tree looks full."

"Yes, but they aren't as sweet as last year."

"Are they ripe yet?"

"No, not for another two weeks."

"Then how can you tell?"

"The birds are leaving them alone."

Madame Pagant and her drinking pal were in the street haranguing old Madame Breton, Gérard's mother, who helped out in the store.

"Port never cost more than 36 francs," the younger one said, her face red. Madame Pagant nodded vigorously. "But you only gave me 10 francs change from the 50-franc note."

"I told you, the price went up."

"It's not right. I always got 14 francs change. You only gave me 10."

Madame Breton stood silent, head slightly bowed. Then Frédéric from the garage passed by and called a greeting. He wore tight jeans and carried a baguette under his arm that waggled as he walked. Madame Pagant dug her elbow into her companion's ample side and cackled. "Not bad, eh? I'll bet what he has is almost that big!"

All three women laughed. Madame Breton went on her way shaking her head, and the other two wandered back to Madame Pagant's house on the corner. Bill trotted up to the closed door, sniffed, then settled himself on the bench for a nap.

Clouds scurried across the sky. A breeze picked up—moist, cool air that felt more like April than June. Down at the cooperative, the door to the salesroom was open. I went in to find Breton joking with a fellow fixing the cash register.

"This machine's so old it doesn't understand new francs," the repair-man was saying. "I hope the rest of the equipment in this place is a little more up-to-date."

Breton poured me a glass of sweet white wine, cool and fruity.

"How are sales?"

"Still slow. Even though we reduced our prices."

"What are you doing around the *cave* these days?"

"Keeping things clean. Making repairs. Bottling a little. *Pas grand-chose.* The wine needs to rest sometimes, just like us."

I wanted to ask if I could taste the '86s, but Breton looked too comfortable. Chiron had more of an academic interest in the wines and would have discussed their progress. For Breton, winemaking was just a job. I couldn't imagine him swirling and sniffing and making compari-sons to fruit and flowers.

The sky was mostly overcast as I left, the wind freshening. I saw the Mayor's car parked beside a hayfield and stopped to see what he was up to.

All three generations of Bonvoisin men were struggling with a baling machine. The hay had been cut and gathered into long rows that snaked around the field. The machine, sputtering and belching smoke, combed the hay, pulled it up a belt, packed it, wrapped it in twine, and expelled the bales out the back, where they tumbled to the ground and broke apart. Each time a bale broke, the men picked it up and shredded it back into the row farther down the line. The wind feathered the edges of the rows and tossed loose straw across the field. Raindrops spattered and hissed on the engine.

"What's happening?" I asked the Mayor.

"We bought this machine to help with the haying," he said. He took off his beret and picked twigs from it. "It's old, as you can see. We're trying to figure out how it works." Claude was swearing; Francis squinted at the darkening sky. The wind whipped the Mayor's thin gray hair across his head. "There's something still escaping us."

A black cloud shrouded the sun, and the breeze loosened a flurry of fat raindrops. I waved goodbye and clambered back to the road. The shower ended as abruptly as it began, leaving the cool scent of ozone. The town seemed as unstable as the weather. Hold on, but not too tightly. Keep busy, stay calm, keep one eye on the sky.

The flowering time for the vines approached and the weather worsened, low rolling clouds and frequent storms. In the midst of one we heard an oddly rhythmic thunder. Ka-BOOM. Pause. Ka-BOOM. The next day in the store I asked Grangier about it.

"That's the cannon," he said. "They use it to drive away the hail."

"Does it work?"

"It didn't hail, did it?"

"Is hail common around here?"

"Now it is. Back when there were more trees and the vineyards were all on hillsides, the vines were hardly ever touched. Now the storms come more often and do more damage. So we shoot at them with cannons. The idea is to break them while they're still over some other town's vines."

One night late we were driving back from dinner in Bordeaux when rain began to fall. It strengthened as we went east, and by Libourne a thunderstorm roared around us.

Bolt lightning streaked the sky at every angle. Thunder crashed. Rain drummed on the roof, the wipers flapped, the motor grumbled till we could hardly hear ourselves speak. We climbed the south bank of the Dordogne at the peak of the fury. Pounding rain as hard as hail. Constant lightning drove back the dark, but the heavy curtain of rain limited visibility to the hood of the car.

We crawled along the ridgetop, hoping the lightning wouldn't find us. It marched along north and west and finally passed over. By the time we approached Ruch, the storm had abandoned the village, the lightning struck south toward Sauveterre and the thunder rolled away behind it. The sky shredded and the full moon slipped from behind a cloud.

There was flooding, scattered showers, gentle mists, nightlong soaking rains. Whole days passed under broken skies as one raincloud after another rolled in from the west, bringing brief storms and fleeting rainbows.

The grass turned green and the gardens grew. After languishing through a cold dry spring, the corn revived. But rain and wind knocked down huge swaths of green wheat. And in the vines, the spiky little flowers bursting from tight green buds were shaken and torn. The growers' shrugs turned to grumbles. *Juin fait le vin,* they said—the weather in June determines the quantity of the harvest. If the flowers didn't bloom, the fruit wouldn't set and the crop would be small. Only the merchants wanted that.

Rain caught me in the street by the *mairie.* I leaned against the tower; the stone was cool on my back. I noticed a plaque set in the wall. "To the memory of Theo Turrier, teacher, killed by the Gestapo March 1 1944 at the age of 25 for the glory of France." One of the streets carried his name, too, but no one talked about Turrier, and his family name didn't appear in the cemetery or the telephone book. I asked the Mayor who he was.

"That poor fellow. He was sent here to teach school because he wasn't fit for the army. Nervous. He carried a gun around everywhere. He told people he was in the Resistance in Bordeaux, and he used to slip across the demarcation line at night. No one knew what he did over there. One day the Germans came around asking for him. He disappeared, and then we learned he was dead. Some said he shot himself because he was afraid of being tortured."

In Ruch, history was a ragged narrative created by the people who lived it and then discussed each experience until some consensus emerged. The importance of an event to the community's self-consciousness determined the depth of the discussion and the endurance of its record. Only rarely did world or even national events intrude on the record; it was a tale of small triumphs and local disasters. Every town needed its martyr. Ruch was fortunate that a stranger had made the sacrifice.

Sometimes disagreement or carelessness became part of the record. According to the war monument, one of the few Ruchelais lost during the Second World War was a Chevillard, listed as an officer in the AEF. In the church, on a wall plaque devoted to the memories of the same dead, Chevillard was placed in the ranks of the AOF. Were they different armies? Which was right? There were still Chevillards in Ruch. Why didn't they correct the error? Perhaps even they didn't know exactly where he served.

One day I was standing on a street corner with Grangier and George Hall when a car crammed with revelers honked through town. Grangier said it was a wedding party; he knew the family. They had taken vows at the *mairie* and were heading to the Blasimon Abbey for the religious rites.

"The bride-to-be lives in Bordeaux, but the family vacations at Faugère."

"Where's that?" I asked.

He looked at me kindly, as though I were ignorant of the simplest things. "Across the road from my house."

"That long, low house? With the ruins nearby?"

"I can see the back of that house from my field," said George. "You know, it was once a monastery, centuries back."

"A monastery?" scoffed Grangier. "That house was owned by the wife of old Petit."

Sara and I entered the region's formal historical record by way of *Notre Vin,* a glossy booklet published by *Sud Ouest* for Vinexpo, the international wine fair held in Bordeaux at the end of June. We were cited in an article by one of the paper's wine writers, Didier Ters. We had met Ters at a wine tasting. We liked each other and he had come to lunch.

"Sara and Thomas share fifty years between them," he wrote to open an essay on "Wine as Civilization." "They're Americans; she photographer, designer, and above all artist; he, merchant, journalist, and above all traveler You'll find them in a presbytère in Entre-Deux-Mers, amid bottles to taste, drawings to finish, and articles to write. The reason for their presence here? Wine. Wine as an object of study, as a cultural reference, as a sacred place in world agriculture. Wine considered as a fine art. Wine as civilization.

"Sara and Thomas had the world to discover. They could have photographed the Amazon basin or New Guinea. They chose Bordeaux."

Vinexpo drew producers and merchants from all over the world, and the paper was full of the fair. It wasn't open to the general public, but at the cooperative a stack of forms invited growers to register for free entry. Sara and I checked the box for independent journalists. We packed our bags and headed into Bordeaux.

The convention center sat west of Bordeaux on terrain once swampy wasteland and now, after massive earthmoving, called Le Lac for the shallow lake that formed its centerpiece. A long box of an exhibition hall paralleled the water, and modern hotels lined the roads that connected it to the city proper. Nothing in the architecture or the landscape recalled Bordeaux, and the everyday life of the city had little hold on Le Lac. But fairs generate life of their own, and Vinexpo created a worldwide city of wine.

Half the great hall was given over to Vinitech, a display of machinery, supplies, and services necessary for the caring of vineyards and the making of wine. The stands were simple and sober, staffed by bored young women and anxious middle-aged men. The few farmers who attended Vinexpo spent their time there, admiring tractors, filters, and bottling lines. Mostly it was deserted.

The other half of the hall was always packed and convivial. Wine producers from around the world had created flamboyant booths to welcome potential buyers and the press. The women who poured the wines were prettier, the men who harangued the visitors more exuberant. This world, Vinexpo itself, spoke the language of marketing rather than production. With a feeling that I was leaving Ruch behind, I spent most of my time with the lively crowd. I tasted wines from Greece and Chile and California. Sara talked with wine label designers, looking for ideas, finding work. The days went by in a happy blur.

Few Ruchelais attended the fair—Chiron and Chatelier from the cooperative, Philippe de Larrard, who called it *grand et beau*. But apart from dreaming over the machinery, and daring a taste or two of lesser wines, they didn't seem connected with the larger world it represented. The flashy booths and exotic technology hardly seemed real compared to Bordas driving his battered truck around the Dordogne to sell his wine. The growers shrugged, as distant from the movers and shakers of the market as they were dependent on them.

Ruch from the north

They talked of summer, which had arrived at last. The wheat changed from green to gold, the fields like vast stretches of sand. The ranks of roses and poppies had thinned, but new flowers were blooming, daylilies and hollyhocks. The late cherries were still ripening, and everywhere ladders were propped against the gnarled stubby trees for children to climb for snacks and their mothers to gather an evening dessert. The late light was richer, more golden as June came to a close, no longer a light-bodied white Entre-Deux-Mers but more a sweet young Sauternes.

The vines were thriving, leafy and vigorous. The *acanage* was finished and the vines trimmed along the top and sides, to direct the plant's energy away from vegetation and into the fruit. The rows looked like long hedges, the fields like gardens. *Sud Ouest* estimated that crop loss from poor flowering would be small, after all. No one complained about the vine work now; when the last spraying was done, it would be time for vacation. In July and August the vineyards could pretty much look after themselves, and their owners would head for the mountains, or the sea.

One warm morning when I stopped into the store Marie-Jo had news. "Did you hear about Monsieur Chiron?"

I shook my head.

"He's leaving the *cave*. He found a job in Castillon, with a fellow who owns four châteaux. They say it's more money, and his wife will be able to work, too. I guess he's had enough of small-town life."

I wandered to the edge of the village and sat on an old wall in the sun. Philippe Sartran was building a new house near his mother's on the village's northern flank. Mounds of earth and stacks of cinder block were freshly loaded onto the lot. But poppies were growing in the kitchen-to-be, and a dog wandered through the bedroom. A small town, on a sleepy day.

14

Fête de Ruch

On Sunday mornings in July, Ruch stayed shuttered and quiet. I wandered late to the store but there was still plenty of bread. Two old ladies visiting family in town complimented the warm weather and each other's grandchildren. They took a long time choosing croissants and sticky raisin buns.

The door opened. We all turned to see Nathalie enter. Did the women notice her black panties, visible through thin cotton shorts, her small breasts free beneath her shirt?

She picked up a stick of butter, stumbled over to the bread rack. Her eyes were thick with sleep. Probably the clothes she wore were closest to the bed; perhaps she had even slept in them. Rumpled and unwashed, she carried a bedroom air of heat and sex.

French farmers' wives all dress alike. They layer aprons, smocks, and old cardigans over print dresses cut like sacks. The fabrics are like tablecloths and blankets. Their physicality speaks more of work than play; they carry their hips and busts like vineyard tools. Rumors of affairs abounded, and the Mayor constantly talked about sex. "I'm fine from here up," he once said to Sara, drawing a line at his waist. "Below, I'm *foutu*. But there are plenty of fine fellows around here who could teach you what a Frenchman knows. Why not try one? *Il faut essayer!"* But the women's dress and behavior could rarely be called provocative. They didn't seem embarrassed by sex, it just didn't have much of an impact on social life.

Once Lacosse and his wife spotted me as I walked past their open door and left the television to chat. Lacosse, always trim and dapper, wore suspenders and a hearing aid, squinting at the world with genial cynicism. While old age was drying him like a nut, his wife was rising like bread dough, soft and ample. The day was warm, and she had left her wrap open; beneath it, her flower-printed housedress strained to cover her bulges. A button had come open at her hips, revealing the top of lacy panties and a few curly black hairs.

There were a few young women in town. Sara went to exercise class with them at the Salle des Fêtes. She said they dressed in sweatsuits and did aerobics to pop music while daughters romped to their own rhythms and laughed at their mothers' antics. The camaraderie was more important than building a better body.

Carole Bonvoisin was one of the bolder girls. The Mayor's eighteen-year-old granddaughter lived in Libourne, but her parents had divorced and she often visited Ruch. She dated Fabrice Lunardelli for a while, and no one seemed surprised when they went off to Africa together for a week. After they broke up, Carole turned to Michel, another soccer player. During one post-game dinner a baguette fell into his lap. She reached for it, fumbled around, then held it up with a squeal of laughter, loud enough for Fabrice across the room to hear. Michel laughed, too, but uneasily, and Carole colored when she saw the stony expressions around her.

But Nathalie didn't fit the pattern. She didn't mind showing her body, or the bawdy play it triggered. Café work was perfect for her. She already seemed right at home behind the bar. One evening the Mayor and I left the *mairie* together and he invited me for a drink.

He pushed open the glass door of the café. *"Bonsoir, Nathalie."*

"Bonsoir, Beber." She leaned across the bar to offer her cheeks to his kiss. "Same old scratchy whiskers. Why don't you ever shave?"

"Then how would you know it was me in the dark?" He greeted three men leaning against the bar. "She knows only boys with smooth faces. My beard is something they can't offer."

"Doesn't your wife complain?" asked Petit.

"She's glad to save the money on razor blades. What are we drinking? A beer for me, Nathalie. The same for Thomas."

The draft beer foamed over the glass; she put it down in disgust and drew another. The men discussed the weather. It had been hot, good for the grapes. Though perhaps a little too hot now, at least with so little rain. Windy, too, it made the vineyard spraying more difficult; young Lunardelli tried to spray upwind and nearly choked to death. Still, the grapes were thickening on the vines. Nathalie swiped the bar with a cloth; the men looked at her out of the corners of their eyes. When the church bell tolled, the men checked their watches. Sunset is already earlier, Viandon said. They drank up and stepped outside. The young man hung back, muttering to the barmaid, but she looked through him and he hurried to catch up to the final goodbyes in the street.

Sometimes the café emptied by dinner. Sometimes people stayed late into the night. Nathalie's sleepy eyes said that this morning had come too soon.

"Business must be good," Marie-Jo said, taking the girl's money. The ladies and I stood back, listening.

"I suppose so."

"It keeps you open late. We heard the clock strike three and we could still hear the music."

"People like to stay on Saturday night. They talk and talk and they won't leave."

"Talking's fine. Everybody talks. But how could they talk with the music so loud? Maybe you could turn it down next time, so they can talk more easily. That way you can close earlier and the rest of us can sleep."

Nathalie mumbled her goodbyes and left, and the ladies closed in on the cash register.

"It's only the *petits Ruchelais,*" Madame Breton said with a shrug. "After all, they have to amuse themselves somehow. But they spend a lot of money there."

"And they don't go to church," added one old woman.

"She's very thin, that young woman. It's not healthy," observed her friend.

"Oh, but look at our American." Marie-Jo pointed at me. "He's thin, too, and everyone knows Americans are the healthiest people in the world."

They turned and stared. I blushed and put my money down. Marie-Jo had an easy way with sexual joking, too. One day she had a stiff neck and couldn't bend to pick up change from the counter. An old man teased her. "Oh, you're getting old," he said. "When you get old, everything gets stiff." She smiled sweetly. "Is that so? I understood that when you got old, certain things got soft." Her saucy eyes were laughing at me. I just said goodbye and strolled back home through the empty street.

Summer deepened. The anticyclone system returned to France and swept the sky clear. No clouds shaded the sun. The air was drenched with heat.

The world's colors changed again, brightened. Sunflowers bloomed, huge fields of them turning to follow the sun across the sky. A second crop of rape flowers bloomed, but the yellow blossoms were modest beside the sunflowers, no longer the vivid startlers of spring. The vines reached full vegetation, deep green and dense. The long fruiting branches had all been attached to the trellis wires, then neatly trimmed into long boxes. They looked like topiary soldiers. The grapes were green pellets, hard and tart.

I saw old Jeanette gardening, cheerful as the flowers she tended. I asked her if the vines liked the heat. Her face fell.

"Too late," she said. "June rains knocked too many flowers to the ground. The harvest will be small this year."

Bastille Day came. It wasn't much of a holiday. *Sud Ouest* noted fireworks in some of the bigger towns, and the military paraded through Bordeaux. In Ruch, the *mairie* raised the flag and locked the door. I didn't see any picnics or parties or sales in the stores. I hardly saw anyone at all save Hélène Delom-Sorbé. She stopped her car on her way through town and rolled down her window. I asked her if her family were celebrating the holiday. Her face tightened.

"Certainly not. The Revolution was a disaster. They killed the best in France, sacked the Church, plunged us into twenty years of war. It was the worst thing that ever happened to this country."

I found George sweeping the gutters, and he complained that the municipal council had given a raise to the woman who cleaned the *gîtes* but not to him.

"All she does is tidy once a week when the people leave. I'm helping them every day. But her husband is on the council. That's how things get done around here. Not fair play."

He fumed and scratched his rake at the curb. "Not only that, she wanted pay for extra hours, too. She told them that the English were leaving the *gîte* filthy and it took her more time to clean it. Completely false, that was, and I told the Mayor so. In her presence." He chuckled bitterly. "That turned a hair or two, let me tell you. But of course the Mayor just ignored it. Just like always. He would never back me up."

Bonvoisin came in for further criticism in the *mairie*. I asked Madame Tallon if Chiron was really leaving the cooperative.

"Of course," she said. "Why would anyone stay in Ruch who had the qualifications to leave? The *cave* is a disaster. Didn't you know? Ever since my Guy resigned as director. First the Mayor took the job for himself, but even he had to admit he was incompetent. Why the man can barely write his name! So he resigned and put one of his henchmen in his place."

"Is that Monsieur Dupuy?"

"Yes, and he runs the *cave* about as well as he runs the soccer team. They both lose. That's why they hired Colette. But he costs more than he produces for them. It's a scandal."

The growers watched the prices for bulk wines rise and fall with an equanimity bred of cynicism. Colette was supposed to sell their wines, but everyone could see he was caught between large supplies and little demand. They grumbled about him, but they grumbled about everything. They commented on the vagaries of the market, then concentrated on their vineyards.

One evening Philippe de Larrard scratched out the economics of grape growing on the back of an envelope. He said a hectare of vines cost 20,000 francs a year to cultivate: 7,000 francs for labor, 3,000 for machinery, 3,000 for chemical treatments and fertilizer, 3,000 for the harvest, and the rest for land costs and materials. The law authorized production of 70 hectoliters per hectare, so when bulk prices reached 6,000 francs per *tonneau* (a standard measurement of 900 liters, representing four of the traditional 225-liter Bordeaux barrels), a hectare generated 45,000 francs of gross income.

Of the 25,000 francs gross profit, the cooperative kept 20 percent for its own expenses and the government took roughly a quarter in taxes. That left 16,000 francs per hectare for the grower. Since the average holding in Bordeaux was just over 5 hectares, that figured out to an annual income of around 80,000 francs.

At an exchange rate of 6 francs per dollar, which held through most of 1986–87, that sum translated to a net income of $13,500 per year. No wonder the growers got anxious when nature reduced the crop yield or the market lowered the prices. Yet they had little control over either force. That bred a kind of automatic pessimism, but somehow it also seemed to free them from driving ambition. Stoic on their tractors, competitive around the soccer field, gruff and wry with drinks in their hands, the farmers casually blamed the larger world, cheerfully cursed its injustice, and hoped for sunshine on the morrow.

By midsummer, my network of magazines had expanded to half a dozen steady customers, who among them assigned two or three articles a month, for an income averaging about $600. Sara added another $200 a month by selling photographs to illustrate my stories, occasional wine label designs, and original drawings. It was almost enough to pay our expenses, and plenty for her peace of mind. But not for mine.

"I need to go to New York," I said one night at dinner.

"In July? I can't imagine a worse place to be." She poured me another glass of wine.

"My portfolio is stronger now. I think I can get new work. And I need to check on the apartment." Three sets of sublet tenants had moved through since our departure. I wanted to reassure the landlord that the situation was under control and evacuate anything valuable that might still be there.

"Are you getting tired of Ruch?"

"Are you?"

"I could stay here forever. I'm not leaving now."

"I miss New York. I want to see what it feels like."

"You better come back."

"I promise. Three weeks. That'll be enough."

New York greeted me with a heat wave. I spent the days crawling over hot concrete and the nights talking late with friends. They were all working hard, making money, getting ahead. They greeted me like an apparition, as if I had somehow broken the laws of gravity to escape the city.

Little had changed since we had left, but everything seemed more intense. I ate in coffee shops, gorging on bottomless cups of coffee and mounds of greasy potatoes. The sidewalks were hard, filled with pushing people. Everyone was busy, everyone was anxious, everyone was shouting above noise from jackhammers, sirens, car alarms, random crashes never deciphered, and music playing everywhere, in restaurants and elevators, blaring from open windows and from huge radios in young men's arms.

I checked on our apartment. The new tenant and the landlord were happy, but the two-room tenement seemed airless and dingy. Could I really move back in there, survive the battered stairway, the barred windows, the trapped feeling that comes from not being able to extend your arms in the bathroom?

One day I found myself in Times Square, dazzled by noise, light, and frenzy. I crossed the street, pausing on a traffic island that was mostly a large, shiny grate, scant security above a dark hole. Most of the pedestrians were avoiding it, but I had lost the habit of automatic prudence. As I moved toward the center of the grate a chiming hum deepened, swelled, until it blocked out all the other sounds of the city. It was so loud, so fundamental, that I almost couldn't hear it, until I moved on and the sound diminished. I moved back, and there it was again. It seemed to emanate from the heart of the earth, almost natural, but clearly too emphatic to be accidental. Was it a problem, an impending explosion? A work of art? There was a steadiness and a peace in the sound that was musical, and a simplicity that was somehow deeper than music. It made me think of Ruch.

During my absence, Ruch celebrated its annual *Grande Fête Locale.* Every town in France throws a party once a year, generally scheduled for a specific Saint's Day to commemorate some miraculous intervention that spared the citizens from siege or plague. The three days of the Ruch fête embraced Saints Frédéric, Arsène, and Marina, but no one had the faintest idea what they had done for the town.

The excitement began to build before I left, with posters in the store and bright orange flyers littering the streets. There would be a skeet shoot, with a Communal Hunter's Trophy awarded to the winner. Bicycle races for three categories of cyclists. Open matches of *boules* and *belote,* the incomprehensible card game whose only rule I could discern was that players must dangle cigarettes from their lips. Each night there would be a Grand Ball in the town auditorium, and Monday's finale would be a fireworks display on the soccer field. Caravans parked in the lot by the café, shuttered and mysterious. Small children hung about hoping to see inside, while strangers came and went on unknown errands.

When Madame Veder talked about Ruch in the old days, before cars and television, the fête assumed mythic proportions. It brought a magical outside world to the village, freaks and strange accents, exotic food and exciting music. Back then, the excitement built for months and sustained the children and the gossips all summer. But when I returned, Sara was a little disappointed in the fair. There had been a lot of noise and smoke, little wonder, and an importunate Moroccan had pestered her at the dance.

Her pictures told the story. At night, the café parking lot became a midway bright with neon and shining eyes. There were the soccer players on the bumper cars, hair flying, mayhem in their smiles. Children rode a carousel, holding tight to the reins of donkeys and bears. Serge leered at the camera, showed off his daughters dressed in pink and bursting with pleasure. In another shot, the two girls swung on the railing by the public toilets, grinning with mischief, their dresses palettes of stains.

In the daytime, on the dirt drive of the cooperative, men in every kind of hat polished and clicked and tossed steel balls in the games of *boules*. They stooped and squatted and twisted to improve their aim, while smug and caustic spectators urged them on.

At the evening balls, colored lights added an exotic note to the Salle des Fêtes, but someone's decision to leave on the overhead fluorescents kept the mood on familiar ground. The band dressed in sober suits, played accordion, electric piano, bass and drums, pounding out café songs and pop tunes with stolid expressions. In one shot, people watched each other. In the next, couples danced close. They dressed to match — here a flowered dress paired with a V-necked sweater, there identical pressed jeans and wine-red shirts. Grangier and his wife stood on the sidelines. Serge's daughters wove their way through the dancers' legs.

And finally, on the soccer field, the fireworks were cascades of light in blue and gold. Was it late when they began? The old people had disappeared, and the few children were snug in their parents' arms. The watchers were bundled in sweaters, hugging themselves against the damp night air. The quick glimpse of the camera revealed girls with hands over their ears, the soccer players eyeing them with wolfish grins.

I imagined the photographer, cold and tired, trying to capture what I couldn't see. Was she having fun? I thought, It must be better than Times Square. But even if she'd rather be in bed, she's determined to do her part. I wished I had been there with her to turn the fireworks from documentary into celebration.

During the fête, Sara had met the two young couples living at Courteillac, the estate on the western edge of town, and when I returned we visited them.

The property belonged to the Dufoussats, the only aristocratic family in Ruch. They had been part of its history since at least the seventeenth

Château de Courteillac

century. The big house, with its turrets and stone-mullioned windows, looked that old, too, but had been built mostly in the nineteenth century. The last baron to live there remained vivid in the town's memory as an eccentric and a bully. Old Dr. Delom-Sorbé claimed he had bought his title but was born a fool. *"Il était baron et con,"* he said with a sly smile. After his death the family scattered and divided the estate. They sold the vines to Stéphane Asséo, who came from the north, and rented the château to Gérard Grieg, a doctor from Toulouse.

Asséo was a shaggy young Parisian who had spent two years wandering Pacific islands before settling in the vineyards. His family helped him buy Courteillac's 15 hectares of run-down vines in 1982; when we met him, he was living with Béatrice and their two small boys. They were rebuilding the winery, and slowly restoring an old stone barn as their house. A new wood stove set in the fireplace could have been in any vintner's home, but no Ruchelais would have furnished his *séjour* with a high-tech sound system, sisal rug, Japanese paper lanterns, and free-form modern sculptures.

"Ruch is fine," he told us. "I don't get involved with the village much, except we enjoy the *quines* in winter. Most of our friends are in Saint-Émilion. But it's open and friendly here. People I know in Blasimon say it's kind of cold over there."

Asséo showed us the vineyards and his winery, diffidence masking deep pride. "The old ones knew where to plant," he said. "Naturally, the aristocrats took the best sites. The soil and exposure here are the best in Ruch. Once there were 160 hectares of vines and a dozen families lived here, but the Dufoussats basically abandoned everything after the war. I bought 50 hectares of land and these tumbledown barns for 800,000 francs. It was *un cadeau pourri,* I guess, a bad deal. But I just fell in love with it. There was no heat or running water, the neighbors had stolen the metal doors from the cement fermenting vats, and that first harvest the vines gave five hectoliters per hectare."

His plan was to concentrate on quality, build a reputation, and establish a niche between basic Bordeaux and pricey Saint-Émilion. The winery was patchwork on ruins, blue sky starring its old wooden roof. But his winemaking methods were closer to the *grands crus* of the Médoc than the *cave* of Ruch. He kept his yields low. He used long macerations to extract the maximum from his fruit. He fermented the grapes from each vineyard block separately, blended only the best lots for his Domaine de Courteillac label, and sold the rest in bulk. He even bought used oak barrels from top Saint-Émilion châteaux to age his red wine. He bottled his wine on the property and sold it through a mailing list to customers all over France.

The 1985 Domaine de Courteillac sold for 30 francs a bottle, almost double the cooperative price. But the difference in taste was just as wide. It was still exuberant with youth, ripe and rich, while the cooperative's 1985 was already mellowing into middle age. The *cave*'s 1986 was straightforward and a little harsh; Asséo's wine was intense and austere.

"How is it that an outsider with no experience in winemaking can take a run-down property and in only three years produce wine like this, when the Ruchelais, with all their tradition and experience, don't make anything like it?"

Stéphane Asséo, Domaine de Courteillac

Asséo shrugged. "Perhaps it's a matter of desire. I know what the grapes are capable of, what the world is looking for. I want to achieve every bit of quality and character I can."

The townspeople were living the lives they knew, but familiarity was no guarantee of understanding. Maybe the *terroir* did have a unique and valuable character that the cooperative was simply not able to articulate. Asséo might be imposing a foreign vision on the place, but his wine tasted authentic, not imported. Perhaps it took an outsider's regard to understand the nature of the place truly.

The relation between insider and outsider came up again as we got to know the Griegs, Courteillac's other couple. One afternoon Sara ran into Gérard in the *mairie* and he invited us to dinner. "There's a Jacques Tati movie on television," she told me. "He thought we might like to watch it with them."

Darkness was falling as we bumped up the dirt driveway to the château. Twilight softened the eclectic architecture, giving its arbitrary extravagance the coherence of a dream. There were turrets and towers, a chapel with stained-glass windows, stone casements, and a massive wooden door. On the side, a simple screen door led into the kitchen, where they greeted us.

Once again, we guessed wrong on appropriate dress. I had put on a coat and tie and Sara wore a dress, but Grieg and his wife, Catherine, a nurse, were both in sweatsuits. For apéritifs, they offered single malt Scotch and tequila. It was the first time we had seen the Mexican spirit in France. They were serious about jazz and the movies, spent their money on audio equipment and art. They found Ruch hopelessly backward, yet loved the landscape; they'd never been to a town soccer game, yet knew intimately the failing lives of the old and the sick.

"Do you think any common maladies can be traced to local conditions of life?" Sara asked.

"*Bien sûr,*" Catherine said. "Problems of the joints, especially in the lower back, from so much work on tractors. Alcoholism, perhaps. Loneliness. Old people love to talk, and their families have left them behind."

They served cassoulet, the stew of duck meat and white beans traditional to Gascony, heated in a microwave. They poured a red 1979 Château Bouscaut from the Graves to go with it. The château lay only a few miles south of Ruch, but sent its wines to American stores.

"What do you think of Stéphane Asséo's wine?" I asked.

"Asséo? Oh, the fellow back there." Gérard jerked his head toward the barns. "Can't say. We've never tasted it." Catherine shook her head. "In fact, we hardly know them. We really should stroll over there one day, see what he's up to. But you know how it is. They're busy, we're busy. Maybe if our children were closer in age . . ."

Dessert was a lemon mousse cake Sara recognized from the bakery in Sauveterre. Then they brought out a bottle of sparkling wine and we settled in front of the television.

In *Mon Oncle,* Tati plays a bemused bachelor who lives in an old, run-down part of Paris where laborers laugh in cafés and dogs run through the streets. He visits his sister and her high-powered husband in their modern house, with its electronic gate and gadget-filled kitchen. Baffled by the mysterious machines, Tati makes a mess of things. Both a farce and a satire, the movie was funny and sad at the same time.

"Ruch is a little like that," I said, "the past at the heart of things, modernity creeping in at the edges. There's Madame Pagant carousing in the center of town and Philippe Sartran building his new house in the suburbs."

"And we're all watching it like a movie," Grieg said. "It's a shame it took us a year to meet."

"We've spent our time getting to know the traditional Ruchelais," I said. "But you and Asséo are as much a part of the town's story as anyone else. Outsiders don't naturally fall together, no matter how much they share."

The sky was deep black. The only light spilled through the kitchen door.

"Looks like rain," Grieg said. "The corn will be happy about that."

We said goodbye and stepped into the night, groping in silent darkness to the car. Then a loud, hoarse, hissing noise came from the tall stone tower, and a ghostly hooting. We jumped into the car and turned on the headlights. A black shadow glided through the shaft of light, white-breasted, fierce-eyed. An enormous owl, then another, the kind the French call *dame blanche*. Broad wings beating, they climbed into the night sky, settled on high branches in an old oak tree, their breast feathers just visible. They hooted again. As we pulled away down the drive, the birds swooped back into the tower. The night fell quiet again, and it started to rain.

15

August

The French don't let ambition overcome their *joie de vivre*. Unlike Americans, whose holiday ration is a meager two weeks a year, most take six weeks' vacation as a natural right. An orderly and convivial people, they all go off together in the summertime. Only waiters and chambermaids and tour guides remain on duty. Their natural resentment of the situation may explain why so many foreign visitors judge the French haughty and irascible.

Even the farmers of Ruch found time and places to go—visiting family in Brittany, joining a group tour to Spain. With the vineyards peaceful and the town empty, Sara and I decided to get away, too.

Friends offered us a condominium in Hossegor, a Basque port two hours down the Atlantic coast toward Spain. The town must have been earthy and picturesque once; now it's overbuilt and overrun during the warm weather. But while the streets were thronged with vacationers, the placid shore absorbed the crowds with indifference. A long stretch of white sand embraced endless waves rolling off the Bay of Biscay. People paddling in the shallow surf and lying on their towels were only tiny markers against the wide beach, immense water, endless sky.

Early in the morning we biked through sleepy streets to a stretch of beach where lifeguards surveyed pretty bare-breasted women. We ate lunch in cafés with Germans and Swedes. Sun-blasted, we wove home through cheerfully anarchic traffic as evening fell, to cook fish and drink cool white wine. We sunned and dreamed, apart from any world we knew. The hot, still days, the strip of white sand between street, sea, and sky offered all we needed. The babble of the waves and the Gascon French around us sent the same message. Here we are, they said. This is enough.

"I could lie on this beach forever," Sara murmured. "Something about the ocean always puts me at peace."

"Time doesn't count here. The waves come in, but they don't add up. I like it, too, but after a while it makes me nervous."

"Nervous about what?"

"Philippe Sartran is building a house and we're building sand castles."

"My sisters and I built wonderful sand castles. We'd spend all day on one, and then after the tide tore it down, we'd start all over the next day."

"When the grapes are ripe, the harvest begins. But nature doesn't tell us when to work. We have to figure it out for ourselves, and I feel like I'm falling behind."

"You think too much about work and not enough about life, Tom."

"I'm afraid that if we don't find more work, we'll lose the life we have."

So we drove back north, crawling through the summer-long traffic. We reached Ruch so gritty and hot the cool sea was only a shimmering dream. We stepped back into our routines—the morning stroll for bread and the paper, the Monday market in Castillon, hours at the desk, meals with friends. But something had changed; we had answered a question. We hadn't just been traveling this time. We had been on vacation, and where vacation ended, real life resumed. This little village in the vines had become more than a base. It was home.

In August, heat settled like a blanket on Aquitaine. The Feast of the Assumption marked the fifth day in a row of temperatures above 90 degrees. Streets and fields were empty for hours. Even Grangier took the day off.

The sunflowers drooped on the verge of harvest. The alfalfa was yellow-brown. In the vines the *véraison* began, grapes changing color from green to black. Merlot bunches changed erratically, hard green berries studding the swelling purple bunches, evidence of the failures of fertilization caused by the cold June. The damage didn't seem catastrophic. The Cabernets, always slower to ripen, seemed even less affected. Lack of water for irrigation was killing the corn, but the deep-rooted vines didn't suffer.

Bordas said that a fine Assumption meant a good harvest. *"Juin fait le vin, Août fait le moût."* August makes the juice, the month's heat and sun building sugar in the grapes, determining the quality of the wine to come. The crop would be small, he said, but maybe the wine would still be fine. There wasn't much they could do now, anyway. Just hope for a fine September and a dry harvest.

Stunned by the heat, we walked around the edges of the day. One twilight we set out among the vines. The earth powdered into dust under our feet. The grass crumpled like paper. Bales of hay strewn in a stubbled field were beaten gold in the dying light, soft purple in the shadows. The whole world was still.

The air was delicious. We couldn't go inside. As night fell we pulled blankets and pillows into a field near the house. The sun set a little after ten, leaving a light blue glow in the sky. The stars multiplied. Then we saw one fall to earth.

"The meteor showers!" Sara cried. "It's mid-August and they're here. Did you use to watch them as a child? We did. We'd lie on our backs for hours, making wishes. For every shooting star, you get a wish."

We hunted the sky for more. The inevitable dogs barked, the only noises in the soft night. We began to pick out planes in the sky, so high they were no bigger than stars, moving rapidly and soundlessly.

"South to north," Sara said. "Where are they going?"

"Madrid to Paris?"

"Madeira to Poland?"

"A safari in the Congo to an office in Brussels."

"The South Pole to the North Pole, and home again."

Another meteor flashed. A plane came by much lower, louder, with lights flashing, bound most likely for Bordeaux. Closer to earth, birds and buzzing bugs followed their own indecipherable flight plans. The dogs settled down, quiet except when a passing truck on the distant highway roused them.

The shooting stars came in bunches, silent arcs you remember as much as see. The air chilled and we snuggled under the blankets. The moon rose red, majestic, dimming the stars around it. Sara fell asleep.

Another meteor. Perhaps two dozen in two hours, hardly more than the planes. Midnight, and all the lights in the village out. Then a rough coughing from behind the moon, and a helicopter emerged low over the ridge and cruised directly above us. It disappeared and the night was whole again. The moon climbed high and hard in the sky. I carried Sara to bed.

"The priest talked about prehistoric times again," Sara said one Sunday after Mass. "You know, we really ought to go see his museum. Come to church next week and we'll ask him for a tour."

Even in late August, the sanctuary was almost as chill as winter, thanks to the insulating power of the stone walls, which must have been five feet thick. The air had the aromatic dankness of a neglected refrigerator. But even the promise of relief from the heat couldn't draw a crowd. The same faithful few took familiar places and pursued impenetrable thoughts as the priest's voice droned through the dim light. After the service, we intercepted him. Would he show us his museum? He proposed that same afternoon.

Blasimon, five kilometers south of Ruch, was also built on a hill. At its foot, the ruined abbey testified to the town's thirteenth-century wealth. Halfway up the slope, a sprawling wine cooperative broadcast the source of its contemporary prosperity. At the top was a pleasant square, ringed with plane trees. The stone arcade around it held a bank, a pharmacy, a bakery, two cafés, the *mairie,* and the priest's museum.

Sunk in heat, the town seemed lost in time. The arcades must have been medieval. A dog sleeping in the shade of a café umbrella looked almost as old. The museum building's gray skin and plain, boxy shape linked it to the local building tradition that had persisted since the Hundred Years' War. A small sign by an open door invited us in, and we climbed a circular stone staircase to the gallery. We were alone. The windows were closed; the air was dusty and stifling. Life was reduced to the lazy buzz of a fly.

The collections filled three rooms. And not just filled them but stuffed them, like old shoeboxes that might once have held a few carefully chosen seashells, then had bright pebbles added, then souvenirs from a trip or two, then finally anything that didn't fit somewhere else, until they were bulging at the seams and you knew that if you picked them up they would split and spill, so you just left them in the attic and gradually forgot about them, until years later a curious grandchild might stumble on a forgotten world.

The rooms themselves had seen many incarnations. Big wooden beams, wide floorboards, and carved stone fireplaces might have graced the office of a powerful official. Spindly tables and tiny chairs were clearly leftovers from a postwar schoolroom. Glass-fronted display cases fitted

The priest's museum in Blasimon

against the walls showed the care with which the collections had originally been installed. But order had become disorder. Hand-drawn posters covered the walls and bits of stone and metal crowded every surface, as obsession wove argument and evidence ever thicker, until it became an impenetrable mass, so heavy, said Madame Barde, that it threatened to crash through the floor.

According to the charts, the exhibits were arranged in rough chronological order, beginning with stones shaped like bear heads dating to the Aurignacian period, thirty thousand to ten thousand years before Christ. We had never heard of the Aurignacians, nor could we really make out the bears in the fist-sized dark, chipped stones. But then, how good was our evidence that any museum artifact was exactly what it purported to be? In the end, we accepted the authority of the curator and the institution. These relics lacked the aura of conventional scholarship. But the narrative thread that linked them was at least as interesting as whether or not the story corresponded to a reality far beyond our grasp.

We found a section of objects unearthed around Ruch. There were shards of pottery, more bits of rock, and a waist-high millstone, most of which were attributed to Roman and medieval periods. A color photo of the church showed the column capitals in the small chapel of Notre-Dame. We were studying them when we heard a shuffling step on the stairs.

The priest stopped in the doorway, breathing heavily. He avoided our glances, as always. Looking past our shoulders into some upper corner of the room, he made a vague gesture with his arm.

"Bienvenue, mes amis. Thank you for your interest in my small endeavors."

"Thank you for taking the time to show them to us."

"There's always time to lead a soul to God."

His shapeless black soutane fell to his feet, to the kind of heavy black leather shoes favored by policemen. The robe parted at his throat to reveal a ragged brown wool sweater, and beneath that a black shirt and a clerical collar. The clothes were shiny with age, spotted with stains, greasy with sweat.

"Shall we begin at the beginning?"

He moved close to me and stared intently at my ear. Sara slipped toward the door to rummage in her camera bag.

"That's very kind of you, but perhaps you don't have the time, as it's Sunday. Perhaps you could just answer a few questions I have about Ruch. These columns, for example . . ."

"Beautiful, aren't they?" He put his face inches from the picture. "Look at the capitals. You can see that there's no cross on them, only flowers and vegetable forms. And this sun with its rays." He picked up a pointer, a long wooden rod as tall as himself. "That suggests they are Merovingian, or perhaps even Visigothic. The columns themselves are undoubtedly Gallo-Roman. Yes, Ruch is a very old site. We have found Roman relics there, and the Romans generally settled where others had lived before them."

"Did you grow up in the country here, to learn so much about its past?"

"No, I was born in a place that will surprise you." For an instant, his eyes sought mine, and he smiled. "Madagascar. It was like the island of Eden. My father was in the diplomatic service."

I tried to imagine him playing beneath a palm tree or sitting with worldly men at a table set with silver and fine wines. It was like looking for the bear's head in the stone.

"I'm afraid we weren't true parents to our colonies." He shook his head sadly. "And I regret that I was not an obedient son to my father. He tried to keep me from the priesthood. But I knew my mission."

He had come to Blasimon in 1958, and taken on the church at Ruch in 1963, during the final illness of Edmond Coudeyre, who had served the parish since 1912. "Blasimon was known as Blasimon the Red then," he said, "because there were so many Communists. But I won them over by going out of the church and into their houses. Many souls have been led to Christ."

"How did you become interested in archaeology?"

He leaned on the pointer. "There was an abbé in Mauriac, Abbé Labré, a great expert in geology. He taught my predecessor here in

Blasimon, who taught me in his turn. In the 1960s, the Church was opening to the world." He turned toward me again, looked past my shoulder. "A priest is baptized like other men. He has the right to enter the world to give service. I opened this museum in 1967. It is my small service to the world."

His voice was a low, rapid mutter, now and then climbing to a rapturous sigh. I had to lean close to make out the words. I could see silver teeth, sleep crusting his pale blue eyes, dust and dandruff on his shoulders. A fine web of red lines patterned his nose and cheeks, like any old vigneron who had drunk his daily ration of wine. He was sweating heavily under clothes meant for stone-cold churches. He smelled like a closet where dogs slept, and I gave ground.

"Does it bother you when people say the only shapes in these stones are in your imagination?"

"They have been certified. Experts from the university have confirmed their existence. The people can rarely see what they don't already know. It is our task to lead them beyond everyday life to catch a glimpse of the mysteries."

He picked up a small piece of slate, knobby and bulging to a point on one side. "Look at this. Try to see the form, not the stone. Can't you see the head of a dog?" He traced the bulge. "This is the muzzle, then the forehead, down here the neck. Isn't that plain?"

Was it? Had I picked it up at random, I would never have discerned a dog. Under his outline, I admitted a dog was plausible, the way a cloud can form a shape that two can share.

"This would date to the Bronze Age," he continued. "The dog-mother represents the earth, the earth-mother well known to Greco-Roman culture." He put the stone down. "The interpretations, of course, are personal, and not exclusive. The theories are my own, from my reading and observation. I am a priest, and some may say these aren't my domain. But we must look beyond the Church in these secular times, to bring the world back when it strays."

The heat was torture. Sara had taken a few pictures, then vanished. The fly found us, wouldn't leave us alone. The priest's complex aroma seemed to intoxicate it, madden it to a suicidal desire. It buzzed in our ears, tumbled past our faces, burrowed itself in the black folds of his clothes. I swiped and swerved to no avail. My fever to kill the fly was so violent I could hardly concentrate on our conversation. But the priest never flinched.

"Doesn't the recognition that other cultures worshipped other gods throw into some question whether Christian culture can claim to know the one true God?" It took some effort to get it into French, and I wondered if he understood.

He came close again, and the fly came with him. He leaned heavily on the pointer, and his breath was raspy and labored. His gaze seemed to pierce the ceiling. He spoke in measured tones, and I could tell he had said the words before.

"These stones tell of our ancient ancestors' faith in the world and life beyond death, a faith that culminates in Christ. The dog is the earth, and the cult of Earth Mother loses itself in the love of the Virgin Mother. Christ absorbs all cults, in his life and love, as we can see in the Paleo-Christian crosses, with the symbols of sun and moon engraved within their arms.

"The many finds itself in the one. It's love that unites us. There is a unity that exists before we exist, but we must work to recover it and realize it in the visible. We see the many become one as the ancient cults become one in Christ, and we can see it in our own lives, as we bring the people together in love. Each time we enlarge the domain of love, the Kingdom of God moves forward. It's slow, but we are on the way."

During the slow summer days, the past seemed more immediate than the present. *Sud Ouest* reported history as news, in stories about Castillon's reenactment of the fifteenth-century Battle of Castillon, its one moment on the world stage.

In most versions of Bordeaux's history, Eleanor of Aquitaine takes the starring role. Headstrong heir to the medieval duchy that stretched from the Pyrénées to Brittany, she became Queen of France by marrying the monkish King Louis VII, then divorced him to marry red-bearded

Henry Plantagenet of Anjou in 1152. When Henry became King of England two years later, Eleanor's dowry—half of France—changed allegiance with her. The two-time Queen finished her life in a convent exile, but her example of independence and romance has come to embody the region's self-image, its vineyards and its wines.

Eleanor's change of heart led to three centuries of English rule over Bordeaux and the development of a strong English thirst for claret. The English kings ruled with a light hand and an eye to commerce, and the Gascons were largely satisfied with the situation. But not the King of France. The two nations fought intermittently for centuries, battles ranging from Poitiers in the north through Entre-Deux-Mers to the Pyrénées. The Hundred Years' War finally ended the struggle for sovereignty in France's favor. The Battle of Castillon, in 1453, ended the Hundred Years' War.

The battle was neither the first nor the last to bloody the town. Yet gradually the event came to define its identity. At the time of the battle, the town was known as Castillon-en-Périgord, after the region that claimed its fealty. Later, as political boundaries were swept away, the town anchored itself to its river, calling itself Castillon-sur-Dordogne. Then in 1953, on the five hundredth anniversary of the battle, the town changed its name again, to Castillon-la-Bataille.

Driven partly by historical pride, partly by the idea that money could be made, the town crafted a reenactment of the battle. Unlike the battle itself, fought by professional soldiers as the peasants huddled within their walls, the dramatization was a full community effort, with townspeople in the roles of their ancestors. Over the years, it swelled from an amateur amusement to a full-blown spectacle. According to *Sud Ouest,* even President Mitterrand attended and was impressed. Tickets cost 150 francs apiece, but we decided we had to go.

The battle took place on the grounds of a seventeenth-century château just out of town, not far from the real battle site. Long lines of cars wound slowly along the narrow roads, parked in an enormous field. The crowds wandered through a "medieval village" of stalls selling snacks and souvenirs, filed into a sizable amphitheater built from planks and metal tubes.

We bought ice cream, ran into friends from Bordeaux, settled into our seats. The real past of the castle and fields, the present of noise and light, and the fantasy of the show all jostled on the stage.

When darkness finally fell at 10:30, tall towers of electronic equipment burst into sound and light. The sprawling set depicted the two army camps, a monastery, a village square, and a winery equipped with a huge wooden grape press. Hundreds of costumed actors peopled the landscape, brilliant in the spotlights or busy on the distant fringes of visibility. The combination of immense stage and high volume sound made the drama hyperreal, a drive-in movie expanded into the third dimension.

History played itself in documented action and invented drama. Soldiers flirted with maidens, peasants brought in the harvest, an old priest celebrated the Mass. Then the French invaded and the English made a last attempt to defend their Aquitaine empire. Armed with advanced artillery and modern strategies, the French troops entrenched themselves and lured the English on to destruction. The climactic battle scene featured dozens of foot soldiers, an enormous cavalry, fireworks, and stirring music. It was thrilling, and when the English general Talbot died on the field, the crowd sighed as one. Shortly after midnight, Aquitaine was French once more, and the pitiless headlights of hundreds of cars wrenched the meadows back to the twentieth century.

The battle scenes were dramatic and realistic, but the quieter scenes in town were more moving. The small business of the actors, working in the vineyards or gossiping in the town square, drew directly from real lives of the present day. The truth of Castillon's experience of the battle and its consequences had less to do with Talbot than with the grape press. The people threw themselves wholeheartedly into their battle, but they didn't trample any vines to stage it. Eleanor of Aquitaine helped define Bordeaux's self-image. The vineyards bordered their daily lives.

By the end of August, the black grapes had all turned red and purple and plump, and their juice was sweet on the tongue. The white grapes were tawny and translucent; if you held one up to the sun, the seeds glowed inside. The farmers stopped grumbling about the size of the crop and began worrying that the heat would shrivel the grapes, or that the fine weather couldn't last and rain would dilute the harvest. One or two tractors still crawled through the vines, spraying, a final insurance treatment against rot. Mostly, the long rows marched up and down the hillsides in splendid isolation and indifference.

Corn filled the meadows in lowland patches around Ruch, and we watched it shoot up, tassel and fruit. The silk began to brown. It certainly looked like the corn that rejoiced our summers in America. Why didn't the French ever eat it? Corn is for pigs, they said. Maybe they didn't know what was good for them. Finally, we gave in to temptation.

I ducked into a field and scavenged half a dozen ripe ears. Shucking them, we were disconcerted to find them hard, the kernels dimpled and reddish like Indian corn. But after ten minutes in boiling water the red faded, the yellow deepened to gold. It smelled like corn, and we slathered it with butter and began to gnaw. Alas, it was tough and starchy. Only a final hint of sweetness confirmed that it bore some relation to the summer corn we craved. We buried the evidence in the compost heap.

Early morning on the last Sunday in August Ruch was as still as the cemetery. The heat had eased and I took a long walk. Only a motorcycle parked by the upper edge of the Vaure woods spoke for humanity. Two baguettes lay across the seat. Hunters, perhaps, checking the tree forts they call *palombières* for the autumn pigeon season. When I returned a bit later, it, too, was gone.

I wandered over to Sartran's construction site. The building had finally achieved house shape, with walls and roof beams and openings for windows and doors. I could make out upstairs bedrooms and a complexly angled roofline. It would be big and sit high in the middle of its lot. I wondered how a fellow who drove a forklift in a wine cooperative could afford such a castle, and why someone so easygoing would build one so assertive. It would certainly change the look of the village from the northern approach.

Clouds gathered in the evening. The sun was hot when it broke through the cover, but when it was hidden, the air was cool and the breeze blew through a cotton sweater. The light had changed. It was longer, thinner, no longer the bright lacquer of high summer but the delicate gilding of fall. Night fell. We watched old Madame Viandon close her shutters. Pulling her shawl close around her, she called, "Autumn won't be long now, children. Throw another blanket on the bed."

16

Second Harvest

The last weekend in August the whole country comes home from vacation. Autoroute toll booths back up for thirty kilometers; the *périphérique* around Paris stands still in both directions. In the provinces, in bottlenecks at bridges and highway connections, people curse in their cars for hours.

There were no traffic jams in Ruch. But Madame Pagant went on a binge, dancing in the street, singing in the cemetery. It ended in the hospital.

"She's killing herself in little doses," Madame Tallon said. "Drop by drop."

The secretary was issuing hunting permits. Men came in, shuffling their feet, and she traded slips of paper for gossip. Autumn chased the *palombes* from the north, the migrating pigeons that make their way over Bordeaux to Spain. The hunters would crouch in huts built high in the trees, talking and drinking and waiting for their chance to shoot.

Old Lacosse came into the *mairie,* natty as ever in suspenders and a straw hat.

"What? You here for a permit?" asked Denise.

"Eh beh non. Let the youngsters shoot each other up. Though I was a pretty fair hunter once."

"Just like Guy. He hasn't fired a gun in years. But he still gets his permit. Just in case the *palombes* decide to roost in our garden. What can we do for you, then?"

"Is Madame Lunardelli coming in?"

"Not that I know of. She's tired, poor dear. She wants to give up the *gîtes,* you know. Why? What happened?"

"The council hired Patrick to replace the roof tiles on the *gîte.* When he got started, there were English there. No one told him."

"Typical."

"They came out and shouted. Of course, they didn't speak French. What was he supposed to do?"

"He was just doing his job."

"They called the *gîte* people in England, and the *gîte* people called their

Monsieur and Madame Lacosse

office in Bordeaux, and Bordeaux called the Mayor and Beber stopped the work. That *gîte* is Madame Lunardelli's concern and we want to know what she intends to do about this. Patrick can't wait all fall."

Lacosse, usually so phlegmatic, was shaking with anger.

Denise, sympathetic as ever, poured oil on the fire. "If Patrick signed a contract based on time, then he has the right to go ahead and work. If he signed one based on an estimate, then he could sue the council for lost wages."

"Well, I don't know about that. But you tell Madame Lunardelli and the Mayor something better happen soon."

Lacosse left, and Denise shot me a triumphant glance. "Our Albert is not a happy man," she said. "There's nothing he hates more than trouble. What he likes is to spend money. Did you know that the council voted to redecorate the office here? The Mayor will have his own little desk and his own little lamp. And he'll do the same thing there he does at that table now." She swept her arm toward the empty desk across the room. "Nothing."

Bonvoisin arranged a subsidy to build a parking lot between the soccer field and the school. Huge trucks rumbled through the village. Men in orange jumpsuits laid asphalt over the dirt field and painted trim white lines.

"The Mayor says it's for the mothers, so they can wait safely for their children," George muttered. "I say it's for the soccer players, and I say it's a waste of money."

Lacosse surveyed the work, too. "When I was a boy, we loved these road crews," he said. "They didn't come often back then. Mother always told us to walk across the hot tar. Our espadrilles were made of rope and the hot tar would stick to the soles. When it cooled, it made the shoes last longer."

The Mayor came by with plastic jugs full of white wine for the workers. "See what progress we can make, even in a town like Ruch?"

"Do you really need a parking lot here? What was wrong with the dirt?"

"Wrong? Old Petit got two flat tires here last year from glass and stones. It's not good to have the town notary upset at the Mayor."

Sunday kicked off the autumn soccer season. The weather continued clear and hot. The men drank beer, women wore fancy dresses, babies crawled perilously close to the field. Ruch won, and Madame Lunardelli invited everyone to an apéritif at the Maison Communale.

When evening fell, the usual crowd gathered. The room filled with smoke and laughter.

"In the old days, we used to celebrate the beginning of the harvest," Viandon said. "The pickers would come from the Dordogne, fifty or sixty for each town. Mauriac didn't have a café, so they would all tramp over to Ruch. There would be pretty girls, and singing and dancing and fighting."

"Then they opened those shoe factories in the Dordogne, and the workers didn't come anymore," Grangier continued. "We brought people from Spain, and the parties weren't the same. Now there's only machines to do the harvests, and we go home when the work is done."

"Things change," said the Mayor. "But it's not always for the worse. My grandfather slept with the pigs and crushed the grapes with his feet. There wasn't enough water in summer or heat in winter, and he was out in the fields at dawn all year round. Remember that, too, when you long for the old days."

One sunny afternoon I wandered down to Vaure, to find the doctor and Nanette sitting in their shady courtyard. Wisteria scented the air.

"Bonjour. Comment ça va?"

"Eh? Foutu, bien sûr," the doctor responded. "That's old age."

"Ready for another harvest?"

"All the noise and commotion! I should never have sold the barns. Those new vats gleam in the sun and blind me even inside the house. And look what they've done to my oak tree!"

Half a dozen new vats extended almost out to the road. I stepped into the cherry orchard beside the house to get a view past the glinting stainless steel. The magnificent old oak tree that had shaded the drive had been sliced down one side, shorn of most of its great limbs. The grotesque shape that remained was pitiful and embarrassing.

Nanette was brisk. "They have to put the new vats somewhere, Papa.

Anyway, it's better now than when we had all those Spaniards on the property. Who cooked their meals? That was no vacation, believe me."

"I remember my first harvest in Ruch," the doctor said. "1922. A broker arranged to sell our entire crop to a Bordeaux wine merchant. My mother-in-law trusted him. They took delivery, then went bankrupt. They never paid us for the wine."

Philippe de Larrard came by to bring them up-to-date on baby Marie, born the end of August. "Harvest is hard on everyone," he said. "But the crop looks pretty good, as long as it doesn't rain."

In the café, Guy Petit clamored for a real rain, to save the grapes from shriveling in the heat and losing juice. The Mayor claimed that rain would be a disaster, because it would trigger the rot that had been lurking in the vines since the *printemps pourri,* the cold and moldy spring.

"You have mold because you're lazy," Petit said. "How often did you spray this summer? You don't care, because you send the grapes to the *cave* and it doesn't matter how they are."

"That's not true," the Mayor protested. "Francis and Claude are out in the fields every day. All you do is sit here in this café."

"You won't even invest in a harvesting machine," Petit countered. "You don't put money into the vines, you just take it out."

"I hire my neighbors to help. It's good for them and more amusing for me."

"You want to buy their votes."

"You're just an old cynic." The Mayor turned to the barmaid. "Don't you enjoy picking grapes for me, Nathalie?"

The girl shrugged. "It was better than waiting tables in Saint-Émilion. But you won't have me this year." She glanced around the room, swiped at the bar with her rag. "This is my place now."

By the opening day of hunting season, Madame Tallon had issued ninety-nine permits. Early the first morning they all fired at once. Every dog in town barked. Another volley echoed over the hills. What sounded like warfare lasted about fifteen minutes, then silence fell again.

"What happened?" I asked the crowd in the store two hours later. "Did everyone get the limit so soon?"

Guy Chatelier snorted. "That's the last thing they got. The first thing was drunk. They fire to prove their manhood, then open the bottles. Hunting's nothing but a way to get away from their wives."

"So that's why you don't hunt," Madame Pagant crowed. "Your wife made the move first and got away from you!"

The old woman had emerged from the hospital pale and drawn. She wanted a bottle of Port. Marie-Jo tried to discourage her. "Never you mind about me," she cried. "If you have the misfortune someday to be as old as I am, you'll have more pity. After all, I'm not a hunter trying to kill some poor innocent animal. Only an old woman trying to kill herself!"

I wandered around by the church and found George mowing the lawn.

"No hunting for you, George?"

"What rubbish. They've long ago killed everything that couldn't escape to Spain. Now they have to raise birds on farms and stock the fields. You see the partridges and pheasants and so forth just before the season starts, stumbling beside the roads. They're all befuddled—they'll come right up to you. Doesn't take much skill to shoot them, does it?"

He glanced toward the *mairie*. "Have you heard about Madame Lunardelli giving up the *gîtes?*"

I nodded.

"I'm applying for the position. Of course, they'll try to figure a way to keep it from me. But I have a weapon."

He drew me into the presbytère and handed me two notebooks. "Read that," he said. "Comments by the guests. All unsolicited, of course. Meant to be useful to the people who come after."

I looked through the entries. Mostly in English, they varied from a brief "Nice spot!" to long commentaries on the local scene and sights. There were recommendations for excursions as far east as Sarlat and south to Pau. In Ruch itself, the visitors had noted the loud church bells that ring "whenever they feel like it," the general store where "fresh bread arrives every morning at nine," and a tendency of the locals to spy on sunbathers. One guest listed the birds she'd seen; a fellow recommended the Scorpion as a place to meet girls. And there were frequent mentions of George—his friendliness, his helpfulness, the usefulness of his English in case of need.

"You see what I mean?" he demanded. "If that doesn't wake up the council, I don't know what will."

He went on with his mowing, and I finished reading through the comments. In one of the longer entries, I came across a reference to "Americans who live in the town. They keep to themselves, but you may run across them in the store. They can be helpful with restaurant recommendations or directions."

I told Sara about the journals over dinner. "We may be foreigners to the Ruchelais, but at least we're Ruchelais to the tourists."

"I feel more at home in Ruch than I ever did in New York," she said. "Don't you?"

"I've moved too often in my life to trust any home."

"Well, I hope you're not in any hurry to leave. I like it here."

September 18 set a record high in Bordeaux, 95 degrees. The village was shuttered and still. The few sounds—a lazy bark, a coughing motor —carried great distances, as if over water. The white grapes were burned brown. The black grapes were hot with sun, thick and sweet as jam.

Sud Ouest announced the official harvest opening dates: September 21 for white grapes, the twenty-eighth for reds. Despite the sunshine, the paper characterized the impending vintage as a race between ripeness and rain. "The uneven flowering resulted in delayed maturity this year. Yet autumn approaches. The choice of harvest dates is not an easy decision for winemakers."

Everybody remembered 1964. The harvest got under way in mid-September. Saint-Émilion and Pomerol, planted largely to early-maturing Merlot, mostly finished by early October. In the Médoc, however, some growers decided to delay picking their Cabernet Sauvignon, hoping for an extra degree or two of ripeness. On October 8 a storm swept in and drowned their hopes. Ever since, connoisseurs have divided the Médoc '64s into those picked before the rain, such as the excellent Latour, and those like Lafite and Mouton-Rothschild, whose wines were diluted and disappointing.

Although each grape grower chooses when to harvest, the authorities give him plenty of guidance. As early as the fourteenth century, local lords and city councils proclaimed the *ban des vendanges* each year; picking early was punished by fines or the confiscation of grapes. In those days, wine production was even more strictly controlled than now—as was most of life, for that matter—and even the closing date was specified.

The regulation helped ensure wine quality, by concentrating the harvest in the period most likely to combine optimum ripeness and minimum risk. The decision-makers paid keen attention to the vineyards, for authorized harvest dates varied from early September to mid-October. Equally important, the regulations helped keep track of a raw material whose finished product, then as now, was one of the region's biggest income producers, through both direct sales and heavy taxes.

With the breakdown of the feudal order and the rise of the great wine estates like Haut-Brion, Lafite, and Latour in the eighteenth century, the *ban des vendanges* lost its authority. By the 1960s, the proclamation of the *ban* became a public-relations event, an excuse for big dinners at celebrated châteaux. But regulation has returned indirectly, as part of the control of chaptalization, the practice of adding sugar to increase alcohol.

In 1979, the Common Market decreed that each grape-growing region must furnish an attestation of grape maturity before it would be allowed to authorize chaptalization. In each appellation of France, a committee of experts agrees on a date of hypothetical maturity, basically the earliest date that will make drinkable wine, and the local prefect officially proclaims the *ban des vendanges* for that date. Growers may pick before that date, but are not allowed to chaptalize the juice from those grapes; as most growers are paid according to the alcoholic degree of the wine, and chaptalization can add two degrees or sometimes more, they have great incentive to wait.

On the official first day of harvest, light rain sprinkled the morning and steamed the hazy afternoon. We took a drive and spotted a few harvesting machines trundling over the hills. A slow start. The next day the paper ran a front-page picture of smiling young grape pickers wearing T-shirts in the vines.

The Ruch cooperative opened on the twenty-fifth. Young men climbed on the new vats, moved pipes, loitered on the front porch of the winery. Chatelier stuck his head out a window and shouted at them. In the kitchen, the black-haired cook was putting groceries away. An iron pot heavy with water heated on the stove.

"Ouverture!" cried someone high on the vats. Everyone gathered on the porch as Philippe de Larrard pulled into the yard. He swung the trailer into position by the press and waited for the green light and horn blast that would signal him to dump his grapes. It didn't come. He dismounted and climbed up to the porch. Jeanne, the woman who had replaced Chiron, came out of the booth.

"Ça va?" he asked her.

"Pas trop." She couldn't get a clear signal. The scales were broken.

"Are you sure?"

"It's not responding."

Breton also emerged from the control booth. "The technician is working on it. Go ahead and dump. That way we can measure the sugar, and you can get back to work."

"And the next guy?"

"We'll worry about him when he comes."

De Larrard's Sémillon slid into the bin. An intern took a reading, then another. "Eleven point one?"

Philippe took the instrument himself. He nodded. "Could be better, but not too bad," he said. "Let's hope the sun keeps shining." He climbed onto his tractor and chugged back into the vines.

The machines began to rumble. Tractors pulled in every ten or fifteen minutes. Engines strained with the winches. The bins roared as the big screws stripped the berries from the bunches, crushed them, and pumped the pulp down to the presses. Pipes banged, men shouted. A tang of sulfur hung in the air, mingled with grapey sweetness and dust.

The next morning, the store was crowded. Nicole scooped fresh mussels from a dripping straw basket, lunch for her crew. Breton listened to an old man boast about his hunting. I picked up my loaf of bread and the paper and got in line. Colette, the cook at the cooperative, was ahead of me. She had two long, dry sausages, three ducks, canned celery, fresh leeks and carrots, a pound of butter, and a dozen loaves of bread. It came to 529 francs, nearly a hundred dollars. Marie-Jo marked the figure in a little book. Behind her, an old man with a liter of wine pried his wallet out of his pocket and pulled out a bill.

"I've already marked it down," Marie-Jo said.

"No, no. I'll pay."

"Oh, don't worry about that." She wagged her finger. "Pay your bills and pass away—the two things there's always time to do."

Then coffee with Sara in the kitchen.

"You were right about the cold. The paper says there was frost in Saint-Pey. It went down to twenty-nine."

The headline said VINTAGE '87: PEU, MAIS BON. Despite the capricious growing season, it looked as if another *été indien* would put the world to rights.

A warm sun shone in a cloudless sky, but a light breeze laid a cool touch on my arm as I wandered in search of the Mayor and his crew. I found them picking Muscadelle, a white grape once favored for sweet wines.

I looked for familiar faces. Sebastián, the mason, and his wife were still working together, and blond Nicole was teamed with Marie-Do again. But Nathalie was in the café, Babette had found work in a clothing factory in Libourne, Marie-Do's son Thomas had moved to Paris to try his luck, and Carole didn't visit Ruch much anymore. Jean-Paul Grangier had been posted to New Caledonia.

Bonvoisin was kneeling opposite old Jeanette, both snipping away.

"Do you have much Muscadelle left planted?" I asked.

"Too much. But what can you do? I'm not going to rip out healthy vines just because they don't pay very well. That's the German way."

A new porter trudged down the row and started to climb the ladder. Francis straightened up.

"*Alors,* Dominique! Hold on there!" he called. "You'll pitch right in the trailer." He grabbed the *hotte* and pushed down; the young man bent over and gripped the edge of the trailer to avoid tumbling. "That's it.

The Mayor and Jeanette

Hold the trailer tight. Dip your shoulder. Let the grapes do the work."

Dominique climbed back down the ladder. "How much does that thing weigh?"

"Oh, maybe forty kilos, if your pickers are working hard. Be thankful it's plastic. In the old days, we carried wooden ones. We used to say they were heavier empty than full."

I asked Francis when he had started in the vines.

He scratched his head. "In 1955, I guess, because it was just before the big freeze. We used horses to plow between the rows then. Some people were still working with oxen." He picked bits of leaf from his clippers. "The work is easier with tractors. Our first tractor ran for twenty-one years. Tractors last. Not like those harvesting machines. Ten years and they're finished."

"And you, Francis?" Jeanette's head poked through the greenery. "How long before you're finished?"

He shook his head and smiled. "Oh, us. You know, old one—for us, the only rest is in the cemetery."

That afternoon, I came across Viandon harvesting an old broken-down field with his bearish friend and a redheaded woman in a silver jumpsuit.

"Want a beer?" Viandon asked.

"Sure."

He pulled bottles from a cooler tucked under his ancient tractor. We all sat down.

"What have you got planted here?" I asked.

"Oh, a little bit of everything." He waved his arm. "There's Sémillon, Muscadelle, Muscat, some old hybrids, and lots of inkvine, little black grapes they used to put in the vats to add color. They're illegal now. We try not to harvest them."

He shrugged and winked. "But sometimes they jump in the panniers." His friends laughed.

"This parcel looks a little ragged."

"Putain!" He croaked. "I don't own it. I just pick it. The vines are all *foutu*. You can't make a living at it, anyway. And it's no fun, either. Twenty years ago there were harvest dances twice a week. Old Chatelier ran them, in a hall that stood right where you park your car. He's gone, the hall's gone, and the dances are gone." He shook his head. "The young people don't know how to have fun anymore."

Around four o'clock the presses at the cooperative broke down.

"How old is this system, anyway?" I asked the Mayor.

"Five years."

"Expensive?"

He shrugged. "They told me a gadget like this would cost *un paquet*. But I said, Go ahead, buy it. I know the farmers around here pretty well. After they harvest their grapes, they like to empty their trailers."

By five o'clock, they had one press working and the tractors began to unload. When the Mayor finally took his ticket, he had been in line two and a half hours, but he was still telling jokes. By six, two dozen tractors were waiting, as the farmers came in with their last loads of the day. By seven, night falling, tractors snaked into the road up the hill. Men stood in small knots, smoking.

Sara and I were sitting on the front stoop, watching the stars come out, when Viandon sputtered by. He parked across the street, then strolled over to visit.

"Nice night, eh?"

We smelled sweet *pastis* on his breath.

"Did you finally get to unload?" I asked.

He pulled his tickets out of his shirt pocket to show us, wrinkled and sticky. He had one for each day: 630 kilos and 505 kilos.

He must have caught a question in my glance. "Eh, oh!" he grated. "Remember, there's only three of us picking!" He shook his head. "They laughed at me down at the *cave*, too. But I don't care. Let them do their work, and let me do mine." Still shaking his head, he made his unsteady way back across the street and home.

The next morning brought a lurid sunrise, blood-colored clouds screaming across the sky. The overcast thickened, then loosened hours of rain. We had invited Philippe and Catherine de Larrard for dinner, and they came discouraged.

"The rain is bad in two ways," Philippe explained. "It dilutes the grapes. And it makes the work harder. Harvesting machines are clumsy. They don't like mud, and if they slip on a hillside, they can tip right over on you."

We served them country pâté and walnut bread from the Castillon market with the cooperative's crisp white wine. Then roast chicken stuffed with fat cloves of garlic and roast potatoes dripping with the garlicky pan juices. A salad of red-leaf lettuce and sweet tomatoes slick with fruity olive oil and spiced with fresh pepper. Nutty sheep-milk cheese from the Pyrénées. For dessert, juicy pears from Lacosse's garden.

Without showing the label, I poured 1985 Domaine de Phillipon, Bordas's red, "What do you think?" I asked.

Catherine protested. "Oh, I know nothing about wine. Before I came here, I didn't even know harvesting machines existed."

Philippe lifted his nose from his glass. "Cathy, your grandfather was a barrel maker in Nantes. You're only a Parisian skin-deep."

"I felt like a real city girl when I arrived," she replied. "I still feel like a foreigner. I come into the village just to pick up a package at the post office or buy matches at the store."

"You should join the choir with me, Cathy," Sara said. "The singing is fun, and now I know all the ladies of Ruch."

"Well, this wine is no *grand cru,*" said Philippe. "But it's balanced and agreeable enough. To me, it smells like Merlot in a ripe year, not young but not old. So I'll say it's a 1985 from somewhere around here, Entre-Deux-Mers or across the Dordogne."

"You're a good taster, Philippe." I showed him the label.

He smiled. "But the *cave* wine is better, don't you think? More concentrated."

"What will happen when Bordas dies? Do you think his children can keep up the property?"

"Why not? Or maybe Pierrette will marry a vigneron."

"Do you worry about traditions fading away? About the property slipping from local hands or vineyards dying out?"

"Not too much," Philippe replied. "Look, AXA, the huge insurance firm, bought Château Pichon-Longueville Baron and now Pibran in the Médoc. Spent millions of francs. They say it's a better investment than Paris real estate. As long as people drink wine, this land will grow grapes. Besides, there are lots of young people taking over vineyards. Look at Claude Bonvoisin. It's a fine life. As long as the rain holds off."

The next day it rained again, and the day after. Saturday, all the bread was gone early at the store. "No one's working," explained Marie-Jo. "They're all home with nothing to do but eat." *Sud Ouest* commented that most of the white grapes were already harvested and that the growers shouldn't hurry their reds. A little rain won't hurt, the paper said. Indian summer will return.

The whole next week it rained, heavy showers driven by a cold west wind. Some days it was steady, and the fields were empty. Some days it came in waves, and when it slackened, men in slickers climbed on steaming tractors and wrestled harvesting machines through the mud. At the cooperative, a pond grew in the middle of the driveway, rippled with rain. The growers grumbled and growled, huddled in the kitchen as they waited their turn to unload.

But the kitchen soothed them. The big stove pulsed with heat, keeping a fifteen-gallon stockpot bubbling with a savory beef stew dark as

Francis Bonvoisin, 1987 harvest

chocolate. A smaller gas burner warmed coffee, and sticky glasses ringed a bag-in-the-box of wine. Bread lay heaped on a table, the heels of all the loaves broken off by furtive snackers. Peeled potatoes soaked in a tub, and under the sink a bag of onions waited to add its sharp sweetness to the pot. In the corner, an overflowing garbage can buzzed with flies.

Next door, the dining room with its long wooden trestle tables was lit by tall windows looking north over the valley toward the Dordogne. Certificates hung on the wall noted medals the wines had won—a bronze in Paris in 1936 for the rosé, a silver for the red in 1985. Old photos showed five trees growing in the driveway where only the mutilated oak remained, and Vaure's scraggly cherry orchard was carefully groomed and heavy with fruit.

The storms broke for two days and the growers brought in 218 loads, over 350,000 kilos of fruit, mostly machine-harvested red grapes. Breton and Chatelier were gray with fatigue and the young workers lost their chatter. I walked back to town in the ragged evening, light dying, and still half a dozen tractors passed me headed toward the winery. Bordas, on his way home, stopped.

"How's it going?" I asked him.

"Oh, could be worse. The wind's so cold it's keeping the mold from spreading. So the sugars may be low, but at least the grapes are healthy. And we'll be done soon now."

Lights glowed in the village. Two tractors with full trailers were parked by the cemetery, half on the sidewalk, motors rumbling. There were cars parked everywhere; the store and the café were bustling. I greeted Madame Cadapeaud and Madame Pagant.

"Did you hear the cranes last night?" Madame Pagant asked me.

"No. Did they go by?"

"And took summer with them. Too soon! Too soon! All that's left is to turn on the heat. Lucky for you, you're young and in love!"

The sky opened to reveal a huge red sun. It torched the clouds, then slipped below the horizon as if into an envelope. The sky's palette deepened from powder blue in the east to lavender and purple in the west, spectacular but gentle. The men on the tractors looked like soldiers in their heavy slickers, but they were smiling in the rosy light.

17

Autumn Storms

October was two weeks gone before the cloud cover broke. I walked home through last light thin as ice and bonsoired Madame Viandon as she pulled her shutters closed. At the little *gîte,* the lamp shone a cheery yellow through the curtains. Sara was making a salad. On the table, a slab of pâté nestled up to a loaf of bread.

"Everyone's much more positive today," I reported. "It looks like they'll get the harvest in before it completely washes away. But the *cave* is a mess, mud everywhere. The crew is exhausted. When the harvesting machines are all running, the grapes just come in too fast to handle.

"Look at this photograph." I showed her the paper: a helicopter hovering low over a vineyard in Saint-Émilion. "This château owner tried to dry his grapes with the wind from its rotors. Would you call that dedication to quality or a publicity stunt?"

I slathered pâté on a slice of bread. "Even the ever-cheerful *Sud Ouest* has about given up on the vintage. They're quoting some guy from the agriculture office in Bordeaux. *'Il a plu, il a trop plu,'* he says. It just rained too much."

Sara didn't want to talk about grapes.

"I was in the store today and Madame Cadapeaud came in with her daughter," she said. "She's very pregnant. All the old ladies gathered around her like a magnet. Madame Barde asked how far along she was, and she said six months. She looked bigger than that to me. Then someone else said she was big for her time. Madame Cadapeaud said at first they thought it was twins, but there's only one heartbeat. But it's in a funny place, the daughter said. Then the woman who lives across the street from the store said, Well, maybe it was twins and one died."

She pulled down wineglasses and I uncorked a bottle of white.

"It shocked me a little that she said that, but it didn't seem to bother anyone else. In fact, they all started discussing the possibility, or what else might cause it."

"Maybe it makes them feel better, as if saying bad things prevents them from happening."

"Maybe. But I hate to think about them. Pour me some, will you?"

She spun around from the cutting board and swept her arm toward me. Her wineglass caught the edge of the table and shattered. She cried out, then bustled for a broom and dustpan.

"Don't worry about that, Sara. Are you all right?"

"Fine. Just a little tense, that's all. Life is so fragile. So short. Let's not just drift through it, all right?"

"What do you mean? We dreamed up this project, pushed ourselves out of New York, and now we're working hard to make it pay off. That hardly seems like drifting to me."

"Working is not the opposite of drifting, Tom."

"Well, what do you want?"

"Oh, I don't know. Nothing. Lots of things. Just for an example, we could get married." She looked up, eyes glistening. "Just for a start."

The next day I was headed for the store when Madame Pagant leaped out of her doorway at me.

"Bonjour," I said.

"Have you heard?" she cried. "Do you know the news?"

"What news?"

"The roadman's wife is dead!"

I shook my head.

"*Mais oui!* You know Monsieur Hall, the roadman."

"Yes, of course."

"Well, it's his wife, Madame Hall. She's dead!"

We stared at one another.

"Madame Hall is dead?"

"*Mais oui!* It happened yesterday." She waved her arms. "Dead!"

"But how did she die?"

"Electrocuted!" She shrieked the word. Then she pantomimed it, bug-eyed, shivering and sputtering. *"Zzzzzzt!"* She broke into a wild laugh and skipped back into her house.

In the store the crowd knotted around Gérard at the meat counter, voices low. I could hear *Estebot* and *mouton*. I edged close to Marie-Jo at the cash register.

"Is it true?" I asked.

She nodded.

"But what happened?"

She told me that the Halls had gone to the Castillon market Monday morning as usual. After lunch, the rain came again and Anice went looking for her sheep in the pasture, to take them back to safety. She found a ewe on the ground, beneath a heavy black power line. She reached to free the animal. The wire was still charged; the shock killed her instantly.

George was in the house making coffee. When Anice didn't return, he followed her into the storm, searching, and found her body on the ground, wet and muddy beside the sheep, the power line still clutched in her hand.

"Fortunately, he realized the danger and knocked the wire loose with a hoe," Marie-Jo concluded. "Or there would have been three bodies lying in the mud."

"Did anyone hear the church bells ring?" asked an old woman.

No one had.

"I wonder if they're Catholic," mused Madame Cadapeaud.

"I never saw them in church," said Chatelier.

Marie-Jo snorted. "No one ever saw you there either, Gitou, except to baptize your children."

"But where will they bury her?" asked Jeanette Barde.

No one knew. I went home to tell Sara the news. We sat in silence for a while. Then Sara said we should take something over to eat, because Anice had done all the cooking. She decided to bake a quiche. I set off for the cooperative.

Random gusts of wind brought intermittent rain, and the sky was shifting through a dozen shades of gray. But color fought through the flat light. Climbing vines painted barn walls and tumbled stone scarlet and rose. In the vineyards leaves were falling from twisted orange branches. The cooperative driveway was a gray mudhole, but along its edges spilled pomace left a vivid purple trail.

All the machinery was working and the workers had become a well-knit team. Tractors came and left, their drivers quiet, hunched under hats. The keen smells of fermenting wine and sulfur solution drifted through the winery. A jug of the new white wine, still sweet and fizzy, lay ignored on the porch bench, a bag of chestnuts beside it.

I found Jeanne in the control room and examined the log. "How's it going?"

"*Pas mal.* Nobody's really happy with the sugars—barely over ten in most of the reds. But the quantities are okay."

"How much longer?"

"The Cabernets could finish this week. Then there's only the Muscat, and there's not much of that left. Everyone will be glad to see this harvest over."

"Did you hear about Madame Hall?"

She nodded. "They say she was quiet and nice. I never met her. Did you know her?"

I nodded.

"Where will they bury her? Back in England?"

"I don't know."

Lunchtime came, and I went home.

"I called George," Sara said.

"How's he doing?"

"He didn't come to the phone. His cousins are up from Les Landes. The ones he always talks about, with the swimming pool. I talked with someone called Jean. He said George was all right. I asked if we could bring the quiche around this evening, and he said yes."

"Did he tell you anything about what happened?"

"No. I didn't ask."

Her eyes were stained with red. I tried to comfort her, but felt numb. We had a quiet lunch, then I decided to visit the *mairie*.

Denise was at her desk; she bristled with energy. I was hardly in the door before she raised her voice.

"Didn't I tell you? Didn't I know?"

"Tell me what?"

"It was an impossible way to live. Hardly human. She lived like an animal and died like one. Horrible, it was just horrible."

"But how do you know?"

"How?" The white foam bubbled at the corner of her mouth. "Dear child, who was the first one there? The first thing he did after he found her was to call me! She was still warm! I helped him carry her into the house. She was filthy, smeared with mud, mud clotted in her hair. It was horrible! And the house—such a shambles. Not fit for a live woman nor a dead one!"

"What happened after you brought the body into the house?"

"The doctor came and pronounced her dead, and the police came and took down the details of the accident. Then they all left."

"And what about the body?"

"It's still there."

"Still there? In the house?"

Denise nodded.

"But what will he do?"

"That's up to him."

"Why didn't they take her away?"

"Take her where?"

"Well, to a funeral parlor, or somewhere."

Denise was doubtful. "I don't believe Monsieur Hall can afford anything like that."

"But what will he do? Where will they bury her?"

She didn't know.

The Mayor sat in the dim café with Guy Petit and Madame Jourdan. He called for a beer for me and another for himself.

"You want another *pastis?*" he asked Petit.

"Who's paying?"

"Listen to him," Bonvoisin said. "Trust and generosity are not in his vocabulary. I'm paying, *putain.*"

"Then I'll have another *pastis,*" he said to Madame Jourdan.

"Such terrible news," the Mayor said. I nodded. "Who would think she'd pick up a power line? Who ever would do that?"

"It would have been easier for you if she had slipped in the mud and broken her neck, no?" said Petit.

Bonvoisin looked sideways at him. "Dying is never easy," he said.

"But now you have the electricity people involved, and that means you have the government." Petit was patient, as if talking to a child. "And if the government is involved, that means you're involved."

"I was nowhere near that field."

"But who is responsible for the fallen power line?" asked Petit.

"Ah, who?" Bonvoisin smacked his forehead with his palm. "That could be a very difficult question to answer."

"And there could be money at stake, if Monsieur Hall knows a good lawyer."

"I don't think he's the kind of person to make trouble like that. Do you?" The Mayor turned to me.

"Well, I don't know. I don't imagine it's the first thing on his mind right now."

"Oh, what I went through over that power line," Bonvoisin moaned. "Between the Englishman and the electricity company, I thought it would never end. He insisted he had to have that line run out there. Who could have imagined it would end like this?" He turned to me again. "Have you seen him yet?"

"No, but we're going over later this evening."

"I hear his family is coming."

"Some of them are already here."

"They can stay in the presbytère if they want to. There's no one there. Free, of course. Make sure he knows that. Will you?"

The vineyards were blue as we drove to Estebot. A Peugeot was parked in the yard, its wheels caked with mud. No one answered our knock, but the door was ajar and we went in. There were dirty dishes in the sink.

They were all sitting in the living room, the three we guessed were cousins and George, in his blue worksuit, face pasty, eyes dull as rainwater.

"*Bonjour,*" we said.

"*Bonsoir,*" the three said, correcting us automatically.

There was a heavy pause. "We're Sara and Tom," Sara blurted. "George's American friends." She moved to George and put her hand on his shoulder. "George, we're so sorry."

"Thank you," he said.

The cousins introduced themselves. I put the quiche down on the table. The gray light of the cloudy evening picked out the stains on the worn Turkish rug. We asked the cousins about Les Landes, the great sandy-floored pine forest south of Bordeaux. Jean had married George's mother's cousin's daughter, as near as I could make out. He told us about the hunting and invited us to visit his *palombière.* He said that George's two sons and their wives were arriving the next day.

"The service is Thursday."

"The funeral?" Sara asked.

He lowered his voice. "The cremation."

"Ah." She paused, then turned to George. "It's good that your sons are coming. Have they visited often?"

"Not too often," George said.

"Well, if they need anything, let us know."

He nodded. I told him about the presbytère, and we went home.

It rained again on Wednesday. Everyone at the store knew about the cremation. She wanted to be buried in England, someone said, and that's the only way they could get her back. Everybody approved, considering the expense. They knew about the crematorium, just outside Bordeaux. No one knew anyone who had actually been cremated, though.

"I saw them sometimes at the market in Castillon," said squinty-eyed Madame Matou. "She was always kind to me."

"Is it true she didn't speak French?" someone asked her.

"Yes, it's true. But she didn't really need to, with the life she lived. She never saw anyone to talk to."

Sara called Estebot. George's sons had arrived. The boys thought it would be good to get George out of the house. Would Sara like to show them Saint-Émilion? She said she'd pick them up in half an hour. I stayed home and worked on a piece about the renovation of the Louvre.

"It was a funny day," she said when she returned. "We all acted just like tourists. Had beers in a café, and I told them about history. And all the time it was as if a black cloud hung low just over our heads. The wives didn't come, and when we got back they were standing beside a bonfire. It was a pile of Anice's things. They wanted to spare George, so while we were gone, they went through her clothes and all and burned everything he wouldn't need. A preview cremation."

The next morning, they called Sara again, to ask her to help drive to the service. She didn't want to, but agreed. I stayed home, citing deadlines, ashamed of myself. I spent most of the day working on the puzzle posed by Anice's life and death.

Fate was the word the Ruchelais were using, matter-of-fact or portentous, depending on the speaker. They didn't expect destiny to be reasonable, or life to be fair. They accepted most events as random elements in the flow of time. The biggest puzzle was why she had picked up the wire, an action so contrary to simple prudence that it became unintelligible.

But if fate had determined her death, something more willful had charted her life. I had seen enough of Ruch to understand how tightly even a small town's gravity held lives in familiar orbits. Anice had traced a path all her own. Either she had been completely unmoored by events beyond her control or there was something in life she wanted fiercely enough to oppose the binding force of common sense. Because the practical, hardworking woman I knew seemed the opposite of a lost soul, I saw her fatal gesture as the culmination of choice, the climax of a life she had plotted herself.

My first theory saw the choice as denial. Her life was like a salmon's path upstream, a long series of self-isolations—from country, family, language. As if she had spent her life hiding from death, from the beginnings that carried within themselves the seeds of ending. And it seemed ironic that death could reach so easily into her sanctuary.

Then, as I tried to hear her giggle, watched her raise a wineglass to her lips, I saw her following a different path. Not fleeing the world, but searching for something beyond it. Not fighting the current, but rushing with the river down to the wide sea. Over the years, in many stages, she had loosened her ties to the world, until only one man and a small flock of sheep stood between her and a kind of freedom the world could never offer. And when she had prepared herself, and the call came, she went out into the storm. I imagined she was calm, even cheerful, clucking to herself about her lambs. Then coming across the fallen creature impetuously, generously reaching to help. And joined it, her journey over at last.

George's family left. The sons would bury Anice's ashes in her family's cemetery in England. George took time off, stayed away from town. We called him a few times, but the phone just rang and rang.

In the store, conversation moved on. The cold weather that had prevented the rain from triggering rot in the vineyards also inhibited the growth of wild mushrooms in the woods. The Ruchelais searched the forests, poking around the old oak trees, but there were few *cèpes* to be found. In the markets, prices were high.

The world awoke from a long bad dream to blue skies, dry air, and crystal light, the sun warm as a distant fire. Only a few machines rumbled through the vineyards. A work gang gathered to work on Sartran's house, building a front porch, happy to have clear skies. We strolled up to watch them as the sun set. A dozen cars rolled by in as many minutes, flicking their lights in greeting. The church bells rang in the evening. Angelus.

The harvest drew to a close. On the nineteenth of October, *Sud Ouest* put another vineyard picture on the front page. The pickers were still smiling, but this time they had on rain suits and big floppy hats. "A Vintage for Noah" read the caption.

The wine writer summarized the vintage in his headline: OUF! He called it the worst since 1984. Maybe the Merlot should have been harvested earlier, he suggested. In such an unstable year, it didn't pay to take too many risks.

In Ruch, the last grapes were picked on Saturday the twenty-fourth, a few loads of Muscat. A hand-picked load triggered a spirited grape fight among the young workers. Chatelier tried to break it up, but Breton and Jeanne held him back. Next week, the crew would disperse. Some of the young men would enter university; others faced the obligatory year of military service. Some would be unemployed. None of them was looking for a career as a winemaker; it was summer work for them, like construction crews for American college students.

"They were good workers, in the end," Jeanne said.

"They always are," responded Breton. "It's the beginnings that are bad."

They cleaned and covered the crushing bins and emptied the control booth of its trophies and paperwork. Jeanne taped a note in the window —"The *cave* will accept no more grapes in 1987"—and locked the door.

Ruch in November

Plenty of work awaited the permanent crew: clarifying and stabilizing the whites, draining the red wine off the skins, pressing the pomace, blending the lots to make the various quality levels, from the Château de Vaure to the *vin de table*. The wine wouldn't sleep in the vats until the new year. But with the harvest in, the greatest dangers had passed.

Every grower with vineyards in Ruch was required to file a harvest declaration at the *mairie*, recording his acreage, volume of red and white wines, and their alcoholic degree. There was no total figure for Ruch itself, because some of those who lived in town owned vineyards in neighboring villages, and some of the vines within the town's boundaries were owned by outsiders. But the cooperative accounted for most of the production both of Ruch vines and of Ruch vignerons, so it served as a fair indication of the town's vintage.

In 1987, the total cooperative volume was 31,750 hectoliters—13,000 hl. white, 18,750 hl. red. That was down 8 percent from 1986, much less of a drop than the experts had predicted. The white wine volume was actually up 8 percent, but that was small consolation, as it brought only 3,500 francs the *tonneau* at best. Still, it was a lot of wine. If the cooperative bottled its entire harvest, it would amount to over 4 million bottles.

The 17 percent drop in red wine volume was significant, but not the disaster the farmers had been expecting. However, much of the extra volume had come from rain diluting the grapes during harvest. The consequence would be less concentration and lower quality, but the Ruchelais could live with that. That's what chaptalization was for, and press wine, and filters—all the improvements of man. Technology couldn't create a great vintage; only nature could provide the precise balance of sun and rain that great wine required. But it could ameliorate a poor one.

For Ruch, compared with the decade so far, 1987 had produced more wine than 1980, '81, and '84. Total vineyard acreage in the town continued to climb, from 665 hectares in 1980 to 870. There had been no miracle in 1987, but farmers don't expect miracles. The eighties had been a boom time so far, and few were complaining, or reading too much into one wet year.

With the harvest over, summer seemed only a distant memory. The village drew back into itself, shutters closing early against lengthening nights. In the mornings, fog wound through the village streets, draped the dull gray countryside. The *palombes* flew south, hidden from the hunters by low clouds.

When the sky cleared, the afternoon light was keen. The low sun cast long shadows past the naked vine trunks; though gnarled and squat, they took on an unexpected grace, like dancers past their prime. Fallen leaves lay in a golden carpet beneath them, swept behind the Bonvoisins' field east across the plateau toward Mauriac. By two empty old houses, side by side across a narrow lane. A persimmon tree stood in front of the larger house, leaves gone, skeletal branches hung with glowing fruit. Three sun-dappled deer burst from the small wood behind the houses. They sniffed the cool, moist air, then dashed across the road.

In the cemetery, the graves threw long shadows, too. The air was cool on bare skin, but the sun-gilt stone wall of the church still warmed the touch. The mason, old Sartran, was stripped to the waist, deep in a hole, methodically laying concrete blocks. Lacosse sat on a nearby tombstone. I asked what they were digging.

"It's a tomb for Monsieur de la Véga," Sartran said.

"I didn't know him."

"You've still got time to meet him. He's not dead yet. Just wants to be ready when the time comes."

"Lives over at Grand Bernat," added Lacosse. "A Bordeaux fellow."

"He did a nice job fixing the old place up, too," Sartran observed. "That cost him some money."

"I'd rather live in Philippe's place," Lacosse said. "That son of yours has the right idea. Build to suit yourself! Why spend new money fixing old stones?"

"Well, he's spending money on new stones here."

The two men discussed techniques and styles. Madame Matou wandered over from the store, her string bag bulging. She wanted to know what they were doing, and then she wanted to know how much it cost.

"Tombstones run well over a thousand francs, even for a simple one,"

Sartran told her. "It all depends on the size and the stone you use. Monsieur de la Véga wants enough room so that if he gets stiff there's space to walk around. This is going to cost him 24,000 francs."

"Then there's the cost of the land," Lacosse added. "You can buy a space for ten years, or twenty, or forever."

"I don't suppose he'll be moving away soon, will he? He'll probably take the long terms," Madame Matou said.

"He probably will, because he's got the money to spend," replied Sartran. "But I'll tell you what, Madame Matou. It's better to buy a good piece of meat and enjoy it while you can."

Now and then a light flashed through the gates: the café door opening and closing. Nathalie was behind the bar, dragging a cloth over the zinc, avoiding her father, who sat silently at one end. School was over for the day, and kids clustered around video machines in the back. They ate peanuts and drank sweet mint syrups, laughing.

"*Bonjour, Nathalie.*"

"*Bonjour.*"

"*Une demie, bien frais, s'il te plaît.*"

"*Un demie,*" she corrected, and drew beer into a mug.

The foam climbed the glass. "What's new?"

"Not much."

"When will your brother return?"

"Next spring, I suppose."

I sipped the beer. She reached down for something below the counter; I glanced, her shirt fell open a little. She kept her head down, looking for something. I could see her small dark nipples. Dust motes swam in a golden stream of sunlight. The electronic noises of the video machines sounded far away; the kids never glanced around. I could be anywhere; she might be anyone. But the dark figure at the end of the bar anchored us in Ruch. Jourdan was too distant for conversation, but close enough to witness. Nathalie fiddled with the radio. I emptied the glass and left.

Late in October, I took the train to Paris again. The wine magazine I had been writing for wanted to add a second reporter to the London bureau. The publisher asked me to interview for the job.

Did I want to leave Ruch? In September, I had billed $1,000 in articles. Sara's photographs were appearing in print. Yet our savings were exhausted, our credit-card bills swelling. Had we turned the corner? Or had we stayed long enough? Sara, optimistic and increasingly rural, believed we could flourish in Ruch. I was more ambitious, and less hopeful.

The appointment was at the Hôtel Crillon. I felt out of place among the sleek-suited businessmen in the lobby. The publisher met me in his suite. A Champagne bottle was turned upside down in a wine bucket. We talked for an hour. He took my portfolio and said he would call. We shook hands, and I found my way out of the hotel.

18

Toussaint

Early one foggy morning a truck rumbled down the street. The noise reached the second-story bedroom and roused me from confused dreams of city life. My eyes opened on floral wallpaper and for a moment I wondered where I was. Then Sara stirred, and I was back in the village in the middle of vineyards in southwestern France. I listened for more traffic, for the sound of Madame Viandon opening her shutters across the street. But there was only silence, so I slipped into sleep again.

By the time I left the house, the shutters were open at the Viandons', a gas burner glowing blue under a saucepan on the stove. Madame Cadapeaud opened her door as I passed and waved. Bill barked and climbed onto his bench.

Chrysanthemums spilled from the store's garage and I realized Toussaint was the next day. I hadn't noticed the flowers in Paris. The Galeries Ruchelaises was busy; there was a crowd around the meat counter and a line at the cash register. The big loaves of crusty bread were still warm. I pulled one from the rack and fell in behind Madame Cadapeaud's daughter-in-law, struggling with ten boxes of long-conservation milk.

"Monsieur Cadapeaud must drink a lot of coffee."

She frowned, then followed my glance to the milk. "Oh," she

laughed. "This is for the schoolchildren. I'm making crème caramel for dessert today."

"What else is on the menu?"

"Vegetable soup. I almost always serve soup in the winter, and it's almost winter, isn't it. Roast pork."

"No salad?"

"They don't like salad very much. I do generally serve it with omelets."

Marie-Jo looked over. "Lunch only costs eight francs, you know. You don't get a three-star meal for eight francs, not even in Ruch."

Outside, tendrils of fog blurred the familiar buildings into soft, dreamy shapes, promising mysteries around unseen corners. In the garage, Antoine bent over a blowtorch, a shadow crouched by a flame. The tourists had finally left the presbytère, and Patrick Lacosse was working on the roof. Caught by the sound of his hammer blows, I lingered, and after a while he climbed down the ladder for a new sling of tiles.

"Ça va?"

"Pas mal. It would be nice if I could see the edge of the roof. That's what happens when you try to do this work in autumn." He shrugged. "At least it's cool."

In the Gironde, churches and châteaux are crowned with slate. Houses and barns are roofed with ocher-colored tiles shaped like half-cylinders. Made from clay quarried on the banks of the Garonne, they have marked the region's buildings since Roman times. The old tiles were simply laid overlapping on the roof. The roofs were all pitched at the angle at which the tiles would hold, giving a pleasing unity to the building's profiles. Then, at the turn of the century, a fashion for more steeply pitched roofs led to the development of flat tiles with hooked bottoms that could hold at greater inclines. House forms began to vary, and the new tiles gave them a peculiar wrinkled look.

In the 1970s, preservationists grew fearful that modern architecture would undermine French character. They formulated building laws to maintain regional styles. In Bordeaux, they mandated a return to the Roman-style canal roof tiles on most residential construction. Since the new canal tiles were equipped with hooks, however, they allowed wide leeway in pitching the roofs, so house profiles remained untraditionally heterogenous. Roofers familiar with the new tiles were in sudden demand. Patrick had made them his specialty.

"The new tiles cost me one franc fifty at the kiln," he told me. "I sell them to my clients for two francs apiece. I save all the old tiles that are still sound and sell them for a franc each to a Parisian who sells them for two francs fifty to people who want their new houses to look old. It works out well all the way around."

The roof was the color of dark rust mottled with mold. It took the midday sun without glare and at dusk softened to the color of dying coals. The tiles' patina married well with the patchy gold and gray of the limestone walls. The small section of new tiles already laid in place was monochromatic in contrast, a bright terra-cotta that lacked depth or texture.

"Will these new tiles ever look like the old ones?" I asked.

"Bien sûr. It takes four or five years, but it'll come. You can't deny nature."

A tile crashed near our feet. *"Eh alors!"* He called upward. A small boy peered over the edge of the roof. *"Doucement, mon petit!"*

"His job is to get rid of the defective ones," Patrick explained. "I hire a different one every day. That's about as long as they want to work. It gives them a few francs to play the games at the café." He hitched the sling and climbed back up the ladder.

Madame Pagant careened around the corner and almost knocked me down.

"Eh hup!" she cried. "Be careful around here, young man. It's dangerous!"

"What's so dangerous?"

"Lacosse up there!"

"Oh, I know. Watch out for those falling tiles!"

She laughed. "Not that, eh? No, not that!" She slapped her buttocks, then cocked her head. The old woman broke into a slow bump and grind; her dress moved like a lumpy bag from which small animals were trying to escape. She slapped her buttocks again. "Don't let him drive your wife off to Libourne!" She turned and swaggered back down the street.

A slow scraping sound from the cemetery drew me to the chestnut path. Water dripped from dying leaves. George was raking the gravel in front of the church.

"Hello."

"Who's there? Oh, it's you, Tom. I thought it might be Madame Tallon, checking up on me. This fog enrages her—she can't see whether I'm working or not."

"How about coming around for lunch today? Sara made a big pot of soup, and it's good weather for it."

"Could do. Round one?"

Sara and I worked at our desks while the sun burned away the fog. By one o'clock, the view was clear across Viandon's run-down vineyard to the Bonvoisins' house. Old Madame Viandon brought out her laundry to hang on the line. I watched George trudge up the street, hail her, stop to chat.

"Here comes George, Sara. I'll go down and put the soup on."

We ate soup every week, but every week it was different. Chicken stock was usually the base, the bones boiled with garlic and plenty of white wine. Sara added whatever vegetables were most abundant in the market, then ran everything through a food mill. The thick savory soup might be green or yellow or orange, might taste of leeks or squash or pumpkin. It was always satisfying.

George knocked on the door. "Anybody home? Ah, that soup smells good."

He pulled off his tall rubber boots and one layer of thick wool socks. "Well, have you heard the latest about Madame Jourdan? It's official. Jourdan found her in the parking lot during a soccer match with Guy Petit. Now Jourdan is sleeping at the café. For security reasons, they say. But these save-face arrangements never last. She'll move in with Petit before the year is out. Mark my words."

Over coffee and Sara's chocolate-chip cookies, George told us that some Sorbier we didn't know had left his wife for Colette Janneteau, the cook for the cooperative. Her husband was killed in a tractor accident, he said. Since Anice's accident, he knew all the stories of sudden death. As he talked, his eyes dropped.

"Anice would have liked these biscuits, Sara," he said. He looked at his watch. "Well, it's after two. Better push along. Thanks for lunch."

In the *mairie,* Denise started when I opened the door.

"These new windows block more sound," she said. "Usually I heard people on the gravel. Now everyone surprises me. But the office will be warmer in winter, I suppose. Not that it matters much to the Mayor." She shook her head. "Nor to me, my dear. Ah, retirement is close now. Ruch will have to get along without me."

I read in the town ledger that Jean Beylot of Peyrat, Ruch, had declared a harvest of 18 hectoliters—2,400 bottles—of red table wine from his half-hectare vineyard. We had seen Beylot and his wife picking grapes from the vines around their house. The ledger said he didn't belong to the cooperative, and I wondered how he made the wine and what it was like. So Sara and I went and knocked on his door.

The Beylots lived in a neat house on the edge of the village. A chicken coop took up half the yard, a vegetable garden the rest. Vine faggots were stacked to the roof of the barn in back. An old well stood by the front door, and a long stone flower pot the priest said was a Roman sarcophagus. Madame answered the door, stout and bright-eyed. Behind her, a little dog barked frantically.

"We're the Americans who have been living here . . ."

"I know," she broke in. "Has it been a good vacation so far?"

"Fine, thank you. We don't want to disturb you, but we're very interested in the local wine and wondered if we could taste—or buy, perhaps—some of yours."

"That's for my husband to say. Why don't you come in?"

She shushed the dog and backed away from the door. We stepped over two pairs of wooden sabots and crouched through the low entryway to the kitchen, where her tall, silver-haired husband was sitting by the fire. "These young people would like to taste your wine," she said. She pointed to the big table in the middle of the room. "Sit down. Please sit down."

The room was squat and a little crooked, warm and cheerful. It felt old. The television, even the electric coffeepot and blender, didn't make it modern. The tiled sink, built low into the front wall, had once been stone and still drained into the yard. A three-legged iron pot stood in the fireplace and gave off a heady aroma of garlic and wine.

"What are you making?" asked Sara.

"Poule au pot," Madame replied. "Some people make it on the stove. In my opinion, it only tastes the way it's supposed to when you make it in a pot over a fire."

The chicken lay on the table, half-plucked. A cake of lard and a bunch of parsley lay beside it. She stripped feathers and began to talk. Her husband was silent. The wine was ignored.

She told us they had both been born in Ruch, a few years into the century.

"At Pelletan, near Douleyzon—do you know the place? No? The house next to the big oak on the ridge."

Her parents had married her young to a man who beat her. She took a job as a servant to a lawyer and he helped her divorce in 1938. She married Jean the next year. He had grown up the son and grandson of bakers in Ruch. In 1940, the Germans took him prisoner and sent him to Russia. When he came back, the government gave him a job as postman. It paid more, and besides, the bakeries were closing. She could remember when there were three in Ruch.

"In the old days, Ruch was hardworking and prosperous. Now there's nothing left."

The chicken was plucked. She ground up lard, parsley, and garlic in the blender, then stuffed the mixture into the bird's cavity and trussed it. She took an iron hook from a peg below the mantel and lifted the cover from the pot, then dropped the chicken inside.

"Later I'll add carrots and leeks," she said. "It'll be ready by the time the grandchildren arrive this evening. Jean, show these young people your *cave*. And bring some wine for the pot."

Jean picked up an empty magnum bottle, slipped on his beret and his sabots, and motioned to us to follow him outdoors. He grinned when Sara put on her beret, too.

"In America, everyone thought I was French because I always wear a beret," she told him. "But in France, they know I couldn't be French because no Frenchwoman would ever wear one. Isn't that right?"

"But it suits you well," he said.

"Where do your grandchildren live?" she asked him.

"In Bordeaux. My son works for Dassault. The company that builds the rockets."

His *cave* was a low building behind the house, stone thinly pasted with dirty cement. He pulled an iron key from behind a board and unlocked the door. Six wooden steps descended into darkness.

Beylot's cave

"My grandfather built this in 1911," Beylot said. "It didn't get much use during the war. My great-grandfather built the house in 1870, just before the Prussians invaded France. The Beylot timing has never been very good." He reached for a hammer and a glass pipette.

As my eyes adjusted to the gloom, I could make out a dozen ancient barrels against one wall, a cement vat in a corner, and a small manual grape press, the kind château owners in the Médoc display as curiosity pieces. All the tools were human-scaled, hand-operated. Everything was black, from the iron tools to the earthen floor. It was a scene from an old photograph, a museum.

He showed us how he crushed the grapes in what looked like a large nut grinder, turned by a hand crank. What about destemming them, I asked. At the cooperative, the destemmer was the weak link in the mechanical system, where debris jammed the screws. Oh, he never bothered with that. The stems added body to the wine.

The juice fermented in the open tank for about ten days. He punched down the cap of skins with a wooden pole every day or so, and when the wine tasted right he drew off the liquid, pressed the skins to extract as much more wine as he could, and piped it into barrels. His brother had been a cooper in Ruch, and some of the barrels were his, half a century old. He racked the wine a couple of times, decanting it from one barrel to another in order to eliminate the heavy sediment, then bunged it tight and drank it, barrel by barrel, until the next harvest.

It was a hybrid method, and I guessed it tended to increase the concentration and tannic content of his wine, enabling it to survive until the next harvest despite the crude sanitary conditions in the cellar. But I doubted if Beylot had reasoned that way. Probably he had just learned here and there, tried this and that, until he found a way to make wine taste the way he liked it.

In the great châteaux, the Bordelais argued constantly over the relative merits of tradition versus innovation in winemaking and wine style. They had invented what was now standard winemaking practice back in the seventeenth century and held up this long history as sacred writ. But spurred by the experimental approach of the University of California, they had invested heavily in laboratories at their own Institut d'Oenologie. In the end, they claimed to maintain the best of the old ways while using the latest techniques where they could improve the wine. The specific elements of "tradition" drifted and fogged. The idea of authenticity became as much a marketing ploy as an actual influence.

Beylot just worked with what came easiest to hand. But despite his unorthodoxies, his method was as authentic as I was going to find. If the long Bordeaux tradition had any validity, the proof would be here. Beylot made wine as wine had been made for centuries, until the twentieth century electrified the operation. No bladder press, no temperature-controlled vats, no spectrographic analysis, no chemical adjustments, no membrane filtration, no sterile bottling. No bottling at all. He just guided the grapes through the basic, mysterious transformation from fruit juice to wine, then let it rest in the cool cellar until he needed it for his table.

My mouth watered as he knocked a bung loose and plunged the glass pipe the French call a wine thief deep into the barrel. I felt a rush of exhilaration as the wine gurgled into the tumblers, glinting garnet in the low light.

This was what we had come to France to find: the past alive in the present. Beylot was drawing up the real, pure thing.

As wine, it would provide a standard of reference for the modern product Bordeaux shipped all over the world, wrapped in its ancient prestige. Tasting Beylot's wine, we would know what Bordeaux used to taste like, how it was meant to taste. Then we could evaluate all the interventions that made wine's adaptation to modern life possible. We could affirm the changes that preserved its essence, and discard those which distorted it.

But the context of the tasting went beyond sensory evaluation. The wine was just a sign, an indication of a whole world, its character a consequence of a way of life. The hand press, the old barrels were only a few of the tools that crafted Beylot's wine. His beret had an influence, and his sturdy wife's *poule au pot*. Even the television, I supposed, helped make it what it was. These things, too, would serve as references for comparison with modern society. If Beylot's wine were good and true, that would justify the life that made it possible.

The old man handed us two glasses. *"Santé,"* he said, and knocked back his own. *"Ah, mais c'est bon. N'est-çe pas?"*

The situation didn't call for the normal analysis of swirl, sniff, spit. I nodded to Sara and raised the glass to my lips.

A sharp aroma, somewhere between sour cherries and salad dressing, hit me first, then a slight fizz on my tongue. The liquid was thin and tart, fleetingly fruity, then bitter as my throat closed. I half-choked, managed to swallow. Sara turned her face away. I forced a smile at Beylot, then drained my glass.

On the second taste, I found the wine. My palate registered the raspberry and herbal notes of Cabernet Franc, the silky mouth-feel of the glycerin, the heat of the alcohol. But these notes were dominated by faults: the vinegar flavor of bacterial spoilage, the mustiness of dirty barrels, the thin sweetness of overenthusiastic chaptalization.

"Well?" Beylot asked. "Isn't that good?"

"It has the real *goût de terroir*," I told him.

It did: it tasted of the earth. In that, at least, it seemed a true reflection of its maker. What could I say? If a sommelier served this wine to me in any restaurant in the world, I would send it back. Beylot drank it with pleasure every day of his life. He seemed at least as healthy and happy as I. So much for the yardstick of authenticity.

"Would you like to take a bottle or two home?"

I was shaking my head when Sara said yes, we'd love to. She said she'd never tasted anything quite like it and how kind he was to share with us. We would always remember it.

So he siphoned off two bottles for us, filled the magnum for his *poule au pot,* and we climbed back out of the *cave*. It was warm outdoors, and the wine was ruby in the sunshine. Beylot tucked the key away and we all shook hands.

"Thank you," we said.

"Not at all. Come back when you want more."

Night fell clear and cool. A light wind chilled me through a sweater when I stepped outside to close the shutters. The moon was a hard, shiny scythe, so bright it hurt the eye, tinting the black sky blue. A dry leaf rustled, and dogs barked in the distance. Headlights flared across the ridge. A mouse skittered around the trash cans. It was 9:30 and the village was silent.

On Toussaint the usual morning fog cloaked the streets, draped the cemetery in a damp shroud. The chrysanthemums were the same colors as the graves they adorned, gray and rust and moss.

Sara and I went to the graveyard around 11:00. We found a dozen people there, wandering the pathways or talking with family. The mood was a cross between visiting hours at a hospital and a field trip to a museum, lively curiosity and even sociability muted by decorum and the edginess of grief.

At 11:15, a troop of nearly thirty people entered the gates, led by the Mayor and his family. We recognized the Lunardellis, the Destrieux, the Grangiers, Dupuy, Sartran—the nucleus of Bonvoisin's supporters, council members, and the soccer crowd. They moved together in a body. It looked like the same program as the year before, but we still had no idea how it was organized or how anyone knew about it. We joined them as they paused at a grave, shook hands all around. Dupuy placed a pot of flowers on the tomb and asked for a moment of silence. Then we moved on to another grave. After a dozen stops, the ragged ceremony was over and almost everyone marched back out the gates.

The churchgoers gathered in the cold sanctuary half an hour later. I asked Madame Le Barazer why none of the Mayor's crowd came to church. "They're Communists," she snorted. "They're afraid God will strike them down." Sara sang with the choir, and I sat with the Delom-Sorbés, who had gathered nearly two dozen strong. The priest was late and raced through the monotonous rites. But when he brought up the ancient ceremonies of the pagan Gauls, as he had last year and probably would in years to come, I felt his chipped stones in my hand.

Once again, the priest led his congregation into the cemetery. Acolytes in white robes swung their censers, smoldering incense mingling with the mist. The priest paused near the large tomb of the Delom-Sorbés and prayed for all the world's dead. He closed with a bit of Latin and the sign of the cross, then marched the acolytes back into the church. The rest of the crowd dispersed at the gates and wandered home to lunch.

The mairie

In the afternoon, the sun burned through the fog, warming the chill air. Sara and I went back to the cemetery. This time she took her camera, and I my notebook, to record the decorations and note whose they were.

The flowers had become radiant, glowing violet, ruby, cream, and gold. Against the gay colors of the petals, the church loomed gray and severe, at once foreboding and reassuring. We wandered around the tombs, trying to make out the names chiseled in Gothic script and now weathered into rude scratches. Some of the graves held remains of families with no living members left in town. Were they tokens of ruptures with tradition, evidence that the town had lost touch with its roots in the past?

No, I thought, not when nearly every grave was heaped with flowers, many with multiple bouquets, and the ground looked like a tapestry of love and respect. The fabric might be worn in spots, but the weavers were still at their looms. "Uncle, we pray for you," read a small marble plaque set on the Sorbier tomb. "At Lourdes, we prayed for you," read a ceramic figure on the Bonvoisins' monument. We hunted till we found the grave of the young man killed in the fight during the 1986 harvest. Grass had grown in and there were fresh chrysanthemums with a tinfoil message: "To our son and brother."

We sat on a low stone wall in the sun. A breeze rustled chestnut leaves along the gravel path.

"Sara?"

"Mmmm."

"I'm glad we came here."

"So am I, Tom."

The air was very clear. A swallow darted into the church tower.

"Sara?"

"Mmmm."

"Maybe we ought to."

"Ought to what?"

"Get married."

She looked over at me, squinting a little in the sun. "Do you mean that?"

"I think so."

She kissed me, a long, happy kiss, then looked up at the church spire, silhouetted against the sky. "I love this place. I could stay here forever."

"Forever?"

"Why not? Remember what the Mayor said? That Ruch had everything we need."

I shook my head. "You know me. I'm restless and hard to satisfy."

She smiled. "But satisfaction isn't the point, is it?" She stood up. "You know that pot of chrysanthemums I bought for the doorway? I think Madame Viandon feels like I put a tombstone outside her window. Maybe it really belongs here. Wait for me."

She slipped through the gates and was back in a moment, placing the flowers by an old, tilted tombstone, with an inscription so faded we couldn't read it to see whose it was. Perhaps that could be our contribution to Ruch, I thought, a gesture to those whom time had made strangers, from two who were almost at home. Then she came and sat beside me again.

The *mairie* bells counted the hour, as if to remind the world that time was passing. But the world didn't care. The streets were empty, the long valley quiet and still. We leaned against the cool stone wall of the church and watched the flowers glow in the sun.